W9-BGQ-133

Praise for previous editions of this book:

"**Fantastic resource on all things Social Security!!!** This is a great book that covers everything you need to know about Social Security. As a Certified Financial Planner®, I have referenced this book numerous times to help plan with my clients. The book is written in easy to understand language and covers pretty much anything you need to know. He uses great examples and provides many links to additional resources. This is a must-have for anyone in the financial services industry or anyone who wants to truly maximize and understand their benefits." ★★★★★—top rating
    Tom Faley, CFP®, http://tomfaley.com/

"**Very useful book!** I've found Andy's book to be absolutely essential for anybody planning their retirement. Andy tells you how to get the most from Social Security, which can add many thousands of dollars to your lifetime payouts. And his info on Medicare helps you navigate the complex rules, so that you minimize your out-of-pocket medical expenses." ★★★★★—top rating
    Steve Vernon, FSA, President, Rest-of-Life Communications and author of *Money For Life* and *Recession-Proof Your Retirement Years*, www.moneyforlifeguideonline.com

"**Great resource for professionals.** This should be mandatory reading for rookie as well as veteran financial planners. The author lays out the often confusing "world" of Social Security in an understandable and entertaining fashion. The book's title says it all." ★★★★★—top rating
    David Koch, CFP®

"**Best explanation of Social Security I've ever seen in print.** I'm a retired Social Security Claims Representative and I rate this book as the best explanation of Social Security benefits I've ever seen. The writer's style is great and he has a nice, friendly approach. It's not an easy subject, but he explains things in a simple, understandable fashion." ★★★★★—top rating
    Amazon.com reader

"**Absolutely fabulous!!** My husband ordered this. He's the "investment guy" in our household and he knows more than most professionals in the field because he's been continuously studying finance-anything for over 40 years because he loves to. This book gave information he had not found anywhere else and now that he's 62, we want to know exactly what our benefits are. We have an adult disabled son and this book explained some critical information that even our attorney did not know (or failed to tell us) that could affect SS benefits (in a positive way) if our son's disability is deemed severe enough for the special rules." ★★★★★—top rating
    Amazon.com reader

"**Good overview and a fairly easy read.** Social Security is complicated because there are many rules and even more personal situations. This book did a good job of giving you the basics so you have an understanding of the general terrain. It may not have a scenario that exactly fits your situation but it will give you an understanding of how to explore your options. It's also well written so most people should be able to understand the subject." ★★★★★—top rating
    Amazon.com reader

"**Social Security Demystified.** I use this book in our Retirement Planning Seminars. This is a fantastic resource on all things related to the Social Security System and how you can benefit from it. Andy Landis is both knowledgeable and concise. A must own." ★★★★★—top rating
    Amazon.com reader

"**Absolutely the best on explaining when to take Social Security.** Excellent book for anyone trying to decide when to begin Social Security. He offers information I had not previously heard about—that age 60 is everyone's base year for computing inflation adjusted earnings. A lot what he explains is not common knowledge. I highly recommend this book as a reference for retirement planning." ★★★★★—top rating
    Amazon.com reader

"**Everyone between 60 and 68 needs this book.** Heard Andy Landis speak, and this book allowed me to get $50,000 more in benefits that I did not know I could get!" ★★★★★—top rating
    Amazon.com reader

"**Excellent. Easy to read. Much helpful information.** Mr. Landis has succeeded in making a very complicated subject comprehensible to the average reader. All my questions about how the system works were answered. I appreciated the fact that Mr. Landis was employed by the Social Security Administration for many years and was able to give an insider's account of procedures and benefits. Many thanks for this very helpful book!" ★★★★—Amazon.com rating
    Amazon.com reader

"**A Perfect 'Layman's' Guide To Social Security.** This book provides a very thorough, yet practical explanation of Social Security in an easy to read format. This is a great guide for almost anyone wanting a better understanding of not only how the program works, but how it will work for them as an individual participant." ★★★★★—top rating
    Matthew P. Jarvis, Chartered Financial Consultant, www.jarvisfinancial.com

"**Buy this if you need to understand SS.** Best of the lot for SS coverage! This book gives all the details, explains it all clearly, details the strategies available to get the most out of SS, and provides excellent links. If you're getting ready to draw SS and don't know much, this is the book. Better than [that other Social Security book] and all the rest." ★★★★—Amazon.com rating
    Amazon.com reader

"**Landis does for Social Security what J.K. Lasser and others have done for taxes**—provide reliable, understandable, and comprehensive guidance."
    Booklist

"In a market full of manuals on Social Security and Medicare, this new book is the first that provides a comprehensive review of the regulations and at the same time explains how the Social Security Administration works."
    Jon Robert Steinberg, *New Choices for Retirement Living*

"Your book will, no doubt, help numerous individuals as they plan for their future. *The Inside Story* is not only full of important information, but also easy to read. You have made a complex subject understandable."
    Horace Deets, former Executive Director, AARP

"For anyone who is approaching eligibility, [this book] is a very useful resource. Recommended."
    Midwest Book Review

"**Andy Landis makes the complexities of Social Security easy to understand.** This well-organized book covers all of the important Social Security topics. The question and answer section and the numerous real-life examples are especially helpful. I highly recommend this expertly guided tour of Social Security."
    Ray Eads, President, Wealth Management Northwest, http://wealth-nw.com/company/

Also by Andy Landis:

When I Retire
The fastest, easiest way to make your retirement fun, fulfilling, and significant

"If you're thinking about retirement, you must read *When I Retire*. This easy-to-read, easy-to-use book will not only inspire you to make your retirement the best it can be, but it gives you practical tools and guidance that empower you to actually make it happen."
    **Steve Vernon, FSA, author, *Money For Life* and *Recession-Proof Your Retirement Years*
www.moneyforlifeguideonline.com**

"Everything you need to think about regarding retirement but didn't know who to ask. I love this book, and recommend it highly if you are (1) thinking about retiring, (2) making plans to retire, or (3) thinking about making plans to retire. The tone of the book is optimistic, encouraging, and non-threatening, without being pie-in-the-sky about retirement. It's a reliable and encouraging companion on the sometimes-stressful road to anticipating your retirement. Don't leave (or stay) home without it!"
    Ed Jacobson, PhD, MBA, author, Appreciative Moments: Stories and Practices for Living and Working Appreciatively. www.EdwardJacobson.com

"Andy Landis has given us the check-lists for the rest of our lives! In a series of bite-sized chapters he offers a series of considerations, lists, resources and quotes from the experts: those who have already retired. They cover every aspect of a life set loose from the constraints, joys and concerns of work. Take a chapter at a time—in your own time—and begin to engage yourself in this next, and maybe even best, part of your life."
    Dan Kennedy, Career and Life Coach, www.ResultsThatMatter.com

"Leonardo DaVinci said, 'Simplicity is the ultimate sophistication.' Andy has the gift of simplifying the very complex in his retirement insights, thereby delivering practical and actionable wisdom. This book is **a must-read for anyone near, at, or in retirement."**
    John Busacker, President, INVENTURE—the Purpose Company, and Founder, Life-Worth, LLC www.inventuregroup.com

"*When I Retire* is a delightful read. Filled with great quotes from retirees' own observations, you'll want to go through it numerous times. It provides excellent lists of things to do and think about, broken down into key categories. Landis nicely adds his own wisdom, covered in 18 short chapters packed with insight, humor, and dreams of adventure."
    Tom Washington, author, *Interview Power*, www.careerempowering.com

"At a time when so much is up in the air and filled with uncertainty, Andy Landis's advice contained in ***When I Retire* offers solid and practical help.** His common-sense recommendations walk you through a confusing maze of retirement planning information and engage you in identifying and executing solutions that work for you. This should be on everyone's nightstand who is contemplating how to make ends meet in a world that fights against that end."
    Lee White, Former Regional Vice-President of AARP

"This is a must-read for baby boomers and those just embarking on a career and preoccupied with the demands of entering the workforce. Never has retirement planning been more crucial to your financial survival in later life. There is no judgment here from Andy Landis; just basic no-nonsense guidance about what to do now! You sense his passion about helping folks steer clear of landmines along the road to retirement. Give this to someone you love."

    Bob McCormick, Host of "Money 101," CBS radio, Los Angeles
    http://kfwbam.com/show/money-101-with-bob-mccormick/

"This book packs so much good information into one place it's like free time in the candy store! I've always wondered when Andy would take all the great knowledge packed in his brain and the fantastic (and sometimes tragic) stories of retirement that he's heard and put them both together in a way that helps individuals and couples plan their sunset years. I wonder no more—here it is!"

    Steven "Shags" Shagrin, JD, CMC®, CFP®, CRPC®, CRC®, RLP®, www.PlanningForLife.info

"Guide to a fulfilling retirement. Andy Landis provides an insightful framework to help arrange your thinking and address those important areas that will make up your retirement life. With broad experience across many years of retirement planning he identifies what to expect from the initial shock of leaving the working world and what that implies to activities you should consider to enhance day to day retirement life. Throughout the book he shares relevant famous quotations as well as real life feedback from retirees "in their words". Beyond just reading, Andy draws you into exercises to help prepare for your own retirement with checklists, recommendations, links and sources of useful information to help you contemplate and navigate your individual journey. As one quote in his book reflects "Don't simply retire from something; have something to retire to." Andy's book can help each of us to do just that." ★ ★ ★ ★ ★—top rating

    Amazon.com reader

SOCIAL SECURITY
THE INSIDE STORY

An Expert Explains Your Rights
and Benefits

2014 Edition

Andy Landis
THINKING RETIREMENT
www.andylandis.biz

Social Security: The Inside Story
An Expert Explains Your Rights and Benefits
2014 Edition
By Andy Landis
THINKING RETIREMENT
www.andylandis.biz

All rights reserved. No part of this publication may be reproduced or transmitted in any form or by any means, electronic or mechanical, including photocopying, recording or by any information storage and retrieval system, without prior written permission from the author, except for the inclusion of brief quotations in a review.

Copyright © 2014 by Andrew S. Landis

Printed in the United States of America.

2014.1

Library of Congress Cataloging-in-Publication Data

Landis, Andrew S.
Social Security: The Inside Story, 2014 Edition: an expert explains your rights and benefits / by Andy Landis. 2014 Edition. Includes index.
$21.95 Softcover
ISBN-10: 1499255233
ISBN-13: 978-1499255232
Library of Congress Cataloging Number (LCCN): 2014907975

1. Social Security—United States—Popular works.
2. Medicare—Popular works. I. Title
HD7124.L36 2010   344.73/02

To Genevieve and Johanna with love,
and with hope that Social Security will be even healthier for their generation
than it is for mine.

Acknowledgements

My primary debt is to the thousands of people I have met through Social Security and retirement seminars over the past 37 years. Your concerns, your tough questions, and your kind attention helped me to see both the details and the "big picture" better, and appreciate the wisdom of Social Security.

Tom Washington, you opened my eyes. Kaycee Krysty steered me by encouragement and example. Ray Larsen gave me an opportunity I will never forget. The fine people at SSA, especially the staffs at the Bellevue and Renton (now Kent) offices and the Auburn TSC, answered my questions and provided invaluable information and materials. Particular credit is due to Kurt Larson, Bill Beineke, Rod Smitkin, Michael Clement, and Kathy Cox for their extensive help and patience.

And to friends and contributors who have gone on, Dr. Ralph Richardson, Ray Larsen, Elwood Chapman, and Andrew Tartella, *Adios. Vaya con Dios.*

This work was greatly improved by the tactful editing of Scott Provence, editor extraordinaire. Special thanks also to Kay Landis and Mary Lou Standerfer for additional editing assistance.

Naturally, any errors are mine.

Disclaimers

Every effort has been made to ensure that the information in this book is accurate at the time of publication. However, each individual case is unique, policies change, and space limitations prevent including every provision of Social Security law and regulations. Only the Social Security Administration can make official decisions. Therefore you should always consult directly with SSA, Medicare, IRS, your employer, or private insurers for individual determinations on your case and your family's.

Examples used throughout this book are fictional. Any resemblance to actual persons, living or dead, is purely coincidental.

The opinions expressed are the author's own. They do not represent the positions of the publisher or the Social Security Administration.

☆ CONTENTS ☆

Today a hope of many years' standing is fulfilled.... We can never insure one hundred percent of the population against one hundred percent of the hazards and vicissitudes of life, but we have tried to frame a law which will give some measure of protection to the average citizen and to his family against the loss of a job and against poverty-ridden old age.

Franklin Delano Roosevelt
Upon signing the Social Security Act
August 14, 1935

THIS BOOK IS FOR YOU

This book will be valuable if you are:

- Retirement age or approaching retirement age and need to know what to expect from Social Security.

- Any age and facing disability.

- Dealing with survivorship issues, either after a death or as part of estate planning for yourself or a family member.

- A taxpayer who wants to know what you're getting for your money.

- A financial services professional wanting improved client service through deeper knowledge of what Social Security does and does not provide.

- An attorney who prepares estate plans.

- A social services provider who needs to know when to refer clients to SSA.

- A human resources professional wanting to serve your employees better by understanding how Social Security benefits relate to your employer plans.

- Just a wonk or a student of public policy wanting in-depth understanding of the program.

In short, this book is for anyone with a stake in Social Security and Medicare, and for those who assist others with retirement, disability, death, or health insurance.

WHAT'S NEW

There have been numerous changes since the 2012 edition of this book:

- **Payroll tax holiday.** FICA taxes came back to the full 6.2% effective January 2013 after a two-year "holiday," during which they were reduced by 2%. The shortfall to the Social Security trust funds was made up by general revenues. (page 247)

- **Personal Statements are back—for some.** SSA stopped mailing Personal Statements in April 2011, as reported in this book's 2012 Edition. In 2013

Social Security resumed mailing annual Personal Statements for select individuals. (page 175)

- **"My Social Security" online accounts implemented.** Personal Statements, earnings records, and benefits estimates are available anytime at www.ssa.gov. And for those getting Social Security payments, online benefits verification, change of address, and change of direct deposit are all available online. (page 175)

- **Affordable Care Act phase-in continues.** The 2010 healthcare reform continues to phase in, particularly affecting Medicare Part C and Part D plans. (pages 160, 165, and 171)

- **Same-sex marriage.** SSA is responding to the U.S. Supreme Court repeal of the Defense of Marriage Act (DOMA) by recognizing same-sex marriage for some spousal and survivor's benefits. (pages 64, 81, 87, and 97)

- **New Medicare taxes.** High-income earners are seeing new Medicare taxes on earned and unearned income. (page 126)

- **Critical ages.** A new "Critical Ages" table is added to Appendix C, pinpointing each important birthday throughout life. (page 271)

- **Visual aids.** New figures like tables and illustrations clarify complex provisions.

- **Editing.** Throughout the book new editing strives for clarity, accuracy, and brevity, including a major re-write of the Medicare and Maximizing chapters.

WHY THIS BOOK

Social Security and Medicare: we all buy them, but who knows what we bought?

For most people, Social Security is the *only* income source that protects simultaneously against inflation risk, market risk (market ups and downs), and longevity risk (outliving your money). All this, with tax benefits! You definitely need to understand how it works.

But during the last 37 years of working with Social Security and Medicare, I discovered an important fact: Almost no one understands them. Where's the information?

You could turn to the Social Security Administration (SSA) itself for help. SSA produces numerous publications and has an incredible website. However, most of the publications are limited to a narrow topic and cannot answer more than one of your questions at a time. SSA does publish a few general booklets addressing more than one topic, but these tend to be *too* general—too brief and vague to answer your specific questions. And the SSA website is comprehensive, but is often overwhelming in its detail and complexity.

Or you could turn to your bookstore or library for information to answer your Social Security questions. But most books on Social Security are disappointing:

- Many are political, typically saying that Social Security should be banned: it's a rip-off; it's a Ponzi scheme; you'll never get paid. (I like to collect the ones from the past that say, for example, that Social Security will be bankrupt by 1977.)

- Some books, intended for legal experts or lawmakers, are too technical for your needs.

- Others, intended for the general reader, lack the insider's understanding of what you need to know about Social Security. Some rely heavily on photocopies of SSA forms that are out of date and will not help you. Others bombard you with details but provide no "big picture" for understanding how the details affect you—leaving you to make sense of the various pieces.

- Some books are simply out-of-date and inaccurate.

- And finally, some give a simple overview but ignore vital details you may need to know to answer your questions.

What the existing books fail to give is *the inside story.* They lack the insider's knowledge.

This book, like my others, addresses that problem. It grows out of my twelve years inside Social Security and my additional years as a speaker and consultant on Social Security and Medicare. This book gives you the clear, inside story.

Like a reference book, it is detailed enough to accurately answer your specific questions about Social Security. It unlocks the Social Security website with links to the exact pages you need. (Remember, weblinks are case-sensitive; you must use upper- and lower-case letters just as shown.) Yet this book also ties the facts together into a sensible and comprehensive whole, shows how different parts of the program work together, and reveals the ideas behind the provisions. And it does so in readable, understandable, non-technical English.

In short, it helps you make sense of Social Security. With this book you will understand what your hard-earned tax dollar is buying, and how to get the most from your stake in the system.

A New Generation

It's time for a new approach for a new generation. My generation was the first to fund Social Security for two generations: our parents and ourselves. We have successfully built a multi-trillion-dollar fund, the biggest ever, for our own future. Now we're entering the time to draw down those investments, and we need to know what's in store for us.

This book gives timely information for a new generation:

- Every computation and numerical fact is updated to 2014.

- The latest provisions are explained, including the Affordable Care Act of 2010 (Obamacare).

- Dozens of web links help you delve deeper into any topic, pinpointing the information you want without endless searching.

- Recent or proposed reforms to the system are explained. Look for *Reform Notes* throughout the text to indicate which provisions may be changed by proposed reforms.

The result is that you are holding the most *up-to-date* book on Social Security, as well as the most comprehensive and accurate.

The Author's Perspective

While reading this book you may detect a bias in favor of Social Security.

I have seen the good and the bad sides of Social Security. Over the course of twelve years inside the agency, I saw it at its best and at its worst. Now outside SSA, I have a different perspective. I now deal with the agency both as a private citizen and as a consultant who needs access to SSA information and materials in order to serve my clients.

Do I still admire the agency? Yes. Call it optimistic realism. Let me explain.

Any government system can be examined at three levels. The first is the *personal* level—how well you are treated when you contact the agency and how easy it is to work with the agency. The second is the *program* level—how fair the rules of the program are and how well the program accomplishes its mission. The third is the *philosophical* level—whether the program's underlying ideas fit well with America's needs and values. Social Security is strong in each of these areas.

Look at Social Security at the *personal* level. Everyone has heard stories of the Administration's fumbles, its delays, its occasional insensitivity in dealing with the American public. But these are the remarkable exceptions. On the whole the agency is very easy, and even pleasant, to deal with. I have seen—and participated in—daily acts of compassion, dedication, expertise and other acts of public service that rise above and beyond all expectations. Polls continue to consistently rank Social Security employees at the very top of all government *and private-sector* workers for public service. And most customers I talk with echo that praise.

At the *program* level, I know there are areas of unfairness or inequity, and areas where people still "fall through the cracks." But for the most part, the program is fair, and SSA is constantly attempting to improve the system, to weed out unfairness and close the gaps that people fall through.

Then there is the *philosophy* of Social Security. It is based on three fundamental American values: work, family, and personal ownership. It is not a handout, but an earned benefit like insurance or pensions. And it retains a strong incentive for individual initiative and enterprise because it does not discourage private investment.

Looked at another way, Social Security balances two natural American values: our *generosity* and our *self-interest*. The manner in which Social Security expresses our American values is one of Social Security's major strengths, and a big reason for its broad popularity and support in the past seven decades.

My perspective is clear then. Despite its flaws, the American Social Security system makes me proud. It's not perfect. But its dedication to public service, generosity, constant improvement, and fairness is impressive. As you read this book you will see some of the reasons for my pride in the system.

TOWARD FAIRNESS AND SIMPLICITY

I intend to inform without bias. Therefore I have attempted to spread my references and examples fairly among people of all backgrounds, a variety of ages, and both sexes. Any bias detected is unintentional.

I sometimes use the (improper but colloquial) "they" to indicate a third person singular of unknown gender, rather than the (correct but cumbersome) "him or her." For example, "Your spouse can file for their own Social Security when they file on your record."

I offer my apologies to grammarians, with whom I usually am allied.

CHAPTER ONE

MAKING SENSE OF SOCIAL SECURITY

Sally Smith has only ten years of part-time work scattered over the years of her life.
She will get Social Security payments.

Bob Johnson had worked only a few years when he had a serious accident. The doctors think it will be years before he can return to work, if ever.
He will get Social Security payments.

Marsha Jones, who worked as a homemaker and volunteer her whole life, has almost no paid work. Her husband John is retiring soon.
She will get Social Security payments.

Frank and Karen Ferguson are in high school. Their father died last month from a sudden illness.
They will get Social Security payments.

Janet Smith was married to Sam for twelve years but is now divorced. She is 62 and wants to retire, but Sam has not retired. Janet does not have enough work to qualify for Social Security on her own.
She will get Social Security payments.

Each of these people was surprised to learn that Social Security is more than just a retirement program for lifelong workers. Social Security is much more, as you will learn from this book.

In coming chapters you will visit each of these individuals, and many others, to discover *why* they are eligible for Social Security and *how much* they can expect. More importantly, you will learn valuable information about what *you* can expect from Social Security for yourself and your family members.

Social Security is a broad and complex program with a rich history. This chapter is an overview of the program and its background, with special attention to

Social Security's strengths and weaknesses, and why Social Security is what it is today.

This chapter will also show you how Social Security works. Reading it will give you a "big picture" perspective to apply to the following, more technical chapters, like quickly looking over a car before inspecting its component parts.

If you cannot wait to learn about the technical aspects of the program, skip ahead to Chapter 2 for retirement benefits, or another chapter that interests you. You can return to this chapter at any time to tie the details together.

SOCIAL SECURITY'S HISTORY

When Franklin D. Roosevelt signed the Social Security Act into law in 1935, it was the product of several years of often bitter controversy, negotiation, lobbying, and compromise. The debate spread through the chambers of Congress, the editorial pages, and the streets and workplaces of America.

On one hand, there were charges that the program would be Communist, that it would lead to social chaos, and that government could not be trusted to pay benefits properly, if at all.

On the other hand was the desperate need to protect workers and their families against grinding poverty following their work years—poverty which, in the depths of the Depression, had already struck millions of working Americans upon retirement and was threatening millions more.

How could such a powerful, popular social program come from such turmoil? FDR envisioned Social Security as a new kind of government program, uniquely suited to its mission of offering protection against family poverty after a worker's retirement or death.

To accomplish its mission, Social Security would draw from two "big three's":

- The "big three" concepts: a powerful underlying philosophy, an independent method of funding, and unprecedented national scope.

- The "big three" partnership: Labor, Industry, and Government.

By carefully harnessing these diverse components into a balanced team, the Social Security program was successfully created.

The philosophy of the program: Social Insurance

The new Social Security program needed to promote, rather than undermine, the work ethic and the dignity of the individual. Therefore, Social

Security was established as a *social insurance* program, not a *social welfare* (or public assistance) program.

Social insurance means that the government acts as an insurance company. It insures your paycheck. Much like a private insurance company, Social Security collects premiums from you the worker, and then pays back to you (or your family) a defined amount when certain events occur. In 1935 the insured event was the retirement of the worker, but insured events now include death and disability.

Payments from Social Security are intended to *partially replace lost earnings.* The payments made are proportional to your contributions to the system (i.e., the Social Security taxes you paid). Those payments, then, are due to you and your family. Your work paid for them; they are an *earned right.* In this way, the system reflects our basic value of *ownership.*

Social Security protects the worker's family as well as the worker. This promotes the American value of *family.*

Social Security payments are most definitely not welfare—not charity, a handout or dole—any more than payments from a private insurance company or pension are charity. And since the payments are earned through work performed, the system encourages productive work, thus promoting another American value: our *work ethic.*

You (or a family member) become eligible for Social Security payments by passing an *insured test.* Work records are checked to make sure you paid into the system. A welfare or public assistance program, on the other hand, requires a *needs test*—every participant must prove that he is so *impoverished* that he qualifies for payments. Compared to a welfare program, an insurance program is less expensive to administer (having no need to prove poverty) and better preserves the *individual dignity* of participants.

By the way, the difference between *private insurance companies* and *social insurance* is that social insurance is run for the entire society, and participation is mandatory, enforced by the tax system.

☆   ***Reform Note:*** Some reform proposals would add a welfare-type means test to Social Security. For example, some propose that retirees with income above, say, $50,000, should have their Social Security reduced or eliminated. This would partially change Social Security from an insurance program to a welfare program.

Examples of social insurance programs include:

- Social Security

- Unemployment insurance (with payments for unemployed workers), and

- Workers' compensation (with payments for those disabled in the workplace).

Independent funding

Social Security is *self-funding*. Much like an insurance company, every dollar the program uses for benefit payments, administrative overhead, or future investment comes from the direct contributions of workers and employers, not from any government subsidies. (Exceptions are Medicare, which is partially subsidized by the government, and the 2011-2012 "payroll tax holiday," with lost payroll tax revenue replaced by general revenues.)

Self-funding lends further respectability and dignity to the program. No Social Security payment can be considered a subsidy or charity payment because of the program's strong independent funding. In this sense, it is supported *by* workers and *for* workers.

Independent funding also insulates Social Security from the vagaries of government funding. Social Security does not reduce benefits during times of government belt-tightening. It is not undermined by the whims of Congress or the President.

The public is well aware of Social Security's independent status, and strongly supports its independence. In fact, Americans loudly question the government's motives when Social Security revenue and expenditures are included in some Federal budget figures. The questioners have a point—there is no sound reason to lump Social Security figures into Federal budget figures because Social Security is independently financed.

☆ **Reform Note:** Many reformers propose direct government subsidies to Social Security. This would change Social Security from a self-funded system to one receiving a government subsidy.

The scope of the program

Some 1930s critics of the idea of a Social Security system raised a pertinent question: Was a national insurance system even *possible?* The scope of such a system—its sheer size and the blizzard of necessary paperwork—was simply staggering, especially considering 1935 technology.

First of all, a system of *record-keeping* needed to be invented. This would have to be a massive system, dwarfing any other program at that time. Just think: for virtually every worker in the nation, a record would have to be kept every calendar quarter. The record would have to reflect every dollar earned from every employer, even if the worker had numerous employers every month (not at all unusual, especially in the Depression), and even if the worker changed names.

The system that was finally adopted required the nation's employers to file the reports necessary for the record-keeping operation. These reports would be broken down worker by worker and quarter by quarter (quarterly reports were replaced by annual reports in 1978). The reports would cover every worker throughout every year of his or her working life. And every employer would prepare and file these reports with no compensation—instead they would be stung with a payroll tax.

The millions of employer reports would be sorted into individual workers' records by the new "Social Security Board" (predecessor to today's Social Security Administration). In order to do so, it was imperative for the Social Security Board to assign a unique *number* to each worker—otherwise it would have been impossible to properly sort the reports into individual records, given the number of identical names, birthdates and birth cities, even within a single large company. Naturally the suggestion of this Social Security Number caused a new round of controversy, with many charging that people were being reduced to serial numbers. (See page 208 for more information on Social Security numbers.)

Even when these tens of millions of records were collected, sorted, and stored in a retrievable fashion, less than half the job was done. The Social Security Board still needed to create a *payment* system to process claims, recall earnings records, compute benefit payments, and maintain monthly payments for the lifetime of every beneficiary.

Recall that the framers of the system were dealing with the technology of the 1930s. There were no computers, magnetic tapes, or electronic data transfers. We're talking about actual paper reports, prepared on manual typewriters, then mailed in and sorted by hand into filing cabinets. Social Security cards were typed by hand and payment computations were carried out with mechanical adding machines and scratch paper.

Needless to say, critics of the new system were sure the program would collapse under its own weight. Few had the vision to imagine the system working, especially since it required the cooperation of three natural antagonists: Labor, Industry, and Government.

Members of the partnership

The Social Security program needed to harness into a formidable partnership the three major sectors of the American economy: Labor, Industry, and Government. And in fact, the Social Security Act succeeded in creating a unique and far-reaching team to provide for the worker in time of need. Each sector was to play a significant role:

- The *individual worker* would make regular contributions to the program through a system of payroll deductions, and cooperate by keeping the assigned

Social Security number. (As noted above, it is doubtful the massive bookkeeping would ever have been possible without the numbers, even with today's computer equipment.)

- *Industry* would match the worker's contribution to the system. Employers would also keep individual records of each worker's earnings and report them to the government.

- *Government* would hire the staffers, issue the Social Security numbers, maintain the national records necessary to compute payments, process claims from retirees, and issue benefit payments.

The system ca. 1937-1940

Guided by this ambitious blueprint, the first Social Security taxes were collected in 1937: 1% of earnings up to $3,000, for a maximum annual tax of $30.00. Only industrial workers were covered—not farmers, the self-employed, professionals, or the military. The first monthly Social Security benefit payments were issued in January 1940. Benefit categories included:

- The retired worker
- The *wife* of a male worker,
- The child under 18 of a retired or deceased worker,
- The *mother* of a deceased worker's child, and
- The dependent parent, 65 or older, of a deceased worker.

These original benefit categories reflect the values and needs of their time. The worker might be either sex, but only wives and widows were considered dependents of a worker; men could not receive benefits on their wives' work records. Children were automatically covered; their dependency on the worker was assumed. However, parents of the worker needed to prove their dependency. In 1940, then, a simple Retirement and Survivor Insurance program, reflecting the work and family values of the era, was put in place.

The system evolves

Incredibly, the overall framework established in the Act in 1935 endures today with only relatively minor modifications. Still in place after 79 years is the *philosophy* of an insurance program rather than a welfare program, the *self-funding* through direct contributions, and the immense *scope* of the system. Even the structure of the three-way partnership among government, industry, and the individual remains intact.

Nevertheless, times have changed and certain portions of Social Security have changed as well. These changes include:

- **New covered workers.** Over the years farmers, domestic workers, the self-employed, the military, professionals, and many government workers have been brought into the system.

- **New types of benefits.** *Disability benefits* were added to the program in 1956, and further expanded in 1960 (they had been proposed since the 1930s). *Medicare* was added in 1965, making health insurance part of the program. (See the "Inside Story" box below for how the Administration's internal jargon has evolved to reflect the benefit types added to the system.)

- **New types of beneficiaries.** *Husbands and widowers* of workers became eligible starting in 1950, joining the wives and widows already eligible.

- **New retirement ages.** *Age 62 retirement* became an option for women in 1956 and for men in 1961. And currently the "Full Retirement Age" (FRA) is rising from age 65 to age 67.

- **Higher benefit payments and taxes.** Over the years benefit payments rose even as the overall population receiving benefits expanded and new benefit categories were added. Today, the law requires that payments must be raised every year to match inflation. These increases and expansions to the program made higher taxes necessary.

- **New information technology.** With the world's biggest record-keeping task, Social Security has always needed the most modern data-processing systems available. The paper files, typewriters, and adding machines have gone the way of the dinosaur, and have been replaced by the largest super-computer network in the world.

Overall, the changes in Social Security in its first 79 years reflect a balance between flexibility and stability. Each decade has brought changes to the program, based on what each generation wanted Social Security to do. Yet the basic structure of the system remains.

This endurance attests to the vision of the original framers of the system. The balance between flexibility and stability gives us some indication of what we can expect for Social Security in the 21st Century: reforms for each generation's needs within a stable framework of social insurance.

Internal names for SSA programs

Over the years SSA has used the initials of its various programs to serve as a kind of "shorthand" in internal communication. As the programs evolved, the shorthand has had to follow suit:

1935-1956	**OASI**	"Old-Age & Survivor Insurance"
1957-1964	**OASDI**	"Old-Age, Survivor, and Disability Insurance"
1965 on	**OASDHI**	"Old-Age, Survivor, Disability, and Health Insurance"
TODAY	**RSDHI**	"Retirement, Survivor, Disability, and Health Insurance"

Today, the Administration's internal magazine is titled *Oasis* in recognition of the original "OASI" acronym. When referring to the various programs, employees group them together using a variation of the old acronyms. For example, when speaking of the retirement/survivor program but not disability and Medicare, you will hear "RSI;" or in comparing the payment programs with the health program you will hear "RSDI."

TODAY'S SOCIAL SECURITY

Many people believe that Social Security is merely a retirement program. However, even from its beginnings, Social Security has always been much more than that. Today it is a comprehensive program of insurance protection, covering not only the worker but also family members. In fact, only about 64% of Social Security payments go to retired workers (see Figure 1.1). Categories of protection include:

- *Retirement benefits*—For workers over 62 who retire. Similar to private pension plans.

- *Family benefits*—For dependent family members of a worker who retires or becomes disabled.

- *Survivor benefits*—For surviving family members of a worker who dies at any age. Similar to private life insurance.

- *Disability benefits*—For workers, widow(er)s, or children under Full Retirement Age who become totally disabled. Similar to private disability insurance.

- *Medicare*—Health insurance for retirees over 65, certain disabled persons, and their dependents. Similar to private health insurance.

Thus, participants in the program are, in the language of insurance, *protected against loss of earned income due to retirement, disability, or death.* This three-fold protection is the mission of the Social Security Administration. In the coming chapters we'll see in more detail how the Administration carries out its mission, extending this insurance coverage to you and other Americans.

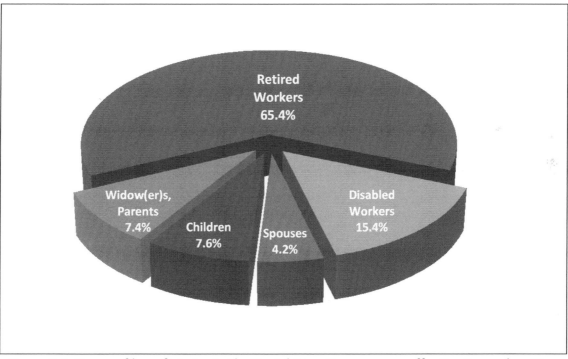

Figure 1.1: Types of beneficiaries in the Social Security program, effective December 31, 2013. (www.socialsecurity.gov/OACT/ProgData/icp.html)

We all hear complaints about Social Security. However, most of the complaints come from younger workers or reformers with an ax to grind. Very few complaints come from actual retirees. Because of the many complaints about the program we tend to forget its substantial strengths.

Maybe it's time to hear some good news. Here are just a few of Social Security's many strengths:

Payments are inflation-proof

Payments from Social Security are inflation-proof. Every year with measurable inflation, the increase in the Consumer Price Index (CPI) is applied to every Social Security payment, with raises effective with the January payments. This is called a *COLA,* for Cost Of Living Adjustment, and has been required by law since 1975.

Without this provision, the buying power of your Social Security payment would steadily erode—exactly the situation for most pensions, which are "locked in" at a fixed dollar amount for life. The erosion can be substantial when compounded over a 30-year retirement.

Some Social Security recipients wondered if COLAs were still in place, after receiving no raise in 2010 and 2011. Quite simply, there was no measurable inflation affecting those two years.

☆ **Reform Note:** Many reformers propose to reduce the COLA to less than the inflation rate (e.g. the inflation rate minus 0.5%), or to measure inflation with an index lower than the CPI, such as the "Chained CPI." Over time this would reduce the buying power of your Social Security payment substantially.

Supplemental payments for family

Additional benefits may be payable to your dependent family members, under certain conditions. Chapter 3, "Family Benefits," gives details on this provision. Under most pension plans the benefits paid are not related to family size, making for tighter budgeting in one-pension families.

☆ **Reform Note:** This provision is also under scrutiny. Many proposals would reduce family benefits.

Insurance, not public assistance

Social Security is an insurance program, not a welfare program. It's a big difference. A welfare program is *needs-based*, meaning that payments from the program are determined by neediness or poverty. "Need" is assessed by investigating all income and assets of the individual or family. The investigation involves a great deal of probing and a great deal of time and paperwork. Therefore a welfare program has steep costs—in speed, money, and the dignity of the claimant.

Social Security, on the other hand, is a *social insurance* program. Payments are based not on need, but on your contributions and age. Contributions and age are concrete facts, far easier to assess than a concept such as need. Thus, Social Security requires far less probing, and is much more efficient to operate, saving money for taxpayers. Most important, individual dignity stays intact—you know you paid for your benefits and own them.

☆ **Reform Note:** Some reformers call for eliminating even this most basic feature of the Social Security system. This usually takes the form of reducing or eliminating benefits for higher-income retirees.

Portability and universal coverage

Ever experience the frustration of losing pension coverage when you change employers? In many cases, thousands of dollars in contributions and a good number of "vesting years" may be lost forever, due to a job change.

Social Security, on the other hand, is totally portable, meaning you carry your coverage with you when you change jobs. And it's a nearly universal pension system, currently covering 94% of all paid jobs in the U.S. (www.ssa.gov/OACT/FACTS/). Your Social Security coverage continues to grow as your career progresses, wherever your career may take you.

☆ **Reform Note:** Most reform plans call for extending Social Security coverage to more workers, making coverage even more universal.

This is a plus for taxpayers as well. Having one large national system provides economies of scale—it is simpler and more efficient to operate than hundreds of individual pension plans.

Financial soundness

The 1980s, 1990s, and 2000s brought a host of financial nightmares. We saw the Savings and Loan Crisis, bank failures, huge insurance companies in receivership, stock market volatility, pension plans going bankrupt, and the "Great Recession."

Social Security had its own financial crisis in the late 1970s and early '80s. Headlines stated the exact month the system was predicted to run out of money. There was tremendous popular protest about the impending failure of Social Security's finances. Congress attempted several fixes between 1977 and 1983. Yet the program continued to operate at a deficit and continued to slide closer to insolvency.

Finally in 1983 the fix worked. The 1983 Amendments to the Social Security Act raised taxes and cut benefits. Since then the system has run a surplus every year, and in fact Social Security is "on track" with 1983's predictions. Social Security is one of our most sound financial institutions.

That doesn't mean that today's surpluses are permanent. Social Security faces another financial crisis in about 2033, and solutions are already being sought. For details about Social Security's long-term solvency, see Chapter 9.

☆ **Reform Note:** The shortfalls predicted for the 2030s are the driving force behind most reform plans.

Political soundness

Where does an 800 pound gorilla sit? Answer: wherever it wants. And where does the most popular government program sit politically? You got it.

If you are a politician, it is very risky to propose anything which would weaken Social Security. The program is just too popular—everyone has a stake. 57 million people (about one in every six Americans) receive Social Security payments every month, and most of them are voters. Right behind them are 163 million other Americans paying into the system and *expecting* a payment someday (www.ssa.gov/OACT/FACTS/). This reality has prompted some observers to comment that Social Security is the "third rail" of politics—touch it and you die.

An example of the political power supporting Social Security: there have been proposals since the late 1980s to reduce or eliminate the annual cost-of-living raises to beneficiaries. Popular opinion won't have it. The annual raises continue as long as there is inflation.

Another example: Congress enacted the Medicare Catastrophic Coverage Act of 1989. Before it was passed—and based on advance publicity—Catastrophic Coverage enjoyed strong support from many retiree groups. Once it became law, and the full costs of the change became widely known, there was a sudden and dramatic reversal in public opinion. Retiree groups called it the Medicare Catastrophe. Incredibly, Congress rescinded Catastrophic Coverage within a year—it was just too unpopular.

The lesson here is that the Social Security program is able to weather political assault. Politicians have learned that if they attack Social Security they need "damage control" to save their careers. Therefore, the various branches of government have no motivation to weaken the system and every motivation to keep it strong. That lends stability to the system, an assurance that problems will be solved and the program will be there when you need it. In fact, the history of Social Security is an example of how our system of government responds to the will of the people.

We should count our blessings. We live in a democracy where the government *really does* have to follow the will of the populace—at least with such a popular program.

WEAKNESSES OF THE SYSTEM

The above section makes it sound like everything is perfect in the Social Security program, like all problems have been solved and every taxpayer and beneficiary is happy.

Obviously that's not so. Here are the principal weaknesses of the program, and some suggestions for how you can counteract them.

Payment amount

The first complaint about Social Security is that payments are not very high. The maximum amount payable to a 65-year-old in 2014 was $2,431 per month (www.ssa.gov/OACT/COLA/examplemax.html). The average retiree draws $1,294 per month. While the average is well above the poverty level, clearly no one is amassing great personal wealth by drawing a Social Security payment. (Age 65 is used here as a common retirement age, rather than the SSA "Full Retirement Age," currently 66. See page 51.)

Of course, Social Security payments were never intended to be your sole retirement income. Rather, Social Security should be considered a *foundation* of retirement income, a base underlying the other assets and other forms of income necessary for a financially sound retirement.

Other forms of retirement income—pensions, investment income, rental income, and so on—do not reduce your Social Security payment. (Remember, this is an *insurance* program, not needs-based welfare.) The *only* type of income which affects your Social Security retirement payment is work income from wages or self-employment while under your Full Retirement Age. (See page 199 for more information on work after retirement.)

The implication for the average retiree is clear: since Social Security alone cannot guarantee a comfortable retirement, you should amass as much as you can in the way of company pensions, personal savings, retirement savings, and any other assets available to you to augment the base that Social Security provides.

Also remember that the average retiree recovers all of his or her Social Security tax contributions in the first two to three years of retirement.

You will learn more about the amount of your Social Security retirement payments in Chapter 2, and will learn how to obtain a personal statement from SSA in Chapter 7.

☆ **Reform Note:** Nearly every reform plan envisions lower Social Security payments in the future. Younger workers should expect to take even more personal responsibility for their own retirement funding.

Complexity—rules and exceptions

There's no question about it. Social Security is a complex program with rules, exceptions to the rules, exceptions to the exceptions, and so on. In fact, Social Security is not a program at all. It is a set of linked programs—a retirement/survivor program with disability and health insurance programs grafted on. It can take years of study to understand the finer details of the system. Claims representatives at SSA are "trainees" for the first three years on the job. Probably no single individual can fathom the entire system in all its complexity.

Is it impossible, then, to understand the program? Not at all. As already noted, the overall structure of the program and its underlying philosophy have been largely stable for over 79 years. That framework can be understood, along with the major exceptions to the general form. A certain order or logic emerges.

As you read this book you will be gaining knowledge about Social Security's rules and practices. Understanding Social Security will enable you to better understand your options and your rights. This in turn will allow you to make better, more informed decisions about *your* Social Security.

A maze of bureaucracy

With over 1,300 offices, some 64,000 employees, and claims manuals that would stack twenty feet high (if printed), we're looking at dense bureaucracy here. Complaints about the bureaucracy range from telephone busy signals, to inability to reach the proper person, to poorly trained personnel. Occasional stories report different answers from different employees to the same technical question. And the more experienced employees are quite accustomed to hearing clients remark, "I'm so happy *you* could finally help me."

Keep in mind that the agency, though large and complex, is still a human endeavor. The Administration is really just a group of people working together with a common mission. There are experienced people, harried people, outstanding people, and newcomers. Being human, they make mistakes. This is especially understandable when you consider the complex rules comprising the program. To their credit, accuracy is over 99%.

There are certain tips for working with this bureaucracy. See Chapter 8, Filing Your Claim, for some ideas. In addition, you have a head start on others dealing with the bureaucracy because you have a strong ally: this book.

FOR MORE INFORMATION...

"Understanding the Benefits"
www.ssa.gov/pubs/10024.html

"A 'Snapshot'"
www.ssa.gov/pubs/10006.html

CHAPTER TWO

YOUR RETIREMENT BENEFITS

Sam Smith is approaching retirement and wants to know how much he will receive from Social Security. When he calls Social Security he is told he can receive $2,067 per month if his payments start at age 65. But Sam is curious. What does his age have to do with his payment amount? Where does the $2,067 figure come from—how is it computed? Is there anything he can do to increase the amount?

Retirement benefits are the heart and soul of Social Security's package of protection. In fact, most Americans think Social Security pays *only* retirement benefits, because most people are not aware of the family, survivor, and disability portions of the program. The retirement program was the pivotal achievement of the original Social Security Act and continues to be the centerpiece of the program.

In this chapter you will examine the retirement program. You will see how you as a worker become eligible for a payment, how your payments are computed, and a few of the special provisions in the program. And, most importantly, you will learn what you can do to *affect* the amount of your payment.

ARE YOU ELIGIBLE FOR RETIREMENT BENEFITS?

General information about eligibility

Sally Smith, Sam's wife, wants to know whether she is eligible for a retirement payment of her own. When she and Sam married, Sally quit her 3-year job. Then she did not work again until the children were grown, and worked only part-time the last seven years. Can she get a retirement payment?

Sally Smith and others with a limited work history need to know whether they can get a retirement payment at all. They need to know the *eligibility rules* for SSA retirement benefits. Eligibility is the first step to understanding Social Security.

The short answer: to get a retirement payment you must be 62 and have at least 10 years of part-time work. The rest of this section gives the details.

Remember, Social Security is a "social insurance" program, and that's a good way to think of it—like an insurance company. Before you can collect on your auto insurance you have to pay the premium and meet certain other requirements. Before your health insurance will pay a medical bill you must be paid up and properly enrolled in the program. Social Security works the same way.

Note that this section deals only with *eligibility* for a payment, not how much will be paid. For information on payment computations see below under "How your payment is computed."

There are two requirements for eligibility:

- You must meet minimum *age requirements*, and

- You must meet minimum *work requirements*.

Age requirement for eligibility

In order to collect a retirement payment, you must "attain" at least 62 years of age. The earliest month you can be eligible for a retirement payment is your first *full* month of being age 62.

Normally this means you are eligible for a Social Security payment the month *after* your 62nd birthday—that is the first month you are 62 for the entire month. So if you turn 62 on June 21, you are eligible for Social Security in July. But there is an exception: If your birthday is the first or second of the month, you are eligible the month of your 62nd birthday. The reason is that you *attain* age 62 the day *before* your 62nd birthday (see "The Inside Story" box below). That

---

☆ THE INSIDE STORY ☆

"Attaining" retirement age

We normally think that we become a certain age on our birthdays. Why does Social Security say we "attain" an age on the day before our birthday?

The story in Social Security training classes: back in the 1800's a man was applying for federal benefits. The law said he had to "attain" a certain age to be eligible. He was born on the first of the month and wanted payments for the month before his birth month. He took the case to federal court and argued that he had lived 365 days on the *day before* his birthday—he had actually lived a year on that day. His birthday, he argued, was actually the start of his *second* year. The judge agreed. Ever since then all federal agencies recognize that you *attain* an age the day before your birthday.

---

exception can result in a slight windfall if you are born on the first or second of the month.

But attaining age 62 is not enough in itself for you to gain Social Security eligibility. In addition you must meet the work requirements.

Sally Smith will be over age 62 when she retires, so she knows she will meet the age requirement. What about the work requirement?

Work requirement for eligibility

In a nutshell you need 10 years of work which pays into the Social Security system to be eligible to receive a payment. The details are a bit more complicated, so let's take a look at the rules.

You "pay your insurance premium" to Social Security by working—or more accurately, working under the system and paying your Social Security (F.I.C.A. or Self-Employment) taxes. The agency keeps a record of your earnings throughout your working life so it can later determine your eligibility and payment amount.

Your eligibility is determined by how many **work credits** you earn. You can earn up to 4 credits per year, so the credits are sometimes called "quarter credits" or "quarters of work." In 2014, for example, you earn one credit for each $1,200 you earn during the year, up to the maximum of 4 credits. Thus, with as little as $4,800 total earnings in 2014, you would earn all four credits for the year. The cost of credits goes up a bit with inflation each year.

For example you could earn $4,900 in January and not work the rest of the year. You would receive all four credits for the year based on your $4,900 earnings even though they were all paid in one month. (Before 1978 you actually had to earn at least $50 in a *calendar* quarter to receive work credit for that quarter. To this day work credits are sometimes called "quarters.")

You need 40 work credits (10 years of work under Social Security) to be eligible, if you were born in 1929 or later. (If you were born earlier you generally need one less credit for each year before 1929—see Figure 2.1. For example, for a birthdate in 1926, only 37 credits are required.) Under current Social Security law, no one will need more than 40 credits.

Bottom line: you need at least ten years of part-time work to qualify.

Sally has a bit over 10 years of work so she almost certainly has the required 40 work credits. Even though much of her work has been part-time, her earnings were high enough to earn all four credits each year because the credits are so "inexpensive."

Date of Birth	Work Credits Needed
1929 or later	40
1928	39
1927	38
1926	37
etc.	etc.

Figure 2.1. Work credits required for retirement eligibility.

Non-covered work. Notice the words "work under the Social Security system" used throughout this section. In some jobs, you do *not* pay Social Security taxes, and that work does *not* count toward retirement eligibility. Examples include most foreign work, work for the Federal civil service (those hired before 1984 only), and certain state or municipal employees whose retirement systems never merged with Social Security. (Local governments were given the option but some chose not to participate in the system.)

Foreign employment. Some people never get a chance to gain retirement eligibility under these rules, because much of their career was outside the U.S.:

William split his career between work in the U.S. and in the United Kingdom. Because of this split, he is not quite eligible for benefits under either system. If only he could combine his work records into one system, and get credit for his work in both countries.

Fortunately for William and others in his situation Social Security has entered into international agreements which provide for just such "totalization" of work records. Currently the U.S. has totalization treaties with many foreign systems, including those in Italy, Germany, Switzerland, Belgium, Norway, Canada (plus Quebec), the U.K., Sweden, Spain, and France. More are added periodically. If totalization affects you because of a foreign career, see "How International Agreements Can Help You" at www.ssa.gov/pubs/10180.html. You might also check with your foreign consulate or with Social Security.

(Note: U.S. military personnel serving overseas are not affected. Full credit for military service pay has automatically been posted to Social Security's records since 1957. For service before 1957, a service pay credit is manually added to the work record. For more information on military service and Social Security, see page 211.)

These *eligibility rules* determine whether you can receive a retirement payment at all, but they do not determine the *amount* of payment. If you have ten years of work under the system, you can be sure of two things: you are eligible for payments, and you will eventually receive them if you simply live to retirement age and apply. Computing the *amount* of your payment is a separate operation, addressed next.

HOW YOUR PAYMENT IS COMPUTED

General information about your computation

Sam Smith is positive he meets the age and work requirements—he has had substantial earnings his entire life—but he still wonders how his payment amount is actually computed, in dollars and cents.

The preceding section explains the rules for becoming *eligible* for a retirement payment. This section explains the method for *computing the amount* of your payment.

☆ Tips For Results: Obtaining Needed Work Credits ☆

If you have too few credits, and no foreign work to add to your work record, you still have two ways to get a payment from Social Security:

- You might have a current or former marriage to someone who is eligible (see Chapters 3 and 4 for details).

- Or you could work the additional years necessary to gain coverage (see Chapter 7 to learn exactly how many credits you need and how many you have). After all, you can earn all four credits available for the year with relatively low earnings— $4,800 earned anytime in 2014 will give you all four credits for the year.

The work credits are posted one at a time on the first day of each calendar quarter. SSA cannot give credit for a future quarter, so the fourth work credit will be posted on October 1.

Example: Suppose you turn 62 in January of 2014, and have 36 work credits counting your work in 2013. You need 40 credits to receive Social Security. You must earn at least $4,800 in 2014, and you will receive your qualifying 40th work credit on October 1, 2014—the first day of the fourth quarter. You would be eligible for Social Security as of October 2014.

Although the computation is fairly lengthy, all you need is grade school arithmetic, and you might enjoy computing your own Social Security benefit. Both the text below and Appendix A give sample computations for Sam Smith.

The short answer: your payment is roughly proportional to your lifetime earnings. In other words, it's proportional to your payments *into* the system. The rest of this section gives you the details.

Your Social Security payment amount is based on only two factors:

- Your *lifetime average earnings* (earnings factors), and

- Your *age when your payments begin* (age factors).

Earnings factors in your computation

Your lifetime average earnings

Most pensions are based on the level of work earnings, and Social Security is no exception. The higher your earnings during your working career, the higher your retirement payment. The amount of your retirement payment is a percentage of your *lifetime average earnings.*

Therefore Social Security keeps an accurate record of lifelong earnings—for you and every other U.S. worker. Your employer reports your earnings to SSA every year, and the Administration keeps a record throughout your lifetime. (If you are self-employed, your tax return includes the necessary report of self-employment earnings.) Your *earnings record* will be used to compute your retirement benefit.

The steps of the computation, moving from your earnings record to your Social Security payment amount, are summarized here and detailed in Appendix A (page 257).

Maximum annual amount posted

There is a cap or ceiling on the amount of earnings reportable to Social Security and subject to the 6.2% Social Security tax. In 2014, for example, the maximum taxable earnings for *Social Security* is $117,000. (There is no ceiling on the 1.45% *Medicare* tax). That ceiling level increases every year with inflation. The maximum earnings level that is taxable each year is called the *taxable earnings base.*

Looking at his earnings record (Appendix A, Figure A-1) Sam Smith sees that Column 2 gives the maximum earnings for each year from 1951 ($3,600) to 2014 ($117,000).

If your earnings are under the annual ceiling, you pay the 7.65% FICA tax on all earnings. In that case, all earnings are posted to your earnings record.

Nationwide, though, about 6% of us earn over the ceiling. If you are one of these high earners, only the first $117,000 of your 2014 earnings would be taxed for Social Security, and only the first $117,000 would appear on Social Security's records. Higher earnings would not increase your eventual Social Security benefit.

Sam's earnings for 1996 were actually $65,000. His earnings record shows only $62,700 in Column 5 because that was the maximum amount that could be posted for that year.

Since there is a maximum of posted earnings, there is also a maximum retirement payment computable from the postings. If a worker had maximum earnings every year and retired in 2014 at age 65, her 2014 Social Security payment would be $2,431 per month. (www.ssa.gov/OACT/COLA/examplemax.html).

The three computation steps

Once your earnings are posted to your record, the Social Security computation proceeds through three steps:

1: An inflation adjustment,

2: Determining your lifetime average earnings, and

3: Applying a formula to that average to determine your full retirement payment amount.

PIA: Your full retirement benefit

The end product of these steps is your *full retirement benefit* or *100% benefit*. This is the amount payable at your *Full Retirement Age (FRA)*, defined below under "Age Factors."

Your full retirement benefit is vitally important. It determines how much you will receive from Social Security, and how much anyone else applying on your record will receive. Think of it as the core or basis for every payment made on your record. Inside the Administration, your full retirement benefit is called your *Primary Insurance Amount* or PIA.

Let's take a look at how Social Security proceeds through the three steps of computing your PIA.

Step 1: Inflation adjustment

     In this step, Social Security applies an inflation adjustment to every year of earnings posted to your record.

     Over the years average wages have steadily risen as our entire economy experienced inflation. The average wages of today would seem like a fortune compared to our earnings in the 1950s and 60s. Similarly, the average wages of the 50's would be paltry indeed compared to today's earnings. For example, 1955's average wage was $3,301.44.

     Would it be fair to compute today's Social Security payment using the much smaller earnings of the 50's and 60's? Most would say no.

     Social Security takes inflation into account when your earnings are reviewed. The first step in computing your Social Security payment is to apply an inflation adjustment to every year of your earnings record.

     What figure does Social Security use to adjust for inflation? The figure used tracks *average wages* over the years.

Sam's computation (Appendix A, Figure A-1) shows the average wages measured by SSA for each year after 1950 (Column 3). In Sam's case each year's average wage is compared to 2009's average wage to determine the proper inflation adjustment (shown in Column 4).

     Why is Sam's inflation adjustment based on 2009's average wages—why not 2008 or 2010? Because the inflation factor in your Social Security computation is always the one in effect the year you *attain age 60*. This is called your *Base Year*. Even if the Social Security computation is not performed until a later year, the adjustment is "locked in" in your Base Year. Using age 60 is reasonable, because then all the computation factors will be known by age 62, when you are first eligible. (Stay tuned for how inflation affects later years.)

     Sam turned 60 in 2009, so that is his Base Year, and all his earnings are adjusted using 2009's inflation figures. If you turn 60 in a later year, for example 2013, then all your inflation adjustments would be based on 2013's higher average wages.

     Note that the inflation factor used for this allowance does not fully cancel out the effects of inflation for high earners:

*Bill Johnson turned 60 in 2009, just like Sam. Bill had **maximum** wages of $14,100 posted in 1975. The inflation factor for 1975 wages with a Base Year of 2009 is 4.7169491 (Figure A-1, Column 4). That means average wages increased by a factor of 4.7169491 from 1975 to 2007. Applying the inflation factor to Bill's 1975 earnings yields the following calculation:*

$14,100 x 4.7169491 = $66,508.98

Bill is surprised. He expected that his 1975 wages—the maximum allowed that year—would be inflated to somewhere near $106,800—the maximum in effect for 2009. Instead, only about two-thirds that amount will actually be available to use in Bill's payment computation.

Clearly, SSA's wage index used does not fully adjust higher earnings. Only if your earnings are exactly *average* would the inflation factor be perfectly fair. What this means is that *even after* the inflation index is applied, *recent* wages are frequently the highest wages.

☆ **Tips For Results: Planning for Early Retirement?** ☆

If you are considering retirement even before age 62, you may be depriving your earnings record of your highest earnings, at the peak of your career. You may also be depriving your record of those years that receive the best treatment in Social Security's inflation computation, if your earnings are above average. (See the Tips for Results below, "Using the Sliding Scale", for more information about the effect of early retirement.)

Be sure to use SSA's online estimators (see Chapter 7) to compare your payments from early retirement versus later retirement.

Step 1 is essential for fairness. When earnings from 30 years ago or more are used for your payment computation, some inflation adjustment is needed. By basing the adjustment on the increase in average wages, Social Security is using the factor that is most reasonable for most workers. And the factor is readily available from SSA's own historical wage records, simplifying the process.

Step 2: Your lifetime average earnings

After adjusting wages for inflation, the second step in computing your Social Security payment is to determine your lifetime average earnings.

What does Social Security mean by your "lifetime" average? Social Security bases your computation on your *best 35 years* of work. (For those born before 1929, fewer years are used, and fewer Work Credits are required for eligibility.)

Most private pensions, on the other hand, are based on the best three to five years of earnings—frequently the last years on the job, the peak of most careers. The Tips for Results section on page 47 explains the advantages and disadvantages of the 35-year computation.

The years used in your computation are the 35 years with the highest inflation-adjusted earnings—in other words, the 35 highest amounts from Step 1 of the computation.

The 35 years chosen do not have to be consecutive nor recent. Wherever the best (highest) years are, after the inflation adjustment, they will be picked—as long as they are after 1950. If you were a child actor, for example, your best years might be very early indeed.

Sam Smith's best 35 years appear in Figure A-1, Columns 7 and 8. Note that his "high 35" years are not a continuous run of years.

Sam is fortunate to have over 35 years of earnings. What if you don't have 35 years of posted earnings? Your *best* 35 years must still be used in the computation, even if some of them are "zero years" (years with no earnings posted to your record).

Sally Smith has only ten years with posted earnings. Yet her Social Security computation must be based on 35 years. Her ten work years will be included because they are her best years. The other 25 years used in the computation will be zero years that will not contribute toward a higher Social Security payment.

Once the 35 years with the highest inflation-adjusted wages are selected, the adjusted wages are totaled and averaged.

Sam's earnings in Figure A-1, Column 8 are totaled and averaged. The total is shown as the "Dividend" in Figure A-2. Sam's dividend is $2,435,501.96.

Social Security actually uses average *monthly* earnings, so the dividend—the total adjusted earnings from the best 35 years—is divided by 420, the number of months in 35 years. The result is called your *AIME*, pronounced like the name "Amy." AIME stands for Average Indexed Monthly Earnings. (The "Indexed" part of the name indicates that the inflation index was applied.)

Sam's AIME, shown in Figure A-2, is $5,798, representing his lifetime average monthly earnings throughout his career, after adjusting for inflation.

Your AIME is your lifetime average earnings, and is used in Step 3 to determine the amount of Social Security you will receive.

☆ Tips For Results: Your 35-Year Computation ☆

Basing your payments on your best 35 years carries certain advantages and disadvantages for most of us.

The **disadvantages** include:

- Your work record may be "spotty," meaning that work may not be posted for every year. This could be due to taking time off work to raise children, working in an industry with frequent layoffs, education years outside the the workforce, immigrating to the U.S. mid-career, taking lower pay while in military service or volunteer work, etc. In such cases, your lifetime average earnings will be lower than the steadier worker, and your Social Security computation will suffer as a result, even if the gaps occurred twenty years ago.

- You may have ended your career at the top of the pay scale, but it may have taken you a long career at lower earnings to climb to that level. If so, your *lifetime average* will be lower than a person who had top wages for more years in his or her career.

The biggest **advantage** is that if you choose to retire early—say, at age 56 or 58—and have a long steady work history, your lifetime average earnings will not be much changed. With 35 years being averaged together, some zeros in the last four to six years will have little impact. You've already established your track record, especially if you had fairly steady earnings over the years, or already have 35 years of work on your record.

Consider Janet Johnson, born in February 1952. She earned maximum wages every year of her work career.

- If Janet retired in February of 2014 at age 62, she would have $1981 per month payable from Social Security.

- On the other hand, if Janet retired five years earlier at age 57 and had *no further earnings*, her Social Security payment at age 62 would be $1929—a loss of only $52 per month. (You can get computations for your individual case, to help you make your own retirement plans. See Chapter 7 and Appendix E for details.)

Janet loses very little Social Security even with 5 years of non-work. The reason is the 35-year average—changing 5 years has little impact on the 35-year average.

Why 35 years? Because Social Security uses your *lifetime average earnings* as the basis of your retirement payments. The 35 years are said to represent the 40 career years from age 22 to age 62, with the lowest 5 years dropped out for equity.

There's a lot of sense in using lifetime earnings. Payments are then roughly proportional to lifetime FICA contributions. Suppose Sam Smith landed a big job with a big paycheck, stayed on the job for three years, and then quit, never to work again. Should Sam get maximum Social Security payments for all the years of his retirement, just because he was highly paid for three years? If the payments were based on his best three years, he'd be guaranteed a high retirement payment as soon as he got his three years in. Most of us would say that wouldn't be fair—to get the maximum, we would say, Sam has to show more perseverance. That's why Social Security uses the "lifetime average earnings" concept.

Step 3: Assigning a percentage

Once the 35 best years are averaged together, a formula is applied to determine your full Social Security payment amount. The formula basically assigns a percentage of your AIME to be paid to you, but there is a twist: not everyone receives the same percentage. It is a sliding scale.

The higher your lifetime average earnings, the higher your Social Security benefit payments, as you might expect. The average worker can expect a Social Security payment of about 41% of her AIME. That percentage is called the *replacement rate* because it shows how much of your paycheck is *replaced* by your Social Security payment.

Interestingly, though, higher earners receive a *lower replacement rate*, with very high earners receiving about 26% of their average earnings. Conversely, a retiree with low earnings can expect a higher replacement rate—up to 90% of the average earnings for very low earners. The computation is *progressive,* favoring lower earners. This is illustrated in Figure 2.2.

2013 Earnings	Social Security Payment	Replacement Ratio
$113,700 (maximum earnings)	$2,431/month	26%
$71,000	$2,018/month	34%
$44,000 (average earnings)	$1,521/month	41%
$20,000	$924/month	56%

Figure 2.2. How average earnings determine Social Security payments, illustrating the "progressive" nature of replacement rates. (Earnings are assumed to be steady at the level shown for life, after adjusting for inflation. Payment amounts are for filing in 2014 at age 65.)

The practice is somewhat like IRS's progressive income tax rates, but in reverse. With IRS, when you have higher earnings you not only pay more total tax dollars, you also pay taxes at a higher percentage rate. With Social Security, when you have higher earnings you get a higher Social Security payment, but it is actually a lower percentage of your earnings.

Why does Social Security use the progressive sliding scale? Because lower earners generally have less opportunity to save for retirement. Those with greater means, on the other hand, require less from the system in their retirement years.

Does this mean that Social Security is not an insurance program? No, it means that Social Security is a *social insurance* program, striking a balance between a purely private enterprise and a social program. In this case, Congress has decided that society's needs are better served by using the progressive sliding scale.

Sam's payment computation in Appendix A shows how the formula used in step 3 results in a lower reward for higher earnings. Sam's actual figures are as follows:

AIME	SSA Full Payment	Replacement Ratio
$5,798	$2,215	35%

Note that the higher your earnings, the higher your Social Security payment will be, even though your replacement ratio may drop. Higher earnings cannot decrease your payment.

This sliding scale has prompted some to observe that *Social Security taxes are regressive, but Social Security benefits are progressive:*

- FICA taxes are *regressive* because they are a fixed percentage for all wage levels and are not paid at all above the taxable earnings ceiling. Therefore lower earners have a larger percentage tax burden than higher earners.
- But benefits are *progressive* because lower earners receive a higher percentage of their taxes back, and there is a ceiling on benefits ($2,431 for a person age 65 in 2014).

☆ **Tips For Results: Using The Sliding Scale To Your Advantage** ☆

The sliding payment scale can work to your advantage if you are considering retirement before age 62. How? Because retiring early lowers your total lifetime earnings, compared to working longer.

- The *bad news* is that this will reduce your Social Security payment.

- The *good news* is that your lower earnings are providing a higher replacement percentage.

The result is that your Social Security may not decline as much as you thought. A 10% reduction in your lifetime earnings might mean only a 7% reduction in your Social Security payments. (See the Janet Johnson example above for an instance of this.)

To summarize: Social Security computes your retirement payment from your 35 best years of work (even if some are zeros), after adjusting for inflation.

That computation determines your *full retirement benefit* at your full retirement age—also called your Primary Insurance Amount or PIA.

You can see that the payment *computation* is totally separate from the 10-year work requirement to become *eligible* for payments.

The only other factor influencing your payment is your age when your payments begin.

Age factors in your computation

Sam wonders why the Social Security representative specified his payment "at age 65." Once he turns 62, does it make any difference how old he is?

The short answer: the earlier you start your Social Security payment, the less you get per month.

The amount paid is based on your birth date and your age when the payments start, so *when you file* will determine how much you'll be paid. Therefore you can affect the dollar amount of your Social Security payments by choosing *when your payments begin.*

Figure 2.3 shows the relationship between age (horizontal axis) and amount paid (vertical axis) for a person born from 1943 through 1954.

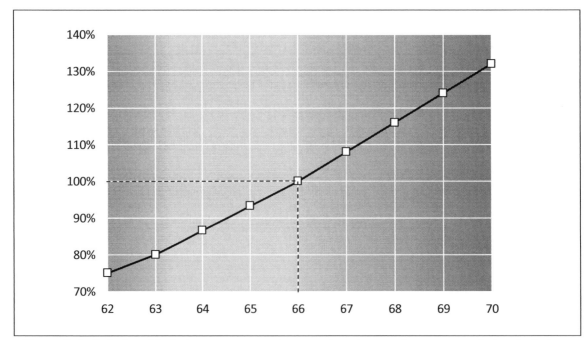

Figure 2.3: Relationship between payment amount and age when payments begin (where Full Retirement Age = 66).

To understand the details, let's start by defining the "Full Retirement Age."

Full Retirement Age (FRA). This is the age at which you can receive a full 100% payment from Social Security—a payment equal to your *Primary Insurance Amount,* defined above. Historically it was age 65, but that has changed:

- Age 67 is being phased in as the new Full Retirement Age.

- The phase-in is based on your birth year.

- Figure 2.4 shows your FRA as determined by your birth date.

You might file for your Social Security to begin at your Full Retirement Age, before it, or after it. Your choice will determine how much your monthly payment is for the rest of your life.

Payments starting at Full Retirement Age: full retirement benefit

The full retirement benefit is payable if your payments start at your Full Retirement Age. You would receive 100% of the computation based on your best 35 years of work—100% of your Primary Insurance Amount (PIA).

Year of Birth	Full Retirement Age
1937 or earlier	65
1938	65 and 2 months
1939	65 and 4 months
1940	65 and 6 months
1941	65 and 8 months
1942	65 and 10 months
1943 - 1954	66
1955	66 and 2 months
1956	66 and 4 months
1957	66 and 6 months
1958	66 and 8 months
1959	66 and 10 months
1960 and later	67

Figure 2.4: "Full Retirement Age"—the age to receive full Social Security benefits. This chart applies to both workers and spouses. See Figure 4.4 (page 88) for widow(er)s.

Sam's birth year is 1949. Therefore his FRA is 66 (Figure 2.4). If his Social Security payments start at that age, he will be paid his Primary Insurance Amount: $2,215 each month. (The $2,215 is in 2014 dollars. Sam could actually receive more due to cost-of-living-adjustments from 2014 to 2015, when he attains his FRA.)

Payments starting before Full Retirement Age—reduced payments for early retirement

You may file for early retirement payments as young as age 62. The catch: your payment amount is *permanently* reduced. The earlier you file the lower your monthly payment for the rest of your life.

The reason is simple. By filing early, you will receive more payments, so the amount must be reduced to equalize your lifetime payments with those of older retirees.

The reduction is computed by counting the months until you reach your FRA. A two-stage reduction applies:

- Stage 1: For the first 36 months of early filing, payment is reduced 5/9 of 1% for each month.

- Stage 2: For any additional early months, payment is reduced 5/12 of 1% for each month.

Example 1: Sally files for Social Security to begin at age 63. Her FRA is 66. Since she files 36 months early, her payment will be reduced 20% (5/9% x 36 months = 20%). She will receive an 80% payment.

Example 2: George, like Sally, files for Social Security to begin at age 63. However, his FRA is 67, so he is filing 48 months early. His payment will be reduced as follows:

20% for the first 36 months of reduction
(5/9% x 36 months = 20%).

5% for the next 12 months of reduction
(5/12% x 12 months = 5%).

Total reduction: 25% (20% + 5%).

He will receive a 75% payment.

Example 3: Fred files for Social Security to begin at age 64 and 6 months. His FRA is 67. Since he files 30 months early, his payment will be reduced 16.67% (5/9% x 30 months). He will receive an 83.33% payment.

We can now understand Sam Smith's payment amount at age 65 (example at top of chapter and Appendix A):

Sam's birth year is 1949. Therefore his FRA is 66 (from Figure 2.4).

If Sam files for payments beginning at his age 65, he will be filing 12 months early (age 66 minus age 65 is 1 year or 12 months).

His payment will be reduced 6.67% (5/9% x 12 months = 6.67%). Therefore his age 65 payment will be 93.33% of his full payment.

His full payment amount is $2,215 (from his lifetime average earnings).

Therefore his age 65 payment will be $2067 ($2,215 x 93.33%)

Payments starting after Full Retirement Age—higher payments for delayed retirement

If you delay filing for payments until after your FRA, you will receive a permanent raise. For people reaching retirement age today, this *Delayed Retirement Credit* is an 8% raise in your payments for each year of late filing. The amount of your "bonus" is determined by your birth year, as illustrated in Figure 2.5.

Year of Birth	Yearly Percentage Increase
1916 or earlier	1%
1917 - 1924	3%
1925 - 1926	3.5%
1927 - 1928	4%
1929 - 1930	4.5%
1931 - 1932	5%
1933 - 1934	5.5%
1935 - 1936	6%
1937 - 1938	6.5%
1939 - 1940	7%
1941 - 1942	7.5%
1943 or later	8%

Figure 2.5: Delayed Retirement Credits.

Our Shifting Retirement Age

Age 65 was originally set as the retirement age in 1935, when the Social Security Act was first written. But why was age 65 chosen as the retirement age—why not 67 or 63? Social Security lore cites two possible explanations:

- Perhaps Uncle Sam wasn't very generous. Life expectancy in 1935 was only about 61. Therefore the odds would be against anyone living long enough to receive full benefits.

- Or perhaps Uncle Sam wasn't very original. Age 65 had already been set as the retirement age in the world's first Social Security system, Germany's, created under Chancellor Otto von Bismarck in the 1880s. This second explanation suggests that the German system became a model program, copied by other nations as the idea of Social Security spread.

Whatever the explanation, age 65 continued to be the Full Retirement Age from 1935 to 1983, when the age limit was raised as part of the 1983 amendments to the Social Security Act. Two explanations were offered for the change:

- First, people are living longer and healthier lives now than in 1935, so an increased retirement age simply reflects the greater life expectancy. In fact, with the current at-birth life expectancy around 79, the Full Retirement Age would have to be about 83 to mirror the situation in 1935.

- Second, raising the retirement age saves SSA money, thus putting the program on sounder financial footing—the key goal of the 1983 amendments.

Age 62 was introduced as the "early retirement" age for women in 1956, and extended to men in 1961. It is retained under present law. However, age 62 payments decrease as the Full Retirement Age increases. Thus, increasing the retirement age reduces payments for nearly everyone, saving money for the system.

Delayed Retirement Credits are actually awarded on a month-by-month basis (similar to early retirement reductions). For each month of delayed retirement, you would receive 1/12 of the yearly percentage increase.

Sam was born in 1949. He could get an 8% increase for every year he delays his Social Security (Figure 2.5).

If he waits until age 70 to file, he would receive an increase for 4 years (age 70 minus his FRA of 66):

4 years x 8% = 32%

Sam would receive a 132% payment. Instead of $2,215 per month he would receive $2,923 per month.

You can file any month

Note that you need not file for benefits in your birthday month, nor on the first of the year, nor in December, as some people believe. There are no such restrictions. You may start your payments in *any* month, provided you are retired and over 62—or over FRA whether or not you are retired.

You should file your claim three months before you want your payments to start. (Chapter 9 defines how much work is allowed in "retirement." Chapter 8 gives details on filing claims.)

Sam was thinking about retiring in June so he could start off with a summer trip. Even though that is not the first of the year nor his birth month, Social Security will compute his exact payment by knowing his exact age.

Once you specify what month your payments should begin, Social Security counts how many months that date is before or after your Full Retirement Age. Then SSA automatically makes the necessary adjustment to your payment amount: a reduction if you are younger than your Full Retirement Age, or an increase if you are older.

How to get the most.

How can you receive the most money overall—by starting your Social Security at age 62, at your Full Retirement Age, or at age 70? Where is the break-even point? See Chapter 10 for answers (page 223).

To summarize: The month your payments begin determines what *percentage* of your full retirement payment you will receive. Your payment could be reduced for early filing, or increased for late filing.

WEP: A Special Computation for Some

All of the above explains the normal process for computing a Social Security retirement payment. However, you might be subject to a different, lower computation.

The people affected are those getting a retirement pension from a job where *no Social Security FICA taxes were paid.*

Generally, this means certain Civil Service workers, including some Federal, State, and local employees whose retirement systems were not part of the Social Security system.

The largest group affected are Federal employees hired before 1984 (those hired later are automatically covered under Social Security, and not subject to this special computation). **Note:** Federal employees in the Federal Employee Retirement System (FERS) are *not subject to this special lower computation.* They are eligible for a normal Social Security computation. The same goes for most, but not all, state and municipal workers.

The number of people affected is very small, and the list of exceptions is long. Check with Social Security to see if you are affected.

The reason

Imagine for a moment how your Social Security earnings record appears if you are one of these Civil Service workers.

For all your Civil Service years, your earnings were exempt from Social Security taxation. None of your Civil Service work is posted to the SSA records. In fact, those years are posted as *zero years* (except in the case of outside jobs concurrent with your Civil Service work). Then you retire from your Civil Service career and start collecting a Civil Service pension.

You might also have enough "outside" work covered under Social Security—10 years—to be eligible for Social Security retirement benefits. But all the years of Civil Service work are zeroes, "hidden from view," since they don't appear on Social Security records. The remaining few years of *covered* earnings look, to a computer's eye, like very low lifetime earnings. This would normally trigger a Social Security computation yielding a very high percentage of average wages, based on the progressive sliding percentage scale (see Figure 2.2, page 48).

That high percentage makes sense in the case of *true* low-wage workers, to compensate for the lack of opportunity to save for retirement. But your earnings aren't really low; they only *look* low to the computer because you were working under a different retirement system, earning a pension separate from and in addition to your Social Security.

In your case, then, the high replacement percentage reserved for low earners would be an unfair *windfall.*

The reduction

Starting in 1986, a solution to the windfall was employed. Called the *Windfall Elimination Provision* or WEP, it eliminated part of the higher percentage bonus for Civil Service workers. It basically removes some of the progressivity in the computation. Under WEP, a modified computation is used, yielding a lower Social Security benefit payment.

If you are affected you will suffer a reduction of up to $408 per month in 2014 dollars. (That's the worst case; the reduction could be less if you have lower Social Security earnings, if you have many years of Social Security earnings posted, or if your non-covered pension is low.) www.ssa.gov/retire2/wep-chart.htm

Betsy had a long career in the federal government. She also worked for several years in the private sector while she was in school. When she retired from her federal job, she became self-employed to supplement her federal pension. By the time she is 65, she will have well over 10 years of work in the private sector under the Social Security system.

At that time she can retire and draw both her federal Civil Service pension and her Social Security. Her federal pension will be unaffected by her Social Security, but her Social Security payments may be up to $408 per month lower because of her federal pension.

Betsy remembers when she requests an estimate from SSA to subtract about $408 from the estimated payment. She knows that SSA's estimates cannot account for her federal pension.

Note that WEP affects *only* your Social Security payments (not your *other* pension). In addition, WEP will affect you only if you are eligible for both Social Security and a pension from a job not covered under Social Security. If your other pension is from work where you paid Social Security taxes, your Social Security benefits will *not* be affected.

*Sam Smith earned a company pension while he worked, in addition to his Social Security. His company pension will not affect his Social Security. He can draw full payments from both the company pension and Social Security because he paid into Social Security the entire time he worked under the company pension plan. He did **not** work under a plan where **no Social Security taxes were paid**. The Windfall Elimination Provision does not apply to him.*

The Windfall Elimination Provision, if it applies to you, affects your Social Security payments made on *your own* work record. A similar provision, called Government Pension Offset, affects your Social Security payments made on *your spouse's* work record, if you get a Civil Service pension. The Government Pension Offset is explained on page 69.

For more information on WEP, go to www.ssa.gov/gpo-wep/ or see the SSA Factsheet "Windfall Elimination Provision," at www.ssa.gov/pubs/10045.html. A WEP calculator is available at www.ssa.gov/retire2/anyPiaWepjs04.htm.

Other special situations

Certain other people have special coverage rules or computations, including:

- Self-employed persons
- Corporate officers
- Insurance sales people expecting renewal commissions
- Farmers and ranchers
- Domestic workers
- Clergy

This book cannot cover the individual rules for these occupations in detail, but SSA produces fact sheets for each of them. If your work appears on the list or if you think another special rule might apply to you, see www.ssa.gov/pubs/index.html, especially under "Work and Earnings," or contact SSA for more information.

RETIREMENT COMPUTATION EXAMPLE

Let's look at another example to help make the ideas in this chapter clear. Meet John. We are going to get to know John better in coming chapters, and learn more about him and his family. But for now we need only the basics.

John is a fairly typical wage-earner. Over the years he has had some prosperous and lean times, but overall life has been good to him. Now that he is nearing retirement age, he wants to know where he stands with Social Security. So he calls the Social Security phone number: 1-800-SSA-1213.

While John is on the phone, the Social Security representative is typing at the computer. She calls up John's work record and an estimate of his full payment amount. On the whole, John's wages have been somewhere between average and maximum. He learns that this means his Social Security retirement payments will be between average and maximum, too. His full payment is estimated at $2,000 per month.

John learns that his Full Retirement Age is 66. He understands that he will get the full $2,000 per month if he waits until then to start drawing his retirement payments, but he wants to know what happens if he starts earlier.

You already know the answer: John learns that he could draw a payment as early as age 62. At 62 he would be eligible for 75% of his full payment amount, or $1,500 a month ($2,000 x 75% = $1,500).

Next, John wants to know what his payment would be if he started his payments somewhere between 62 and 66—for example, at 63 or 64. He learns that at 64, his payments are reduced for 24 months at 5/9 of 1% per month:

24 months x 5/9% = 13.33% reduction.

This leaves him with an 86.67% payment, since 100% - 13.33% = 86.67%.

$2,000 x 86.67% = $1,733.40

Similarly, John learns that his average-to-high lifetime earnings will yield him the following benefits:

Age 66	100% payment	$2,000 per month
Age 65	93.33% payment	$1,866
Age 64	86.67% payment	$1,733
Age 63	80% payment	$1,600
Age 62	75% payment	$1,500

. . . and he may file in any intervening month, for a proportional adjustment.

We'll learn more about John and his family in the following chapters, as we examine family and survivor benefits.

FOR MORE INFORMATION...

"Retirement Benefits"
www.ssa.gov/pubs/10035.html

"Social Security Retirement Planner"
www.ssa.gov/retire2/

"How International Agreements Can Help You"
www.ssa.gov/pubs/10180.html

"Windfall Elimination Provision"
www.ssa.gov/pubs/10045.html

"Information for Government Employees"
www.socialsecurity.gov/gpo-wep/

"Your Retirement Benefit: How It Is Figured" go to
www.ssa.gov/pubs/index.html, select "Retirement" in the radio buttons, find the
title, and select your birth year in the drop-down box

CHAPTER THREE

FAMILY BENEFITS

BACKGROUND INFORMATION ON FAMILY BENEFITS

Sam and Sally Smith (page 37) are concerned that Sally's payment on her own work record may be very low. Is there some way she could draw part of Sam's payment?

Yes. One of the key strengths of the Social Security system is the provision for *family benefits* for the families of retired or disabled workers. Under certain circumstances, your dependent family members are eligible for Social Security payments—payments *in addition to* whatever payments you receive yourself.

These additional payments, called *auxiliary benefits* inside the Administration, recognize the greater financial need inherent in a larger family. They also acknowledge the support you receive from your family during your work years—support such as homemaking assistance, transportation, help with child rearing, and other personal maintenance we need to perform at your best. All this support increases your productivity and deserves the special recognition given by the Social Security program.

Eligible family members are:

- your child(ren)

- spouse, and

- former spouse(s)

Family benefits are additional payments made to members of the worker's family. They do not reduce the amount paid to the worker.

As mentioned, payments can be made "under certain circumstances." Is this a catch? Not really; the rules will be explored in this chapter, but they are fairly reasonable on the whole. The most important rules are these:

- *A family benefit will be paid unless you (the family member) are eligible for a **higher benefit** on another work record, including your own.* In other words, if you are eligible in two ways—as a family member and as a worker in your own right—Social Security will generally pay you the *higher* of the two benefits.

- *For you to draw a family payment on a worker's record, the worker must be retired or disabled, and drawing a Social Security payment of his or her own.* An exception for former spouses appears below. Another exception is when the worker *suspends* his or her payments (page 232).

- *To be eligible, you must be retired.* Family benefits are intended to replace earnings lost due to retirement or other periods of non-work. That means your earnings must meet the same limits as those used for other Social Security recipients. The limits, and an exception if you are over FRA, are described on page 199.

We'll see how these rules work in examples throughout this chapter, and more examples appear at the end of the chapter. Figure 3.1 gives a summary of family benefits, with more detail in the text.

Are you currently unmarried? Read on, because family benefits include payments for *former spouses*. In addition, any children you have might also be eligible. If you are a widow or widower, see Chapter 4 for details on survivor benefits.

BENEFITS FOR THE WORKER'S SPOUSE

Spousal benefits are the most common family benefit paid. Here we will closely examine the rules governing spouse payments, giving particular attention to:

- the definition of a spouse,

- age rules, and

- payment amounts,

to see if you or someone in your family might qualify for spousal benefits.

Definition of Spouse

A spouse can be either sex—a wife or a husband. A spouse may be *currently* married to the worker, or may be a *former* spouse, i.e. divorced from the worker. There are a few special rules for former spouses which we'll look at in a moment.

A spouse must be (or have been) legally married to the worker. Generally, if state law recognizes a legal marriage relationship between individuals, then so does Social Security. There are a few special areas described below.

PERSON	BENEFIT AMOUNT (Percentage of worker's Full Payment Amount)
SPOUSE	
Full Retirement Age or older	50%
Age 62 (assuming FRA of 66)	35%
Any age, caring for the worker's entitled child under 16	50%
Requirements: • Worker must be on Social Security (or have suspended payments) • Claimant must be age 62+, or caring for worker's entitled child	
FORMER SPOUSE	
Full Retirement Age or older	50%
Age 62 (assuming FRA of 66)	35%
Requirements: • Worker must be age 62+; not necessarily on Social Security • Marriage lasted 10 years or more • Claimant age 62+ • Claimant currently unmarried	
CHILD	
Any age	50%

Requirements:
• Worker must be on Social Security
• Child must be unmarried and either:
  • Under 18, or
  • Under 19 and in high school, or
  • Adult but disabled before age 22.	

NOTE: Family maximum may reduce total amount payable to family.	

Figure 3.1: Summary of benefits for family of retired or disabled worker.

Common-law marriages

Common-law marriages are recognized if they are legally entered into. Common-law marriages are legal in several states, and once entered into are recognized by other states and by Social Security.

Legal impediment

John and Marsha apply for Social Security as a married couple and provide a marriage certificate as proof. Only then do they realize that the certificate was not properly recorded with the state.

In cases like this, SSA looks for "good faith" on the part of the married couple and in most cases will determine a spousal relationship exists, and award spousal payments.

Same-sex spouses

Spousal benefits for same-sex couples are available in certain circumstances. The marriage had to take place in a state that then legally recognized same-sex marriage, and the worker must reside in a state that recognizes same-sex marriage at the time of filing. Claims previously put on hold awaiting policy decisions are now being processed.

For any marriage, if there is a question about your legal status you should discuss the question with Social Security now to clear up any possible problems. There is a good likelihood that SSA will rule in your favor.

Special rules for former (divorced) spouse

If you apply as a former (divorced) spouse, you must meet the same marriage requirements as the worker's current spouse (shown immediately above). In addition, you must meet three special requirements:

- You must be at least 62. This age limit means you cannot qualify at a younger age even if you have the worker's child in your care.

- You must be *currently unmarried*.

- You must have been married to the worker for *at least ten years* before the divorce. The ten years run from the date of marriage to the date your divorce was final. To prove the length of marriage you usually need to supply a marriage certificate and divorce decree.

Sam Smith's former spouse, Janet, may qualify for former spouse benefits on Sam's work record. Janet is over 62, retired, and currently unmarried. She was married to Sam for 12 years. When Janet applies for her own Social Security, SSA will automatically check to see if she can draw more on Sam's record than on her own record, and pay her the higher of the two.

These *former spouse benefits* acknowledge the fact that in a ten-year marriage, an economic union was established between the members of a couple, and that this union persists even after the marriage ends. There are other areas of American law where this idea is expressed. For instance, a divorce decree with

---

☆ THE INSIDE STORY ☆

Why Special Rules for Former Spouses?

Note that the worker must be 62, but need not be on Social Security for a former spouse to be eligible (page 66), if the divorce is over two years old. This is different from the rules for current spouses, where the worker must have applied for Social Security.

Before 1985, divorced spouses were subject to the same requirement as a current spouse. That is, a divorced spouse could not draw spousal payments until the worker applied for Social Security. Why did Congress change the rule? What problem prompted the change? Consider the following example:

*When George, a worker, went to file for his retirement payment in 1983, he was told that his former spouse, Eunice, could draw Social Security on his record. Carrying a grudge for many years, George responded that, in that case, he would **never apply**.*

Under the old rules, Eunice would have waited and waited for a Social Security payment based on their ten-year marriage. Eunice might be impoverished, perhaps eligible for public assistance, but would basically be held hostage by George's retirement decision, over which she had no influence.

Therefore, an exception was made. Effective in 1985, Eunice could draw on George's work record if George was over 62, even if George never applied for Social Security. The divorce must be final for at least two years.

Is this unfair to the current spouse who must wait for the worker to retire? Generally not, since a *current spouse* has access to the worker's current earnings; the *former spouse* does not. So the former spouse's eligibility should not be blocked by the worker's earnings.

provision for spousal support or alimony shows that an economic union persists beyond the divorce date.

Another special rule for a divorced spouse is that *you need not wait for the worker to retire* if you have been divorced at least two years. As long as you are 62 and retired, you can draw payments on the worker's record as soon as the worker reaches age 62, whether or not the worker retires and whether or not the worker applies for Social Security.

Janet is already 62 and retired. Her former husband Sam is 62 but still working and not drawing Social Security. Nevertheless, Janet applies for Social Security on Sam's work record and her payments begin, years before Sam is ready to retire.

Further illustration of these rules will be found in the "Examples" section below.

Age rules for spousal benefits

There are really only two rules about age eligibility for spousal benefits. The first rule is that you must be at least 62, just like a retiring worker.

The second rule is an exception to the age 62 rule (and a big exception it is). You may be eligible at *any* age, provided you have a child of the worker in your care. The child must be:

- under age 16 or disabled, and

- drawing Social Security payments on the worker's record.

Note that the age 62 exception does not apply to divorced spouses. If you are divorced from the worker, payments are possible only if you are over 62—even if you are caring for the worker's child.

The first rule means that if you have reached the early retirement age of 62, you are potentially eligible for payments on your spouse's or, if currently unmarried, your ex-spouse's work record. You might also be eligible for payments on *your own* work record.

The second rule means that if you are caring for your young or disabled child, and your spouse is retired or disabled, *both you and the child* may be eligible for Social Security payments. This is true even if you are well below retirement age—say, 35 years old. Keep in mind you will have to meet the same work limits as most other Social Security recipients; see Chapter 9 for details.

Fred Ferguson retires at age 62 and applies for Social Security. He learns that his 14-year-old child, Frank, will also receive Social Security. In addition,

Fred's wife Fran, 52, will get Social Security because of Frank's entitlement. Her payments will continue, as long as she meets the earnings limits, until Frank turns 16. Then she will have to wait until she turns 62 to become re-entitled.

Payment amount for spouses

If you are eligible for spousal benefits, you will receive a certain percentage of the worker's *full payment amount* (the benefit payable to the worker at 66 or other full retirement age). Your payment is computed on the *full payment*, not on what the retired worker is *actually receiving*.

Fred's 100% payment is $1000 per month, but he draws payment at age 62, with a 25% reduction for early retirement. His payment is then actually $750 (75% x $1000 = $750). However, the spousal benefit for his wife Fran is computed as a percentage of his full $1000 payment, not the $750 he receives. Fran's payment is determined only by Fran's age and Fred's full benefit amount, regardless of Fred's age and payment amount.

If you are eligible for spousal benefits because you are *caring for the worker's child,* you will be paid 50% of the worker's full payment amount, regardless of your age.

Fran's payment is 50% of Fred's full payment amount. 50% of $1000 = $500 per month. Fred will draw a 75% payment at the same time Fran draws a 50% payment.

If you are eligible for spouse benefits *only because of your age* your payment computation is a little more complicated.

Payments starting at Full Retirement Age—50% payment

If you are at least age 66 (or other Full Retirement Age—see page 51) when you first apply for payments, you will be eligible for the full 50% of the worker's full payment amount. There is no increase for filing after FRA.

☆ **Reform Note:** Some reform proposals would reduce the maximum spousal payment to 33% of the worker's payment.

Payments starting before Full Retirement Age—reduced payments for early retirement

You can file for early retirement spousal payments as young as age 62. Early payments are reduced as follows:

- Stage 1: For the first 36 months of early filing, payment is reduced 25/36 of 1% for each month.

- Stage 2: For any additional early months, payment is reduced 5/12 of 1% for each month.

This payment reduction is very similar to the way a retired worker's payments are reduced (see page 52). The same Full Retirement Age (FRA) is used for workers and spouses; see Figure 2.4 (page 51). Note that the first stage, using 25/36 of 1%, is a slightly different reduction rate than retired workers (5/9 of 1%). The second stage is the same reduction rate.

John Jones is retiring at age 66 with a $1000 full payment amount. His wife Marsha is turning age 62, and files for Social Security on John's record. Marsha's FRA is 66.

Marsha's payment will be reduced as follows:

- *25% reduction for the first 36 months of reduction (25/36% x 36 months)*

- *5% reduction for the next 12 months of reduction (5/12% x 12 months).*

- *Total reduction: 30% from the full 50% spouse payment.*

Marsha's payment amount will be computed as follows:

- *50% payment = $500 ($1000 x 50%).*

- *$500 – 30% = $350.*
  Marsha will be paid $350 per month, starting at age 62.

In addition to monthly cash payments, spousal benefits can include Medicare at age 65. See Chapter 6 for details.

Dual entitlement

As noted above, if you are eligible both as the spouse of a worker and as a worker in your own right, you will receive the *higher* of the two payments. You cannot receive both added together.

If dually entitled, your own retirement payments have priority. You will be paid your own retirement benefit first. Then, if you can get more as a spouse, your own payment will be supplemented up to the level of the spousal payment.

Sally Smith can draw $300 on her own work record at age 66. Sam Smith's full payment amount is $2,215, so Sally could draw $1,107 as Sam's spouse (50% of $2,215). She will draw her full $300 on her own record and have an additional $807 added to her payment from Sam's record. Her payments will not affect Sam's payments in any way.

If you are eligible for more on your own record than as a spouse, spousal payments are impossible. No spousal claim will be taken. You will draw only your own retirement payment.

If you are under FRA, you will be *required* to apply for both your own retirement and your spousal payment, if a spousal payment is possible. This is called *deemed filing,* i.e. you are *deemed* to file for both benefits when you file for one. If you apply under FRA, your own benefits and your spousal benefits are like a bundled package.

If you first file at FRA or above, deemed filing no longer applies. You can file for "Spousal-Only" payments without filing on your own work record, holding you own higher payments in reserve. The two benefits are "unbundled." That allows you to draw first one payment and then the other. You can use this as a strategy to maximize total lifetime Social Security benefits (see Chapter 10).

GPO: A special computation for some

If you receive a pension from *work not covered by Social Security,* i.e. a government pension, your government pension may reduce your Social Security benefits. Your pension may reduce Social Security payments on *your own* work record; that reduction is called the *Windfall Elimination Provision,* and is described on page 55. Your government pension also reduces, or *offsets,* Social Security *spousal* payments you get on your spouse's work record. The provision for reducing your spousal benefits is called *Government Pension Offset (GPO).*

Government Pension Offset affects Social Security spousal and widow(er)'s benefits. The amount of the reduction is equal to two-thirds of the amount of your government pension.

The Government Pension Offset was enacted to provide *equity* in the amount of your spousal benefits. Consider the fact that Sally Smith cannot receive full payments on her own work record, plus full spousal benefits on Sam's work record; she gets the *higher* of the two, but not *both.* The total amount payable to Sally is limited. Similarly, the Government Pension Offset limits the total amount payable to a person eligible for both a government pension and a Social Security spousal benefit.

Sally's neighbor, Grace, is a retired federal employee. Grace receives a Civil Service pension of $300 per month. Grace's husband Gus has the same full Social Security payment amount as Sam Smith: $2,215 per month. Therefore, Grace would normally be eligible for a $1,107 spousal payment from Social Security (50% of Gus's $2,215). However, due to her government pension the $1,107 will be offset, or reduced, by $200 (two-thirds of her $300 government pension). Her spousal benefit will be $907 instead of $1,107.

This is similar to Sally's example (in the section above titled "dual entitlement"). Sally is eligible for $300 on her own work record, so her spousal benefit from Sam's record is limited to $807.

Notice that Grace's total income of $1,207 ($300 federal pension + $907 spousal Social Security) is greater than Sally's $1,107 ($300 own Social Security + $807 spousal Social Security). Even with the GPO, government pensioners are financially advantaged compared to workers under Social Security. Only two-thirds of their government pension counts against their spousal benefits, compared to 100% of Social Security.

For more information on the offset, see the SSA Factsheet "Government Pension Offset," available at www.ssa.gov/pubs/10007.html. A GPO calculator is at www.ssa.gov/retire2/gpo-calc.htm.

To summarize: You can receive payments on the work record of your spouse or former spouse. If you are dually eligible as a spouse *and* as a worker in your own right, you can draw the higher amount. For more information about how spousal benefits will work in your case, see the "Examples" section below.

BENEFITS FOR THE WORKER'S CHILD

Is a minor child going to be part of your retirement? Are you disabled and raising children? Or are you concerned about your disabled adult child in your advancing years? If so this section will be very important to you.

Child's benefits are commonly paid by Social Security, yet they are little-known and even less understood. The general idea is that SSA will pay benefits for your child if you are retired or disabled, so long as the child meets certain requirements.

This section will be especially important if *you* are a minor or are disabled and your parent is retired or disabled. If so, you will learn exactly how you can receive payments on your parent's work record. (If the worker is deceased, see Chapter 4, Survivor Benefits, for more information.)

Definition of child

For your child to qualify for child's benefits, *you* must be eligible for your own Social Security payments as a retired or disabled worker, and your *child* must meet the definitions in this section. The child must be:

Your child, and
Unmarried, and be:
- Under 18, **or**

- Under age 19 and a full-time elementary or high school student, **or**

- Age 18 or over and under a total disability. The disability must have begun before age 22. For details see page 117.

The child is your child if she is:

- Your legitimate child,

- Your natural child (if acknowledged as your child in writing or in legal proceedings),

- Your legally adopted child, or

- Your stepchild.

The rule of thumb here is that if State law would recognize the child as your heir in its intestacy inheritance laws, then Social Security will recognize your child as well.

There is also limited provision for a grandchild or step-grandchild to receive payments on your work record. The grandchild's parents must be deceased or disabled. In addition, the grandchild must be your dependent.

Examples

Fred has a natural son Frank and a stepdaughter, Karen, both in their teens.

Both will be eligible for child's payments on Fred's record once Fred is eligible for Social Security retirement or disability.

Karen is a high school senior when she turns 18. Her Social Security payments do not stop until June, when she graduates.

Frank turns 19 shortly before his own graduation. His payments stop when he turns 19.

Payment amount for child's benefits

If eligible, your child is entitled to 50% of your full payment amount, regardless of what percentage you, the worker, receive. Thus, the child's computation is similar to a spouse computation, as described on page 67. However, there is no reduction for a child's age.

Fred's 100% benefit is $1000. Karen is entitled to $500 per month.

If you have two eligible children, they might *each* receive $500 per month. However, there is a limit to total family benefits, known as the *family maximum payment.*

FAMILY MAXIMUM PAYMENT

Kathy has a large family. At 66, she applies for a 100% Social Security payment on her own record. Her husband will get a 50% spousal payment on Kathy's record. And each of her 5 minor children is eligible to receive a 50% payment. Could Kathy's family receive higher payments under Social Security retirement than they ever received in wages while in the workforce?

In fact, there is a limit to the benefits payable to Kathy's family members. A *Family Maximum Payment* is factored into every Social Security computation. The family maximum ranges from 1.5 to 1.8 times the worker's full payment amount, based on a complex four-stage formula.

Once the maximum is being paid to a household, no higher payments will be issued, even if another individual becomes eligible. If, say, another child is added to a record already paying the maximum, the same dollar amount is simply divided into smaller shares to be distributed to the new, larger household.

In other words, if someone else sits down to dinner, almost everyone receives a smaller slice of the pie.

There are two kinds of benefits *not* affected by the family maximum: Payments to *workers* and payments to *former spouses.*

- The worker's payment remains a fixed amount no matter how many other family members are added to the payment record; the worker is *primary.*

- Former spouses are not considered part of the family unit, so their payments do not affect anyone else on the record.

Let's look at our example family to see how the family maximum works.

Kathy is receiving a $1,200 age-66 payment. Her family maximum is then $1,992, an amount computed from her $1,200 full payment (using the 2014 formula).

If Kathy has one eligible child, the child is entitled to $600 (50% of Kathy's full $1,200). Total family payments are then:

Kathy	$1,200
+Child 1	+$600
Total	$1,800

Since this total payment is under the family maximum, the entire $1,800 is paid.

What if Kathy has two eligible children? Without a family maximum, the computation would have looked like this:

Kathy	$1,200
Child 1	$600
+Child 2	+$600
Total	$2400

But since this exceeds the $1,992 family maximum, the children will **not** receive full payments. Instead, two steps are used to compute the children's benefits, while still ensuring that Kathy **gets the full amount she is due**:

Step 1:

Family Maximum:	$1,992
—Kathy's share:	—$1,200
Amount available for dependents:	$792

Step 2:

Amount available for dependents:	$792
Divided by number of dependents:	÷2
Amount for each child:	$396

Then the final payment schedule is:

Kathy	$1,200
Child 1	$396
+Child 2	+$396
Total	$1,992

Similarly, if we were to add more children, or a spouse, to Kathy's eligible family, the $792 available for family members would simply be split among them, in smaller and smaller shares. Kathy would always be eligible for her full $1,200, and all other family members would split the $792 evenly.

Former spouses and the family maximum

The family maximum rules *do not apply to former spouses.* If Kathy has a former husband eligible on her record, for example, he will get his full $600 payment (50% of Kathy's $1,200) even if Kathy's immediate household family is already receiving the family maximum.

Why? Because the ex-spouse is considered a separate family unit. By treating former spouses as separate family units, Social Security does not get in the middle of conflicts between former spouses.

Combined family maximums

A child is sometimes eligible two ways: as the child of both a working father and a working mother. Which of the two family maximums should be used—the mother's or the father's? In that case, the payment rule is a bit more complicated than simply using the higher of the two. An additional computation is performed, yielding a *combined family maximum* for the child and any siblings. This combined family maximum can be as much as the sum of the two maximums together, but with a combined maximum limit.

Callie is eligible for up to $600 as Kathy's daughter. But because her brother Carl is also drawing on Kathy's record Callie can only receive $396.

Later Callie's father, Ken, starts receiving Social Security. Because Callie and Carl are eligible on Ken's higher record as well as Kathy's, their family maximums can be combined. The children each receive $650 instead of $396.

EXAMPLES

John and Marsha

John and Marsha Jones are married. Both have a Full Retirement Age of 66, and John's full payment amount is $1,000. Let's take a look at spouse benefits for this couple, using a variety of different work histories for Marsha.

Let's take the basic case first. Assume that John and Marsha are both 66. That makes John eligible for his full $1,000 payment. Marsha's payment depends on her own work history. Here we will consider four different possibilities, summarized in Figures 3.2 - 3.5:

Both age 66.

(1)   If Marsha is *not eligible* on her own record: $500.

Marsha will be eligible for a spousal payment of 50% of John's full payment, even if she is not eligible for any payment based on her own work record (in other words, she lacks the required 40 work credits from 10 years of work— page 39) . Marsha's payment is *in addition to* John's, and does not reduce John's payment. Therefore Marsha will receive $500 per month (50% of John's $1,000). John and Marsha together will receive a total of $1,500 per month (John's $1,000 + Marsha's $500).

(2)   If Marsha is eligible for a *smaller* payment on her own work record: $500.

For instance, let's say Marsha has worked enough to be eligible for a $400 Social Security payment in her own right. That makes her eligible two ways: as a worker and as a spouse ("dual entitlement"). Social Security must pay her the *higher* of the two. She will receive the $500 spousal payment because it is higher than her own benefit. John and Marsha will receive a total of $1,500 per month altogether, just as in the previous situation.

Note: If Marsha were under her FRA of 66, she must be paid any benefits on *her own* record before drawing spousal payments ("deemed filing," see page 69). This means that she would actually draw her own $400 benefit, with an additional $100 spousal benefit from John's record added into her monthly payment. Since she is already age 66 in this example, deemed filing does not apply; she could draw the spouse benefit without filing for her own payment.

(3)   If Marsha has substantial work: She will draw her own payment amount.

For example, suppose Marsha's own work record yields a $800 payment for her. Since the $800 is higher than the spouse payment ($500), she will receive the $800. John and Marsha will receive a higher total of $1,800 per month together.

(4)   If Marsha out-earns John: She will draw her own payment amount.

Let's say Marsha earns more than John, so that her own Social Security payment is $2,200. Like the previous example, she will then receive her full payment on her own record, since it is higher than the spousal payment. John and Marsha will receive a total of $3,300 per month together. The total will be $3,300, not the expected $3,200, because John will get a spousal payment of $1,100 (50% of Marsha's payment).

Note: No gender bias is intended in these examples, nor is any bias inherent in the way Social Security performs these calculations. If John's and Marsha's work histories were reversed, John would be eligible for exactly the same benefits listed above for Marsha.

Figure 3.2 summarizes the four spouse cases just described.

BOTH AGE 66			
John's Own Payment	Marsha's Own Payment	**Marsha's Payment**	**Family Total**
Example 1: Marsha not eligible for her own payment.			
$1,000	$0	**$500**	**$1,500**
Example 2: Marsha eligible for $400 on her own.			
$1,000	$400	**$500**	**$1,500**
Example 3: Marsha eligible for $800 on her own.			
$1,000	$800	**$800**	**$1,800**
Example 4: Marsha eligible for $2,200 on her own.			
$1,000	$2,200	**$2,200**	**$3,300**

Figure 3.2: Summary of John and Marsha's benefits at age 66 (or other FRA). Note that in Example 4, John will receive a 50% spousal payment of $1,100 (50% of Marsha's $2,200).

Both age 62

Next, our example becomes a bit more realistic, and a bit more complex.

Perhaps John and Marsha are not yet 66. If they are both 62, John is eligible for 75% of his full $1,000. John's payment would be $750.

At 62, Marsha's *spousal* benefit is 35% of John's *full* $1,000. That makes her spouse payment $350.

The Marsha in Example 3 would then be eligible for more on her own record than she could get on John's. At 62 she can get 75% of her own $800 full payment, or $600.

The Marsha in Example 4 would be eligible for 75% of her own $2,200 full payment, or $1,650. John would be eligible for a spousal payment of $770 (35% of Marsha's full payment amount of $2,200).

Figure 3.3 summarizes these four cases.

BOTH AGE 62				
	John's Own Payment	Marsha's Own Payment	**Marsha's Payment**	**Family Total**
Example 1: Marsha not eligible for her own payment.				
	$750	$0	$350	$1,100
Example 2: Marsha eligible for a full benefit of $400 on her own.				
	$750	$300	$350	$1,100
Example 3: Marsha eligible for full benefit of $800 on her own.				
	$750	$600	$600	$1,350
Example 4: Marsha eligible for full benefit of $2,200 on her own.				
	$750	$1,650	$1,650	$2,420

Figure 3.3: Summary of John and Marsha's age-62 benefits, assuming FRA of 66. In Example 4 John will receive $770 spousal payment (35% of Marsha's $2,200).

Mixed ages

What happens if John and Marsha are not the same age? If John is 62 and Marsha is 66, John's work record might pay $750 to him (75% of his full retirement benefit of $1,000) and $500 for her (50% of the same $1,000).

Note that Marsha's spouse benefit is computed on John's *full* age-66 payment, even if he is drawing a reduced payment because of early retirement. Each person's payment is computed based on *that person's age when that person's payment begins*, regardless of the other spouse's age or payment.

Figure 3.4 summarizes this information.

MIXED AGES				
	John's Own Payment	Marsha's Own Payment	**Marsha's Payment**	**Family Total**
Example 1: John age 62 and Marsha age 66.				
	$750	$0	**$500**	**$1,250**
Example 2: John age 66 and Marsha age 62.				
	$1,000	$0	**$350**	**$1,350**

Figure 3.4: Summary of John and Marsha's benefits with mixed ages. (Examples assume Marsha is not eligible on her own work record.)

Madam X

When John and Marsha apply for Social Security payments, their Social Security representative or online application asks, "Did you have any previous marriages?" Their prior marital history must be determined, to see if anyone else might be eligible on their work records.

John responds that, yes, he had a former wife, Madam X. The representative inquires, and John confirms that he and Madam X were married for ten years and Madam X is over 62. This is a *claims lead* that Social Security must resolve by either paying Madam X or determining that no payment is possible. The Social Security representative must attempt to locate Madam X to see if payments are possible.

When Social Security contacts Madam X, she confirms that she was married to John for ten years, that she is currently unmarried, and that she is 66 and retired. Therefore, Madam X could be eligible for former spouse benefits, depending on how high her own payments on her own work record might be.

Quite logically, she either will be paid her own payments in her own right, or spouse payments on John's record, whichever is higher. This means that Madam X is eligible for exactly the same payment schedule as Marsha (Figure 3.5). Since she is over 66, she might even file for "Spousal-Only" payments (see page 237).

Note that payments made to Madam X will have no effect at all on payments to John and Marsha, and vice versa. Furthermore, they are considered separate family units so the Family Maximum will not apply. In fact, because of the Privacy Act, John and Marsha will never know if Madam X is on John's record, and Madam X will never know about John and Marsha's payments.

FORMER SPOUSE "MADAM X"		
John's Own Payment	Madam X's Own Payment	Madam X's Payment
Example 1: Madam X not eligible for her own payment.		
$1,000	$0	**$500**
Example 2: Madam X eligible for a full benefit of $400 on her own.		
$1,000	$400	**$500**
Example 3: Madam X eligible for full benefit of $800 on her own.		
$1,000	$800	**$800**
Example 4: Madam X eligible for full benefit of $2,200 on her own.		
$1,000	$2,200	**$2,200**

Figure 3.5: Madam X's payment schedule at age 66 or other FRA.

Another important point: In order to draw on John's record, John's current wife Marsha must be retired and must *wait for John to start receiving his own Social Security.* (See Chapter 9 for working in retirement.) But unlike Marsha, Madam X can draw on John's record as soon as she is 62 and retired, *whether or not John retires,* as long John is 62 and the divorce was final at least two years ago. This special eligibility rule for former spouses is explained on page 66.

Tom & Harry

Shall we make our example even more complex? When Madam X applies for Social Security, *her* marital history must also be established, to see if anyone might be eligible on her work record, or if she might be eligible on someone else's record. Therefore the Social Security representative asks, "I understand you were married to John for ten years. Did you have any other marriages?" Madam X responds that, yes, she was married to Tom for eleven years and Harry for twelve years.

How will Social Security handle this situation? Will Madam X be eligible under the record of the most recent husband? The longest-lasting marriage? The first marriage?

The solution is simple: she will be paid on whichever record *pays highest.* Therefore, Madam X now has *four* work records to choose from: her own, John's, Tom's, and Harry's. Madam X will be paid from whichever record pays the most.

The "best" record might change over time. For example, Madam X might be drawing a $500 benefit on John's record. Then, at a later date, Harry turns 62. Suppose Harry had higher lifetime earnings than John—Harry's age 66 payment is $1,800 compared to John's $1,000. Therefore when Harry turns 62 Madam X should switch to *his* payment record to receive $900 per month. Thus, it pays Madam X to keep track of former spouses, since Social Security may not know about the higher eligibility, and the higher benefits are not payable until Madam X actually files a claim for them.

Madam Y and Z

Let's add one more detail to our John and Marsha example. Suppose John had a number of ten-year marriages—not only to Madam X, but to Madam Y and Madam Z as well.

In that case, current spouse Marsha, and former spouses Madam X, Madam Y and Madam Z could *each* draw $500 payments on John's work record. There are no family maximum considerations because each spouse is a separate family unit. The former spouse payments, then, would not affect Marsha's payment amount, nor would they affect each other.

Other Examples

Marsha may have ex-husbands, just as John has ex-wives. Mr. A, B, and C, if we call them that, might be eligible for payments on Marsha's record, assuming that Marsha's payments are high enough and assuming they are not eligible for a higher payment on another record. The rules would be exactly the same as those for Madam X, Y, and Z applying on John's record.

Here's a quiz: could John or Marsha become eligible on the records of *their* former spouses? Why or why not?

The answer is that neither John nor Marsha are eligible on other records because they are currently married. You must be *currently unmarried* in order to draw benefits on a former spouse's work record.

These examples are chosen because you may be a John, a Marsha, a Madam X, or a Mr. A, and you need to know where you fit into the Social Security program. Furthermore, these examples illustrate an important philosophy of the Social Security Administration: It is SSA's *duty* to pay you the highest payment you are entitled to. If a possible higher benefit is overlooked, it is charged as an

---

☆ THE INSIDE STORY ☆

Examples vs. Real Life

The examples used here are not far-fetched. I remember too well my first day of "real" claims, as part of Claims Representative training. My fellow trainees and I had practiced on textbook cases. We had role-played retirement interviews. We felt our instruction and testing had prepared us for the real world, so we were given some hand-picked "simple" cases to process.

In no time, our eager confidence was knocked down a notch or two, as the "simple" cases revealed complex former spouse issues, earnings problems, special computations, or any of the thousands of other complications that arise when working with real people.

That day I learned an important lesson. There is a tendency in government to have a rule for every situation, a category for every individual. But that is impossible. No matter how complex the government makes its rules and categories, the next person to walk through the door will have a life much more complicated than the rules. The examples above, with their Madam X, Y, and Z, are actually much simpler than any number of cases Social Security deals with every day. If you work with people, you know this is true. What a marvel of diversity real life is.

employee error and back pay might be issued to you. Every possible way to determine your highest legal payment must be explored.

There are reasonable limits to this policy. If you refuse to apply for benefits, you can't be paid. If you delay filing, no back pay can be issued. But once you telephone or otherwise contact SSA, the Administration must pursue every possible payment for you. By reading this book, you'll know why SSA asks about former marriages, and you can help SSA search for every possible chance for payment without overlooking a higher payment on another record.

The next section deals with a subject which touches every one of us, though it can be difficult to contemplate: death. Specifically, we will explore what Social Security benefits are payable to those left behind after a death, focusing on *who* is eligible, *when* they are eligible, and *how much* their payments can be.

FOR MORE INFORMATION...

"Retirement Benefits/ Family Benefits"
www.ssa.gov/pubs/10035.html, and scroll to "Family benefits "

"Retirement Planner: Benefits for you as a spouse"
www.ssa.gov/retire2/applying6.htm

"Same-Sex Couples"
www.ssa.gov/same-sexcouples/

"Benefits for Children"
www.ssa.gov/pubs/10085.html

"Government Pension Offset"
www.ssa.gov/pubs/10007.html

"Information for Government Employees"
www.ssa.gov/gpo-wep/

CHAPTER FOUR

SURVIVOR BENEFITS

Fran Ferguson is desperate. Her husband Fred died last month from a sudden illness. Her son Frank and her daughter Karen are still in high school. Fran does not work. How will she pay her bills?

Fran learns that she and Frank can get Social Security survivor payments. Karen, as Fred's stepdaughter, will also be eligible.

BACKGROUND INFORMATION ON SURVIVOR BENEFITS

Did you know that when you pay your Social Security taxes, you are also buying protection for your family in case of your death? This protection is called *survivor benefits*, and works somewhat like life insurance. It can be worth hundreds of thousands of dollars for your family members if they are left without your support.

Survivor benefits are similar to family benefits except they are payable after your death. Like family benefits, your eligible family members will be paid a monthly payment proportional to your earnings level, and there is a family maximum payment which limits the amount payable to larger families. However, compared to family benefits, each survivor can get a higher percentage of your full payment amount. In addition, larger families will receive higher individual payments because your absence keeps total family payments lower compared to the family maximum payment. Figure 4.1 summarizes the types of payments available.

The Four Types of Survivor Benefits

Payments to your widow or widower, and/or your former spouse.

Payments to your surviving unmarried children.

Payments to your dependent parents.

A one-time, lump sum payment to your spouse or children.

Figure 4.1. Types of survivor payments.

Each of these four types of benefits is detailed in the sections below.

Here is a very important feature of survivor payments: *In order for your survivors to be eligible for survivor benefits, you do **not** need to be drawing Social Security payments, **nor do you need to reach retirement age**, before you die.* Even if you die well before retirement, say at age 35, your family will receive monthly Social Security payments until the children are grown, provided you meet the work requirements.

Harold died at the age of 28, leaving his wife, Hannah, age 27, and two minor children. Hannah and the children will receive Social Security payments until the children are grown (provided that each individual meets the work limits described on page 199). Hannah will again be eligible for payments when she reaches age 60.

WORK REQUIREMENTS FOR SURVIVOR BENEFITS

Before your family members can be eligible for survivor payments, you the worker must earn coverage through working.

Your work is measured in *work credits.* These are the same credits used to establish your eligibility for Social Security *retirement* payments (see page 39).

Recall that you must have earned 40 work credits to be eligible for retirement benefits. But consider that those who die at a young age have less opportunity to obtain the full 40 credits required for retirement:

When Harold died at 28, he had only 30 credits on his work record, because of his schooling and a few years of low earnings. Hannah is concerned that she and the children will not be eligible because Harold has fewer than 40 credits.

To account for younger workers having fewer work years, fewer credits are required to ensure your family's eligibility in the event of an early death.

There are, in fact, *two* ways to meet the work requirement: *fully insured status* or *currently insured status.*

Fully insured status—comprehensive protection

"Fully insured status" is the most comprehensive coverage for your family. Fully insured status means you have earned enough work credits to provide Social Security payments to your survivors of *all types*—spouses over 60, younger spouses caring for your children, your children, and your dependent parents.

Work Credits Needed for Survivor Benefits (Fully Insured Status)	
Death at age	**Credits Needed**
28 or younger	6
29	7
30	8
31	9
32	10
33	11
34	12
35	13
36	14
37	15
38	16
39	17
40	18
41	19
42	20
43	21
44	22
45	23
46	24
47	25
48	26
49	27
50	28
51	29
52	30
53	31
54	32
55	33
56	34
57	35
58	36
59	37
60	38
61	39
62 or older	40
See text for exception to these requirements.	

Figure 4.2. Work credits needed for survivor benefits (fully insured status).

The number of credits you need for your survivors to receive benefits depends on your age when you die. The older you are, the more work credits required to ensure benefits for your survivors, up to the maximum of 40 credits. Figure 4.2 shows the number of work credits that you the worker need in order to attain fully insured status. Note that once you earn 40 credits, you have earned *permanent* protection for all your family members.

Since Harold was 28 when he died, he needed only 6 credits for fully insured status for survivor benefits, not the full 40 credits required for retirees. His 30 work credits ensure that Hannah and the children will be eligible for Social Security.

Fred Ferguson died at 62. He needed 40 work credits to make Fran and his children eligible for Social Security.

Currently insured status—fallback protection

"Currently insured status" is a special rule for those who do not meet the requirements for "fully insured status." Think of it as a backup provision which provides only limited or partial protection for your family. If you are only "currently insured," *only your children and your spouse who is caring for the children can be eligible*. To qualify, your spouse must be caring for a child under 16 and the child must be receiving Social Security. No payments will be possible to your parents or your surviving spouse not caring for children.

You are currently insured if you die with at least 6 work credits in the previous 13 calendar quarters—in other words, at least 1-1/2 years of work in the 3 years before your death. However, remember that this rule applies *only* when surviving children are involved, or for the payment of the Lump Sum Death Benefit (described below). It will neither ensure benefits for your spouse without children in care, nor for your dependent parents.

*Ken died at age 32 with only 8 work credits. He is not **fully** insured because he needed 10 work credits for fully insured status (see Figure 4.2). However, 6 of his work credits were earned in his last 3 years; therefore he meets the **currently** insured status. His children can receive Social Security on his work record until they are grown. His wife Carol can also get Social Security while she is caring for the children, until the youngest is 16.*

*When the children are grown and Carol reaches retirement age, she will not be eligible for widow benefits on Ken's record because his **currently** insured status does not provide for that type of benefit.*

Ken's family will probably receive low payments because of his limited work history.

If you meet the work requirement, your survivors may be eligible for Social Security. The following sections describe in detail the various types of payments, their special requirements, and the amount paid.

BENEFITS FOR WIDOWS AND WIDOWERS

The most common type of survivor payment is for the widow or widower after a worker's death. If you are a widow(er), this section will tell you if and when you are eligible for a payment and how much to expect. Figure 4.3 summarizes available benefits.

Definitions of widow, widower, and surviving divorced spouse

The definition of a widow(er) is nearly identical to the definition of a spouse for family benefits (see page 62). Basically, if you were married to the worker for at least 9 months at the time of his or her death, you will meet the definition of a widow(er).

Same-sex spouses may be eligible for widow(er)'s payments. The marriage must have taken place in a state that then recognized same-sex marriage, and the worker must have resided in a state that recognized same-sex marriage at the time of death.

If you were divorced from the worker at the time of death, you might still qualify for Social Security payments as a *surviving divorced spouse.* Again, the requirements are similar to those for family benefits: your marriage to the worker must have lasted at least ten years. (The ten-year marriage requirement is waived if you are caring for the worker's eligible child who is under 16 or is disabled.)

Eligibility rules for a surviving spouse (survivor benefits) differ from the rules for a spouse of a living worker (family benefits) in two important ways: different remarriage rules and different age requirements. These are discussed in the next two sections.

Remarriage rules for surviving spouses

One important rule applies to all widows, widowers, and surviving divorced spouses: you must be currently unmarried *or remarried after age 60.*

Maud, age 62, draws a widow's payment on the record of her deceased husband. She and Greg are in love and wish to marry. If they do, Maud can continue to receive her widow's payment because her remarriage is after age 60.

*Hannah, age 58, wishes to draw a widow's payment on Harold's record when she turns 60. She also wishes to marry Hank. If she marries Hank before she turns 60 she cannot draw a widow's payment on Harold's record. (But she could draw a **spouse** payment on **Hank's** record when she reaches 62.)*

Age requirements for widow(er)'s benefits

Normally, you must be at least *age 60* to be eligible for widow(er) or surviving divorced spouse benefits. This age 60 requirement is unique. For other retirement or spouse benefits you must be age 62. The younger age limit for

PERSON	BENEFIT AMOUNT (Percentage of worker's Full Benefit Amount)
WIDOW OR WIDOWER	
Full Retirement Age or older	100%
Age 60	71.5%
Any age, caring for worker's entitled child under 16	75%
Requirements:	
• Must be currently unmarried **or**	
• Remarried after age 60	
SURVIVING DIVORCED SPOUSE	
Full Retirement Age or older	100%
Age 60	71.5%
Any age if caring for worker's entitled child (child under 16 or disabled)	75%
Requirements:	
• 10-year marriage **or** have child in care, **and**	
• Currently unmarried **or** remarried after age 60	
NOTES: Family maximum may reduce total amount payable to family. If the worker was eligible for a reduced retirement payment before death, a survivor payment may not exceed the reduced payment amount or 82.5% of the full payment amount, whichever is greater. Surviving spouses or surviving divorced spouses who are fully disabled may be eligible at ages 50-59; see Chapter 5, Disability.	

Figure 4.3. Summary of benefits for surviving spouses.

survivor payments can help to alleviate what is a difficult situation for many widows and widowers.

Maud lost her husband Mark when she was 57. Her children were grown. She had been a homemaker and volunteer for years with little or no paid work. She lived on life insurance proceeds and savings, plus some part-time work, after she was widowed. She was relieved to start drawing Social Security on Mark's record at age 60.

☆ THE INSIDE STORY ☆

Remarriage Rules for Widow(er)s

There is a good reason for the rule permitting remarriage after age 60. In the 1970s a widow(er)'s remarriage was never permitted; Maud would lose her widow's payment if she married Greg. Thus, there was incentive for them to live together without marrying.

The media trumpeted the situation. Newspaper headlines read "Government forces seniors to live in sin."

Needless to say, Congress, acting to prevent political embarrassment, amended the Social Security Act to allow remarriage after age 60 without endangering widow(er)s' payments.

There is an exception to the age 60 rule. You may qualify for widow(er)'s or surviving divorced spouse payments at any age, provided you are *caring for the worker's child*. The child must be under age 16 or disabled, and must be drawing Social Security payments on the worker's record. This exception to the age 60 rule provides for Social Security payments to millions of young widows and widowers, many in their 20s, 30s, or 40s.

When Harold died, Hannah was 27 and caring for their two children. Because the children got Social Security, Hannah also qualified for payments. She drew Social Security payments for two years until she returned to work. The children's payments continued through high school.

Note that you can qualify with a child in care whether you were married to or divorced from the worker at the time of death. (If the worker were still alive, a *former* spouse must wait until age 62 to be eligible.)

*John and Irene were divorced when John died. Irene was raising their son,
Bill. Irene and Bill can each draw Social Security on John's work record.*

One special payment category should be mentioned here: you may draw a
disabled widow(er) benefit at age 50 to 59, provided you are fully disabled within
7 years of your spouse's death. This is detailed in Chapter 5, "Disability."

Payment amount for widow(er)s

Like family benefits, widow(er)'s benefits are computed as a percentage of
the worker's full benefit amount. There are three differences, though, between
family benefits and widow(er)'s benefits:

- First, the worker may not have lived to retirement age (see the next section
  immediately below). In the event of a younger death, a full benefit is
  computed *as if the worker were Full Retirement Age (FRA) at the time of
  death.*

- Second, the percentages paid to survivors are higher—up to 100% of the
  worker's full payment, as shown in Figure 4.3.

Year of Birth	Full Retirement Age
1939 or earlier	65
1940	65 and 2 months
1941	65 and 4 months
1942	65 and 6 months
1943	65 and 8 months
1944	65 and 10 months
1945 - 1956	66
1957	66 and 2 months
1958	66 and 4 months
1959	66 and 6 months
1960	66 and 8 months
1961	66 and 10 months
1962 and later	67

*Figure 4.4: "Full Retirement Age" for widow(ers). Note slight differences from Figure 2.4
(page 51), FRA for workers and spouses.*

- Third, the Full Retirement Age for widow(er)s is slightly different from the FRA for workers and spouses, with a later phase-in to age 67, as shown in Figure 4.4.

If you first draw a widow(er)'s payment at your FRA or older, you will receive 100% of the payment the worker *was receiving,* with a minimum of 82.5% of the full payment amount. The payment will get no bigger after FRA, except for Cost of Living Adjustments (COLAs). If the deceased worker was receiving a reduced payment because of early retirement (page 52), your payment will be reduced to that level or 82.5% of the full payment amount, whichever is greater. If the worker was receiving a bonus for Delayed Retirement Credits (page 53), your payments will reflect that bonus. If the worker died before ever receiving Social Security payments, you will receive 100% of the full payment amount (see next section).

Frances lost her husband Tom when she was 68. Tom's full payment amount was $1,600, but he was receiving only $1,200 (75%) because his payments started at 62. Frances' widow's payment will be $1,320 (82.5% minimum).

Sharon lost her husband Shel when she was 68. Shel's full payment amount was $1,600, but he delayed retirement until he was 70. Because of his delayed retirement, Shel's Social Security was actually $2,112 (132%). Sharon's widow's payment will be $2,112.

You should note that when you opt for a reduced early retirement payment, you are also limiting your surviving spouse to that same reduced payment or an 82.5% payment, whichever is greater.

When Tom opted for a reduced age-62 retirement payment, he was also opting for a reduced widow's payment for Frances, whether he knew it or not.

Thus, your choice of a reduced payment has far-reaching financial planning implications, which can extend to your survivor in the case of your death.

If you first draw a widow(er)'s payment before your FRA, and *not* caring for the worker's eligible child, you will be paid a smaller percentage of the worker's full payment amount. The amount will be proportional to your age when your widow(er) payments begin. The reduction amount is varying, and always results in a 71.5% payment at age 60, no matter what the widow(er)'s FRA is.

The amount of the reduction for each month is derived by dividing 28.5 percent by the number of months from age 60 to the widow(er)'s FRA. (If you are eligible at age 50 - 59 due to disability, there will be no further reduction below the age 60 payment amount; you'd get a 71.5% payment. See Chapter 5, Disability.)

For example, if your FRA is age 66, you could be entitled up to 72 months before FRA (age 66 – age 60 = 6 years or 72 months). Each month of early payments therefore causes a reduction of 28.5 percent divided by 72 (or 0.00396).

Eugene was retired and 59 when his wife Eunice died. Eunice was already 66 and drawing a full 100% Social Security retirement payment of $600. When Eugene turns 60 he can draw a widower's payment of $429 (71.5% of $600).

Maud started drawing a widow's payments on Mark's record when she turned 60. Mark's full payment amount was $800, but he was only receiving $600 because he chose a reduced age-62 payment. Maud's widow's payment is $572 (71.5% of the full $800). If Maud postponed her payments until FRA, she could be paid $660 (the minimum of 82.5% of Mark's full payment amount.)

If you are eligible because you are caring for the worker's child, you will receive 75% of the worker's full benefit amount.

Note: If you receive a *pension from work not covered by Social Security,* your widow's benefit may be reduced by the *Government Pension Offset,* described on page 69.

What if the worker never received Social Security payments?

You may be eligible for survivor payments even if the deceased worker never received Social Security, and even if the worker never reached retirement age.

This provision is particularly important if your working spouse dies at an early age, leaving you with young children to raise. In this case, the children would receive payments until they are grown (see details below) and you could receive payments as the children's parent until the youngest child is 16. The amount paid is based on your spouse's full benefit amount, which would be computed *as if he or she were Full Retirement Age at the time of death.*

These payments could easily amount to tens or hundreds of thousands of dollars while your children mature. The Social Security payments offer substantial protection to help offset the loss of your spouse's wages.

Be sure to consider these Social Security payments when you make your life insurance decisions. Social Security will provide a foundation for survivors' income, with pensions, life insurance and savings providing the rest.

Hannah drew payments for herself and the children years ago, following Harold's death. When the children were grown, the Social Security payments stopped. Now that Hannah is 60 and retired she is re-applying for widow payments. Harold's full payment amount is now $1,000—it has been automatically adjusted *for inflation over the years. Hannah will receive $715 (71.5% of Harold's full payment amount).*

BENEFITS FOR SURVIVING CHILD(REN)

Definition of surviving child

The definition of a surviving child is the same as the definition of a child used for family benefits: he or she must be unmarried and the worker's legitimate child, natural child, legally adopted child, or stepchild. He or she must also be:

- Under 18, **or**

- Under age 19 and a full-time elementary or secondary school (high school) student, **or**

- Age 18 or over and under a total disability that began before age 22.

Fred died when his children were both minors—Frank was 17 and Karen, his stepdaughter, was 15.
Karen is still in high school when she turns 18. Her Social Security payments do not stop until June, when she graduates.
Frank turns 19 shortly before his own graduation. His payments stop when he turns 19.

Henry is disabled. His mother died while he was still in high school. Henry drew survivor payments on his mother's work record.

UNMARRIED CHILD	BENEFIT AMOUNT (Percentage of worker's full payment amount)
Under 18 (or 19 if in high school)	75%
Disabled before age 22	75%
NOTE: Family maximum may reduce total amount payable to family.	

Figure 4.5. Summary of benefits for surviving children.

*Henry's payments continue after high school because of his disability. He is still drawing payments when he turns 30 and becomes married. Then his payments must stop because he is no longer an **unmarried** child.*

There is also limited provision for a grandchild or step-grandchild to receive payments on the deceased's work record. The grandchild's parents must be deceased or disabled, or the grandchild must be adopted by a surviving spouse of the deceased grandparent. In addition, the grandchild must have been dependent on the deceased.

Payment amount for surviving child

A surviving child is entitled to 75% of the worker's full benefit amount. (As noted above, if the worker never received Social Security payments, his full benefit amount is computed as if he died at Full Retirement Age.)

*Fred's full 100% benefit was $800. Frank and Karen will **each** be paid 75% of that, or $600, per month.*

Henry's mother had a $1,000 full payment amount. Henry was paid 75%, or $750, per month until his marriage made him ineligible.

The **family maximum payment**, described on page 72, may limit payments to three or more persons enrolled on one work record.

BENEFITS FOR SURVIVING DEPENDENT PARENTS

Definition of surviving dependent parent

Figure 4.6 summarizes the benefits payable to the dependent parents of a deceased worker. To qualify for these parent payments, you must meet certain requirements:

- You must be the *parent* of the deceased worker. You will qualify if you are the natural parent, or if you became the worker's stepparent or adopting parent before the worker reached age 16.

- You must be *dependent* upon the deceased worker. This means you received one-half of your support from the worker before he or she died (or before he or she became disabled, if applicable).

- You must be at least *age 62.*

Payment amount for parent

Your payment amount is based on the worker's full payment amount (PIA), like other survivor payments. If one parent is enrolled, the payment is 82.5% of the worker's PIA. If two parents are enrolled on the same earnings record, the payment is 75% of the PIA for each individual. Payments may be less if the **family maximum** is involved (see page 72).

Parent benefits are rarely paid because of the *dependency* rule. Still, this is an important benefit that could help you in a difficult time. If you think you might be eligible, contact SSA for details.

Before Don died he had been supporting his father, Tom. Tom had a very small Social Security payment; Don's support was well over 50% of Tom's total income.

When Don died Tom qualified as his dependent parent. Tom's small Social Security payment was raised to 82.5% of Don's full payment amount. Since Don's full payment was $1,500, Tom was paid $1,237.

Lynn was supporting her two parents before she died. Her full payment amount was $1,600.

Each parent will receive 75%, or $1,200, from Lynn's work record, for total Social Security income of $2,400 per month.

DEPENDENT PARENTS	BENEFIT AMOUNT (Percentage of worker's full payment amount)
One parent over age 62	82.5%
Two parents over age 62	75% each
NOTE: Family maximum may reduce total amount payable to family.	

Figure 4.6. Summary of benefits for surviving parents of a deceased worker.

DUAL ENTITLEMENT FOR SURVIVORS

You may be eligible for payments under your own work record as well as survivor payments on a different work record. In that case, you will be paid the *higher* of the two amounts (unless you request otherwise). This is the same rule as for family benefits (see page 68).

Tom (above) had received $500 Social Security on his own record until his son Don died. Don had provided most of Tom's support. Tom's payment was raised to $1,237 because Tom's payment on Don's record was higher than the payment on Tom's own record.

If you are eligible on more than one record, you might draw on one of them first and then switch to the other. For example, if you have lost a spouse, you might be able to draw survivor payments from age 60 to 62, then change to your own record if a higher payment is possible there. *Deemed filing* (see page 69) does not apply to survivor payments.

SPECIAL ONE-TIME DEATH BENEFIT

The various kinds of *monthly* payments available for survivors are not the only payments possible. You may also be eligible for a special one-time payment called the *lump sum death payment*, or LSDP.

The LSDP is a one-time payment of $255, made in addition to any monthly benefits that may be due. The payment amount may appear to be small—it has been the same amount since the 1940s—but it can help with funeral expenses or other final expenses after a death.

The LSDP can be paid to you under three different circumstances:

1. If you are the worker's surviving spouse, and you were *living with the worker* at the time of death, you may claim the LSDP. You are considered to be "living with" your spouse even if there was a temporary absence from home for reasons such as work or medical treatment.

2. If you were married to but not living with the worker at the time of death, the LSDP can be paid to you—but only if you were *eligible for survivor benefits* on the worker's record in the month of death. (You are *eligible* for benefits if you could have filed for and received payments. You need not be actually *receiving* payments.)

3. Finally, if there is no spouse to receive the LSDP, you may claim it if you are the child of the deceased worker, but again, only if you were *eligible for benefits* on the worker's record in the month of death. If there are other such children, you will split the payment proportionally with them.

Note that the LSDP cannot be paid to a former spouse. Nor can it be paid to a funeral home, even though that was the general practice some years ago.

You must file for the LSDP within two years of the worker's death, or show good cause for late filing. The application is filed like any other Social Security application—see Chapter 8 for a full description. *Exception:* no application is needed if you were already receiving spousal benefits from the deceased at the time of death.

When Harold died and Hannah applied for survivor benefits for herself and the two children, she also filed for the Lump Sum Death Payment. It was included with her first payment.

To summarize: Social Security survivor payments provide valuable benefits for family members following a worker's death. Surviving spouses, children, surviving divorced spouses, and dependent parents can receive payments. Survivor benefits provide valuable protection for the worker's family members—protection similar to life insurance, paid for by Social Security taxes.

Note the previous three chapters, on retirement, family, and survivor payments, describe the "core" of the early Social Security system (originally planned as "OASI" or "Old-Age and Survivor Insurance"). In the next two chapters you will explore newer, more recent additions to the system: disability and Medicare protection.

FOR MORE INFORMATION...

"Survivors Benefits"
www.ssa.gov/pubs/10084.html

"Social Security Survivors Benefits"
www.ssa.gov/ww&os2.htm

"Survivors Planner"
www.ssa.gov/survivorplan/ifyou.htm

"Important Information for Same-Sex Couples"
www.ssa.gov/same-sexcouples/

☆ NOTES ☆

CHAPTER FIVE

DISABILITY BENEFITS

GENERAL INFORMATION ON DISABILITY BENEFITS

Sheila is very sick. Her doctors say she may never return to work. How will she support herself and her family?

According to the Social Security Administration, a young worker has a 30% chance of becoming disabled before retirement age. Can Social Security help if you become disabled during your working years?

The answer is yes. If you become disabled before retirement age, SSA can provide a package of protection to partially replace your lost wages, which can include:

- Monthly disability payments for you,

- Monthly payments for your spouse and children, and

- Medicare health insurance, after 2 years of disability benefits.

Currently over 8.9 million American workers receive monthly Social Security disability payments, with another 2.0 million family members eligible because of the worker's disability.

If you are disabled and do not qualify for disabled worker benefits, you might still qualify as a disabled widow(er) of a deceased worker, or as a disabled child of a worker who is retired, disabled, or deceased. These types of benefits are outlined later in this chapter.

Few people know about Social Security disability, but it is yet another kind of "insurance" you are buying with your Social Security FICA taxes, much like the retirement insurance, survivor insurance, and health insurance provided by the program.

ELIGIBILITY FOR DISABILITY BENEFITS

In order to receive disability payments, you must first meet the eligibility rules for the program. The eligibility criteria are more restrictive for disability, partly because disability is more difficult to define than, say, retirement or death. Basically you must meet both the *work requirements* and the *medical requirements* detailed below.

Age at disability	Lifetime Work Credits Required	Recent Work Credits Required
24 or less	6	All earned within last 3 years
25	8	All earned after age 21
26	10	
27	12	
28	14	
29	16	
30	18	
31-42	20	20 earned within last 10 years
43	21	
44	22	
45	23	
46	24	
47	25	
48	26	
49	27	
50	28	
51	29	
52	30	
53	31	
54	32	
55	33	
56	34	
57	35	
58	36	
59	37	
60	38	
61	39	
62 or over	40	

Figure 5.1. Work credits required for disability eligibility at various ages.

Work requirements for disability eligibility

The work requirements for disability payments consist of two standards: you must have both *substantial lifetime work* and *recent work* to be eligible for disability. If you become disabled at age 31 or less, both these standards are combined into a *special age 31* requirement. Figure 5.1 summarizes the work requirement for those who become disabled at various ages.

Substantial lifetime work standard

To meet this standard, you must have between 1-1/2 and 10 years of work under the Social Security program, depending on your age when your disability begins. Your work is actually measured in Work Credits, just as it is for retired workers (see page 39 for details).

The idea here is that a younger worker does not have as much opportunity to build up work credit as an older worker, so fewer credits are required for the younger worker.

The lifetime work required is shown in the second column of Figure 5.1.

Sheila is 35. She had 12 years of part-time and full-time work before she became disabled. Since she needs only 20 credits (5 years of work) she meets the substantial lifetime work standard.

Recent work standard

In addition to the total number of lifetime credits required, some of your work credit must be recent. In the 40 calendar quarters (10 years) immediately preceding the onset of your disability, you must have earned 20 work credits (5 years' credit). To meet this requirement, you must have worked sometime in the last 5 years before your disability, or at least have worked steadily up to a point 5 years before. The recent work requirement is shown in the third column of Figure 5.1.

The reasoning here is simple: Social Security insures you against *loss of earned income due to disability.* If you were not depending on current or recent earnings, then your disability did not really cause you an insured loss. The "20-40 rule"—requiring 20 work credits in the last 40 quarters—is a quick, simple test to see if disability caused you any actual loss of earnings.

Sheila became disabled in 2014. She had nearly steady work from 2002 to 2012—she had some time between jobs, and a maternity leave, but she earned 4 credits in each year. Therefore she meets the recent work standard. Since she meets the substantial lifetime work and recent work requirements, she meets all work requirements for Social Security disability payments.

George became disabled this year. He has over 40 work credits. However, he retired 6 years ago, and hasn't worked since. He does not meet the recent work standard (5 out of the last 10 years must be work years). Therefore he does not meet the requirements for Social Security disability payments. He can receive retirement payments when he reaches early retirement age at 62.

Special age 31 rules

The two work requirements above are combined into a unified rule if you are under age 31 when your disability starts. In that case, you need credit for having worked half the time between your 21st birthday and the time you become disabled. The *minimum* requirement for those under 24 is 6 work credits in the last 3 years. For example, if you are age 25, you need credit for two years of work (out of the 4 years since age 21). If you are 19, you need to meet only the minimum requirement of 6 credits in the past 3 years.

This opens the door to very young workers receiving disability payments. The youngest I know of was this example, a true story:

*"Ken," a 14-year-old boy, suffered an accident resulting in permanent disability. However, he had had a paper route for two years, and had earned Social Security work credits by paying his taxes. He applied for and received monthly Social Security disability payments **on his own work record** for the duration of his impairment.*

There are thousands of other examples like his—I personally assisted many people of all ages, ranging from their teen years into their sixties, to become entitled to disability payments.

Medical requirements for disability eligibility

In addition to meeting the work requirements above, you must meet strict medical requirements. Among the many definitions of disability used in government, insurance, and industry, Social Security's is perhaps the strictest. SSA defines disability as:

The inability to engage in any Substantial Gainful Activity by reason of any medically determinable physical or mental impairment which can be expected to result in death, or which has lasted or can be expected to last for a continuous period of not less than 12 months.

"Substantial Gainful Activity" is defined as earnings of $1,070 per month (or $1,800 for blind individuals) in 2014.

In short, you must have a medical condition that prevents virtually all work (severity) *and* it must be expected to last at least a year or be terminal (duration). When you examine this rule—or live by it, as Social Security representatives and beneficiaries do—you discover just how strict the definition is. Examples abound.

Patty lost her ability to practice her skilled trade because of a serious illness. She can never again perform her accustomed work. She finds that all she can do is a part-time job in a fast-food restaurant, making $1,200 per month.

*When Patty applies for Social Security disability, however, her claim is denied. Why? She does not meet the **severity** rule. The definition of "substantial gainful activity" is earnings of $1,070 per month ($1,800 for blind) in any work, whether or not it is her accustomed work. Since Patty is performing substantial gainful activity, she cannot meet the definition of disability.*

Greg was in a severe automobile accident. He will be hospitalized for 7 months and have another 4 months of daily therapy after that. He will be restricted to part-time work for another two years after his course of therapy.

*However, Greg will not qualify for Social Security disability, since he can return to part-time work within a year—he does not meet the 12-month **duration** rule.*

The point is this: you must be *totally and permanently disabled*, or nearly so, to qualify for Social Security disability. There is little or no provision for partial or temporary disability, as there is under Veterans Administration benefits, certain State plans, and many private insurance policies. Because many people do not understand this, they apply even though their impairments are partial or temporary. In fiscal year 2011, only 35% of disability claims were approved, largely because of this misunderstanding.

That same year, over a million disability claims were approved for payment. Here are some examples of impairments which do or do not meet the standards:

Cancer

Numerous claims are filed for cancer, but few are approved. Patients typically claim disability payments shortly after detection or during medical treatment. However, at such a point the chances for recovery are high enough that most claims must be denied.

If a malignancy has *recurred* after medical treatment or is *untreatable*, and limits daily activities, the claim may be allowed. Also allowed are cases where the medical treatment itself, or the treatment combined with the disease, causes inability to work for at least a year.

Coronary disease

This is also an area where many claims are denied, usually because the disease still allows some low-stress work activity, or because the acute phase of the illness is not expected to last a year. Extremely serious coronary disease which truly and permanently prevents all work will, of course, be allowed. In order to qualify, though, the severity must be documented with specific X-ray, ECG, or blood chemistry evidence.

☆ THE INSIDE STORY ☆

How Your Disability Is Evaluated

Social Security employees don't directly determine whether your condition is disabling. Rather, SSA contracts with state governments across the nation to make these determinations, with SSA providing the rules, training, and quality reviews to ensure compliance with federal regulations. This "Disability Determination Service," usually part of the state department of health, is also charged with making disability determinations for state programs such as vocational rehabilitation and workers' compensation.

The state disability evaluator obtains and weighs extensive evidence in your case, including:

- Your first-hand reports on your medical condition,

- Your medical records from your doctor, hospital, or other care provider, and

- Your vocational and educational background.

Whether your doctor does or does not subjectively believe that you are disabled is not material. Rather, your medical records must show objectively that your condition meets certain standards, or *listings,* which specify precisely how severe an impairment must be to be disabling.

For example, the listing for emphysema may include requirements for X-ray evidence, lung capacity tests within certain parameters, and tests for blood gases with certain values.

The disability evaluator must order any tests that are either missing or not current, then determine whether the severity of your impairment meets the disability listings. Your vocational history and education are generally taken into account to determine your suitability for retraining for other types of work.

In many cases, keen judgment is necessary. For example, you may have a combination of impairments; perhaps no one of them alone is disabling, but in combination they are.

Approximately 65% of claims are denied at the initial claims level. Many of these denials result from public misunderstandings about SSA's requirement for near-total, near-permanent disability. (For example, many people file claims for a broken leg or for a temporary severe illness.)

If your claim is denied—or *any* time you receive an "adverse determination" from SSA—you may file an *appeal* to have a new decision made by a different person or team. Among disability claims pursued to the *hearings level (*a higher and more elaborate level of appeal; see page 195) more than half are approved for payment.

Expect the process to take a long time. In 2012, the average disability claim took about 4 months to be decided. Appealing to the hearings level took 382 days on average in 2013.

Back injury

"Back pain" can be severe and totally immobilizing. The difficulty is that SSA requires medical documentation, and this is sometimes hard to obtain. Claims with X-ray evidence of arthritis or osteoporosis, or with persistent motor, sensory, and reflex loss, are allowed for disability. Some of these claims are initially denied but awarded at a higher level of appeal where an individual's level of pain or suffering is assessed in person by a judge.

AIDS

Infection by HIV (the AIDS virus) is not by itself considered disabling. However, a number of conditions associated with HIV can qualify if very severe, including:
- Pulmonary tuberculosis resistant to treatment
- Kaposi's sarcoma
- Pneumocystis carinii pneumonia (PCP)
- Carcinoma of the cervix
- Herpes Simplex

- Hodgkin's disease and all lymphomas
- HIV Wasting Syndrome
- Candidiasis
- Histoplasmosis

Loss of limb

Loss of a limb—or loss of use of a limb, e.g. after a stroke or spinal cord injury—is generally not by itself sufficient for a disability allowance. Exceptions are made for loss of a leg with other complications. Loss of function in *two* limbs, e.g. paraplegia or double amputation, is considered disabling.

Psychiatric disorders

Impairments such as depression, agitation, or hallucinations can be difficult to assess. These are considered disabling if they result in persistent marked restriction of daily activities, constriction of interests, and a seriously impaired ability to relate to other people. In these cases, Social Security takes a close look at your daily living patterns to determine the severity of the impairment.

Black lung

Special rules govern disability benefits for miners suffering from pneumoconiosis (black lung). To be found disabling, black lung must be diagnosed by X-ray, biopsy, or other medically accepted means; must meet particular medical descriptions of severity; and must prevent comparable and gainful work.

These examples should help shed light on what is and what is not considered disabling. As you can see, the decision process is a detailed and objective process of assessing whether the impairment will prevent substantial work for at least a year.

To summarize: The twin hurdles of a stiff work requirement and a severe medical definition of disability act as a substantial barrier to many claims. Nonetheless, you may, like millions of other claimants, meet these strict standards and receive disability benefits. The payments and other benefits you could receive are detailed in the next section.

DISABILITY BENEFITS: PAYMENTS AND MEDICARE

Once approved, Social Security disability entitlement offers three kinds of benefits: cash payments, Medicare eligibility, and a chance to return to work without immediately losing your disability payments.

Cash payments

The first benefit of disability entitlement is monthly cash payments from Social Security.

Your cash payments are computed much like retirement payments as if you were Full Retirement Age. The average disability payment in 2014 is $1,148 per month, about the same as the average retirement payment. The maximum is about $2,600—again, like retirement payments.

In addition to your own disability payment, family members like your spouse and child(ren) may also be eligible. Family benefits for a disabled worker are paid just like family benefits for a retired worker (see Chapter 3).

Waiting Period

There is a "catch." Your cash benefits begin only after a *five-month waiting period.* During the first five full months of your disability, no payments can be made to you or your family members. (Since the five months must be *full* months, it is more accurate to say the waiting period is six months; see "The Inside Story" on this topic.)

Sheila became disabled on January 10. Her waiting period runs from January 10 to June 10—five full months later. Her first month of eligibility is July, the first month after the waiting period.

Back pay

Although no payments are possible during the 5-month waiting period, you may qualify for *back payments,* also called retroactive payments:

- You can qualify for up to 12 months of payments *before the month you file* your Social Security claim, assuming that you became disabled at least 18 months before filing your claim (to allow for the waiting period).

- When your first payment comes, it can include the back payments for up to 12 months *before* you filed your claim, plus payment for any months you have waited for your claim to be processed *after* filing.

The Five-Month Waiting Period

The five-month waiting period might more accurately be called a *six*-month waiting period, since only "full" months count.

To illustrate, suppose your disability onset is April 4. (Your onset is generally the date your impairment first made you unable to work, or when you stopped working.) You will have waited five full months on September 4, so you would first be entitled to Social Security disability payments in October. The October payment is paid in November, meaning you waited six months for eligibility and nearly seven months for payment.

Note that disability *entitlement* does not begin until the end of the waiting period. Therefore, if you recover or die within the five months, no disability payments are due, even as "back pay," either to you or your survivors. (Your survivors may be eligible for survivor payments from Social Security, but that is different from disability payments during your lifetime.)

The waiting period saves Social Security money. Some private insurance policies, whether for health coverage, disability, or nursing home care, specify a waiting period of days, months, or years. A longer waiting period makes the insurance policy much less expensive, since fewer benefits will be paid. SSA says that the waiting period ensures that no payments will be made to those with an unexpectedly rapid recovery.

- Note that no more than 12 months of back payments are possible, so if you have been disabled for over 18 months you should file your claim *as soon as possible* to avoid loss of payments.

Sheila became disabled January 10. She did not file her Social Security claim until September and it took until November to process her claim to payment.

On November 15, she received her first payment and a letter to explain the payment. The payment included full back payments for 4 months (July, August, September, and October). Sheila cannot be paid for her 5-month waiting period (January 10 to June 10), but she can be paid back payments for July and the following months. All these payments can be made because Sheila applied within 18 months of her disability onset.

Sheila's next payment will be in December, when she is paid for the month of November.

John became disabled January 15, 2010. He waited two years to file for Social Security, finally filing on January 5, 2012.

John's claim took 3 months to process. His first payment arrived in April 2012 and included payments for January 2011 through March 2012. He can get back payments only to January 2011—12 months before he filed his claim—plus the three months of processing time after he filed his claim. Social Security cannot pay John for months before January 2011 because back pay is available only for the 12 months before his claim was filed. John will never be paid for the earlier months he was disabled.

John's next payment will arrive in May, when he is paid for the month of April.

Other government benefits

Your Social Security disability payments might be affected by other government benefits. The exact effects depend on the type of government benefit you receive:

- *Pension from non-covered work.* Your disability payment may be reduced if you are eligible for a pension from work not covered by Social Security, just as your Social Security retirement payment can be reduced. This is called the *Windfall Elimination Provision (WEP)* and is explained on page 55.

  Harold received a Federal Civil Service retirement pension before he became disabled. He can still receive Social Security disability but he is subject to a special computation and lower payment amounts from Social Security.

- *Government pension for disabled widow(er).* Social Security disabled widow(er)'s benefits are subject to being reduced by two-thirds of the amount of a *government pension.* This is called the *Government Pension Offset (GPO)* and is explained on page 69.

  Grace receives a Civil Service pension of $600 per month. She is also eligible for disabled widow's benefits of $715 per month from Social Security. Two-thirds of her Civil Service pension—$400—will be counted against her widow's benefit, leaving $315 payable on her Social Security ($715–$400).

- *Workers' Compensation.* If you are disabled due to a job-related injury or illness, you may be eligible for *workers' compensation* payments. If so, there is a limit to the total amount payable to you and your family. Total compensation from workers' compensation and Social Security is capped at 80% of your "average current earnings" before your disability. Either your SSA or your workers' compensation payments may be reduced, depending on your local laws.

John has been receiving a workers' compensation benefit and his claim for Social Security disability has been approved. His combined income from the two programs cannot exceed 80% of his "average current earnings" from before he was disabled. An adjustment will be made either to his workers' compensation or to his Social Security to bring his total benefit under the 80% limit.

- *Other disability payments.* Certain *disability* payments from *Federal, State, Civil Service, or military programs* may trigger a similar limit. Total compensation from some such programs, combined with your Social Security benefits for you and your family, is capped at 80% of your "average current earnings" before your disability.

If any of these provisions affects your payments, your Social Security representative will discuss the limit with you.

Employer or union disability payments

Your employer or union may provide disability payments while you await your Social Security disability:

- Sometimes your *accumulated sick leave* can support you during the claims process and waiting period.

- Some employers offer *temporary disability benefits* in addition to sick leave. These typically last for six months—just enough to get through the Social Security waiting period.

- Large employers sometimes provide *long-term disability benefits*, but beware: many such plans require an SSA disability approval to trigger employer benefits. Your employer may also subtract your Social Security payment from your employer payment. That means (1) you must wait for SSA's decision, (2) you could be denied employer benefits if you do not meet SSA's strict definition of disability, and (3) you might receive little or no employer money above and beyond your Social Security payments.

Every employer or union plan is unique. To get details on how your organization's disability coverage works, and how it fits with Social Security, ask your benefits office for information. And be sure to apply for any employer or union benefits if you become disabled.

Medicare

In addition to your cash payments, you will also be eligible for Medicare health insurance. You become eligible for Medicare after you have been entitled to disability payments for 24 months. Note that you must be *entitled to payments*, so the 24-month period starts after the five-month waiting period.

Sheila became disabled January 10, filed her claim in September, and received her first payment on November 15. She was paid back pay to July, since July 1 is the date she became entitled to payments. Two years later, on July 1, she will be covered by Medicare.

John became disabled January 15, 2010. He filed for disability two years later on January 5, 2012. His back pay is computed from January 1, 2011 (12 months' back pay). His Medicare is effective January 1, 2013—two years after he is entitled to payments.

Your Medicare coverage is exactly like Medicare for age-65 retirees. See Chapter 6, Medicare, for details.

Some large employers or unions will extend your group medical insurance until Medicare starts. This means that if you become disabled, you will not have a period without health insurance. Check with your benefits office for their policy.

Sheila stopped work due to disability on January 10. Her Medicare starts in July two years later.

Sheila's employer provided medical coverage until her Medicare coverage started.

WORKING WHILE DISABLED

One of the valuable features of the Social Security disability program is that it encourages you to work whenever you are able. Many determined individuals return to work despite disability.

SSA's policy is to help you return to work *before* stopping disability payments and Medicare benefits, in order see if the work attempt is successful.

The programs that help you return to work are called *work incentives.* They include:

• Continued cash benefits,

- Continuation of Medicare coverage,

- Help with disability-related work expenses, and

- Access to work training or other rehabilitation services.

The general idea is that anyone wishing to return to work should have a number of months to try and do so without immediately losing all support from Social Security. In other words, your Social Security and Medicare eligibility can be *extended* when you return to work.

Your *medical* disability must continue for you to qualify for the eligibility extensions described below. SSA will periodically review your medical condition to ensure that you still meet the medical definition of disability. *If your impairment is no longer disabling,* SSA must stop your payment three months later. An exception is made if you are engaged in a *vocational rehabilitation program,* including the SSA "Ticket To Work" program, when your medical condition improves. If so, your payments can be continued until the rehabilitation services are completed or until you discontinue receiving services. The rehabilitation program must be expected to enable you to return to work permanently, and you must be making timely progress.

The following extensions of eligibility serve as work incentives.

9-month Trial Work Period.

If you return to work, SSA will continue your payments with no reduction or other penalty for a minimum of nine work months, called a "Trial Work Period." The rules are as follows:

- To count as a Trial Work month you must earn $770 or more (2014 figure), and/or have 80 hours of self-employed work. Lower earnings do not count in any way—you could have unlimited months of earnings below the Trial Work limits without affecting your disability payments.

- The nine Trial Work months need not be consecutive. They may be scattered over many years of brief work attempts.

- All nine Trial Work months must occur within a 60 month (5 year) time span to complete your Trial Work Period. This is termed a *rolling 60-month* Trial Work Period. In short, if you never complete nine Trial Work months within a 60-month period, the Trial Work Period will continue indefinitely.

When all nine months have been exhausted within one 60-month span, your work activity will be evaluated to see if it indicates an ability to perform "Substantial Gainful Activity" (generally, this means work averaging over $1,070 per month, or $1,800 for blind individuals, in 2014). If you have demonstrated such ability (e.g. your substantial earnings continue), your payments may be stopped after a one-time grace period of three consecutive months.

This means that you could make many work attempts, each lasting several months, before SSA would closely examine your work activity. It also means that even after you started a steady, well-paying job, you could receive another year of Social Security payments—nine trial work months plus the three-month grace period.

Sheila makes several work attempts, each lasting only a few months. After three such attempts in three years, she still has used only 8 of her 9 Trial Work months. Her disability payments continued without interruption or reduction.

John makes several work attempts and uses 7 Trial Work months in the space of two years. After these short-term attempts, he succeeds at a steady, well-paying job. The first 2 months at his new job use up his last 2 Trial Work months. His third, fourth, and fifth months of work use up his 3-month grace period. His Social Security payments stop after his fifth month on the new job.

36-month Extended Period of Eligibility

What if your disability payments do stop after your Trial Work Period, and then your earnings decline or end? Do you need to re-apply for your disability payments?

Probably not. Once you complete your nine Trial Work Period months, SSA keeps your claim open for an additional three years. During this 36-month *Extended Period of Eligibility,* your disability benefits can be paid for any month your earnings are below the Substantial Gainful Activity level, but cannot be paid for any month your earnings exceed that level. Basically, your Social Security payments start and stop depending on your work amount.

The 36 months of extended eligibility are consecutive calendar months, starting with the month after the ninth Trial Work Period month (see Figure 5.2). The Extended Period of Eligibility acts as a safety net in case your work attempt does not lead to permanent, substantial employment.

After a year at his new job, John's condition worsens and he must stop work due to his impairment. Since he is still in his Extended Period of Eligibility, John does not have to repeat the extensive disability application process. He notifies SSA that he stopped work and his Social Security starts the next month.

Six months later, John returns to work with substantial earnings. His Social Security payment must stop for every month his earnings are substantial.

After another year of work John must again leave his job due to his impairment. John is still in his Extended Period of Eligibility, so his Social Security again resumes when his work stops.

Expedited reinstatement

If your benefits are stopped because of substantial earnings, you have access to expedited reinstatement during the next five years. If your condition again prevents your working, you can re-file for Social Security disability. Your payments would begin immediately while your medical condition is reviewed, assuming you meet other requirements.

John returns to substantial work two years later, after his Extended Period of Eligibility has ended. His Social Security payments must be stopped. However, his work again ends three years later due to his impairment. He contacts Social Security. Since he is within five years of his benefit termination due to work, his payments begin immediately under expedited reinstatement, without even re-applying for disability.

93-month Continuation of Medicare Coverage

Your Medicare will also continue in force during your Extended Period of Eligibility, at least 93 consecutive months after your Trial Work Period (36 months corresponding with the Extended Period of Eligibility, plus a 57-month additional period).

After the 93 months, your Medicare will stop unless you opt to purchase the coverage with a monthly premium. 2014 premiums for Part A Hospital Insurance are:

- $426 per month for those with under 30 SSA work credits, or
- $234 per month for those with 30 or more work credits.

Part B Medical Insurance costs $104.90 per month, or more for high-income individuals (see Chapter 6).

Purchasing Medicare makes good sense—it is not as expensive as some private insurance policies, offers basic coverage, and can be supplemented with additional coverage.

Remember, these extensions are possible *only if* your medical impairment continues. If you recover from your disability, your payments must stop within three months. Also note that SSA depends upon you to report *all* work activity so that your SSA representative may properly tally the months of your extended benefits.

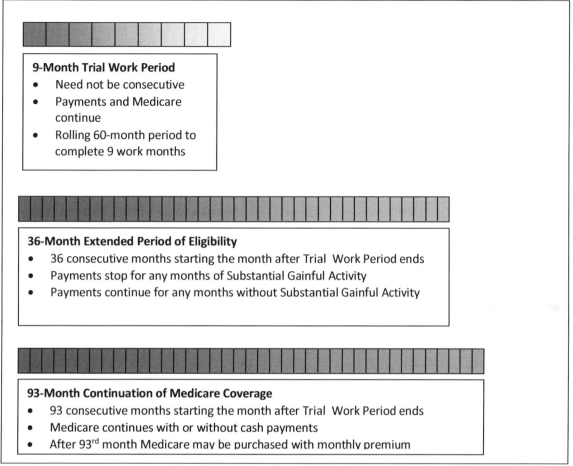

9-Month Trial Work Period
- Need not be consecutive
- Payments and Medicare continue
- Rolling 60-month period to complete 9 work months

36-Month Extended Period of Eligibility
- 36 consecutive months starting the month after Trial Work Period ends
- Payments stop for any months of Substantial Gainful Activity
- Payments continue for any months without Substantial Gainful Activity

93-Month Continuation of Medicare Coverage
- 93 consecutive months starting the month after Trial Work Period ends
- Medicare continues with or without cash payments
- After 93rd month Medicare may be purchased with monthly premium

Figure 5.2. Summary of the Trial Work Period, Extended Period of Eligibility, and Continuation of Medicare Coverage.

OTHER DISABILITY BENEFITS: WIDOW(ER)S, CHILDREN

General Information on Disabled Widow(er)'s and Disabled Child's Benefits

The provisions described above allow you to receive disability payments on *your own* work record. That is, you apply on your own record and payments are proportional to your own work history.

Social Security provides two other disability programs:

- If you are a disabled widow or widower, you can apply on the work record of your deceased spouse.

- If you are an adult, disabled since before age 22, with a parent who is a retired, disabled, or deceased worker, you can file on your parent's work record.

In these cases, you may have had little or no opportunity to build disability protection under your own work record, so Social Security extends eligibility to you through your family relationship to the worker. These additional disability programs supply monthly payments and Medicare to many individuals who would otherwise be ineligible.

Disabled Widow(er)'s Benefits

If you are a disabled widow or widower, you may be eligible for this type of disability payment.

Payments can be made on the earnings record of the worker (your deceased spouse or former spouse). Payments are proportional to the deceased worker's lifetime earnings. You would be paid 71.5% of the worker's full benefit amount.

Mimi worked and supported her disabled husband, George. Mimi died when George was 52. He had no means to support himself.

George discovered that he could receive disabled widower's payments. Mimi's work yielded a full payment amount of $800. George is eligible for 71.5% of the $800, or $572 per month. With this Social Security money, plus some life insurance and pension payments, George is able to make ends meet.

The general requirements are largely the same as for other widow(er)'s benefits, described in Figure 4.3 on page 88. You must have been married to the worker at the time of death or, if divorced, you must have been married for at least 10 years and be currently unmarried. In addition to the general requirements shown in Figure 4.3, you must meet these special requirements for disabled widow(er)s:

- You must be at least *age 50.* (Since you are eligible for regular widow's payments at age 60, this effectively limits disabled widow(er)'s benefits to ages 50 – 59. See below for an exception regarding your Medicare eligibility.)

- Your disability must have started before the worker's death or *within 7 years* after the worker's death. Alternatively, if you were previously eligible for Social Security payments because you were caring for the worker's child (see page 89), your disability must start before those payments end or within 7 years after they end.

- You must meet the same definition of disability as a disabled worker.

In other words, to qualify for disabled widow(er)'s payments you must be within a certain age range, your disability must start within a specified period, and your disability must be severe.

If you qualify, your payments will begin after a 5-month waiting period (see page 107).

Two years after your payments begin, you will be eligible for *Medicare,* just like a disabled worker. Under a special provision, you can also get Medicare from age 60 - 64 because of your disability. At 65, you will be eligible for Medicare based on age rather than disability.

Disabled Adult Child's Benefits

If you are the disabled adult child of a worker who is retired, disabled, or deceased, you may be eligible for this type of disability payment. In order for you to be eligible, your parent must be entitled to Social Security retirement or disability payments or, if deceased, your parent must have been "fully" or "currently" insured for Social Security survivor payments (see pages 84-86).

Payments will be made on the earnings record of the worker (your parent), and will be proportional to his or her lifetime earnings. You will be paid a percentage of your parent's full benefit amount—50% of a living parent's or 75% of a deceased parent's full benefit.

The general requirements are the same as for other child benefits (see page 70). These include the requirement that you must generally be unmarried to receive child's benefits.

In addition you must meet the *disability requirements:*

- You must meet the same definition of disability as a disabled worker, and

- Your disability must start or have started before you reach age 22.

The age requirement raises certain issues. If you are already receiving Social Security child's payments at an early age, payments normally stop when you turn 18 or leave high school. If you are disabled, however, your payments can continue past 18 and you will be eligible for Medicare coverage as well. You would want to file a disability claim shortly before turning 18, to ensure that your payments continue.

Ted received child's benefits on the record of his retired mother, Irene. Normally Ted's benefits would stop when he turned 18 or finished high school. However, Ted qualified for disabled adult child's benefits. His "child's" benefits continue into his adulthood until he marries, recovers, or proves an ability to perform substantial work.

RIB, DIB, DAC

SSA staffers need a shorthand language to refer to the various types of claims and benefits. The result is an interesting vocabulary that sounds like a variation of Pig Latin:

RIB   Retirement Insurance Benefit. "She should file for RIB at 62."

WIB   Widow(er)'s Insurance Benefit. "He could have gotten WIB but his own RIB was higher."

DIB   Disability Insurance Benefit. "He filed for his DIB right after his accident."

DWB   (Pronounced "dwib.") Disabled Widow(er)'s Benefit. "Her DWB was denied because of the 7-year time limit, but her DIB will be allowed."

DAC   Disabled Adult Child. Officially this should be "CDB" for Childhood Disability Benefit, but no one knows how to pronounce that acronym.

Overlapping eligibility rules make for interesting choices of benefits, and this makes for interesting language at SSA. Examples: "He was 62 and disabled so we filed a RIB-DIB. Then I found out he had a disabled child so we turned it into a RIB-DIB-DAC." "She could get RIB or WIB but we took a DWB to get early Medicare."

If Irene dies at some date in the future, Ted's payments continue but are raised from a 50% payment to a 75% payment.

Another possibility: You may be disabled at an early age, but your Social Security payments cannot begin until your parent retires and files for Social Security—that might be the first time you are eligible on any work record. At that point, you can start receiving *child's* benefits, even though you may be in your 30s or 40s, because you are a *Disabled Adult Child.*

The difficulty then is how to prove that you are not only disabled, but *have been* disabled since before age 22. Sometimes medical records from 20 years ago can be difficult to locate. However, Social Security will extend every effort to help process the claim.

Heather is 35 and has been disabled since birth. When her father, Greg, retires at age 62, his SSA claims representative asks if he has any disabled children (this question is always part of the application).

Heather applies for disabled adult child's benefits and her medical records prove she has been disabled since before age 22. Her claim is awarded and she is paid 50% of Greg's full payment.

Jay became disabled in an auto accident when he was 21. He is 40 when his mother dies. As a surviving child Jay can receive 75% of his mother's full payment amount because he has been disabled since before age 22.

If you qualify, your payments will begin *without* a 5-month waiting period—unlike worker's or widow(er)'s disability payments. Just like those programs, however, you will be eligible for Medicare two years after your payments begin.

EXAMPLES OF DISABILITY PAYMENTS

The specific examples below will illustrate the age, work, and disability requirements described in this chapter. Here you will see how some of the rules work together in individual cases.

Example 1: Disabled Worker

Fred is a 42-year-old machinist who works full-time for a large aircraft manufacturer. He is married to Jane, 41, and has two children living at home. Derek, 14, is Jane's son by a prior marriage, and Amy, 10, is Fred and Jane's daughter. Jane works part-time as an accounts clerk for a bank.

On March 5, Fred is driving to work when he is hit by a truck that lost its brakes. Fred suffers a back injury resulting in paraplegia. His company benefits office puts Fred on sick pay and his company medical plan covers most of the doctor bills.

In May, Fred enters rehabilitation and calls the company benefits office. He learns that his company will continue his sick pay and medical insurance for some months, but he must apply for Social Security disability for extended coverage.

On May 20, Fred calls Social Security's toll-free number to start the application process. His application is completed by telephone and mail on June 7. By August 3, SSA obtains the necessary medical documentation and certifies that Fred meets all work and medical requirements for disability payments. His disability onset is set at March 5, the day of the accident. His first Social Security payment arrives on October 3, based on this calendar:

March 5 - August 5	5-Month Waiting Period (No payments possible).

| September | First month of eligibility. |
| October 3 | Payment issued for month of September. |

Fred's monthly payments are $1,600. His payment amount is proportional to his wages over his work years—wages which were higher-than-average because of his work as a skilled machinist, but with gaps due to periodic layoffs.

Derek and Amy will also be eligible for payments from SSA, Derek as Fred's stepchild and Amy as Fred's natural child. They are each eligible for *up to* 50% of Fred's payment amount.

However, Fred's family maximum is 150% of his payment, or $2,400. Since Fred will draw $1,600, that leaves $800 for Derek and Amy to split. Each will receive $400 per month on Fred's record.

Payments will be made payable to either Fred or Jane as the parent of a minor child.

Each child's payment will continue until age 18 (or 19 if still in high school). Note that once Derek's payment stops, Amy's will no longer be limited by the family maximum payment, so her payment will rise to the full 50%, or $800. Thus, the family will continue to receive the same $2,400 total payment.

Jane is also potentially eligible. However, she decides not to apply when she learns that her own part-time earnings would reduce her Social Security payment, and that the total amount payable to the family would be the same $2,400 whether she applies or not, because of the family maximum.

Medicare. Two years after his first Social Security eligibility, in September, Fred will also be eligible for Medicare. In the meantime Fred learns that his company medical coverage will continue until the Medicare begins. Furthermore, the company can provide a small disability pension to supplement the Social Security payments. (Many employers' health and disability benefits are designed to dovetail with Social Security in this manner.)

Outside income. Fred also receives a large settlement from the trucking company which caused his injuries. Since Social Security is insurance, not welfare, that settlement does not affect Fred's SSA payments. The interest he receives by investing part of the settlement is also not counted against his payments. Similarly, Jane's paycheck is not counted against any of the three Social Security payments.

Example 2: Disabled Widow

Jean was 52 when her husband George died. Since the children were grown no Social Security was payable to the children, nor to Jean, since she was not yet age 60. Jean managed to live on George's life insurance proceeds and a part-time job she started once the children were on their own.

Now, a second disaster has struck. At age 54, Jean has a serious bout with cancer which causes her to quit work in February. Surgery, chemotherapy, and a long recuperation are expected to keep Jean out of work for at least a year, and perhaps permanently. The social worker at Jean's hospital recommends that Jean apply for Social Security disability payments.

When Jean contacts SSA, she is initially concerned because they tell her she probably cannot qualify for disability payments on her own work record (she does not meet the requirement for 5 years of recent work). However, she might qualify under the record of her deceased husband, George, as his disabled widow between 50 and 59.

Jean's widow's claim is approved. Her first payment arrives in September (following her 5-month waiting period). She will receive $1,287 per month, which is 71.5% of George's $1,800 full payment amount. She will also be eligible for Medicare two years later.

Jean has a chance for medical recovery, to the point that she might be able to return to work next year after her long recuperation. Because of this, SSA flags her case for a medical review in 18 months. At that point, and again in future years, SSA will re-contact Jean and her doctors to see if her disability continues. If she recovers, her payments will be stopped three months later. If that happens, she would have to wait until age 60 to receive regular widow's payments based on her age.

Example 3: Disabled Child

Hal is 35 and has always had a developmental disability. His IQ is in the low 60's and he has some difficulty caring for himself on a day-to-day basis. He lives in an Adult Home not far from his parents' house, and he is enrolled in a special training program to develop his daily living skills. Most of Hal's income comes from SSI (a federal public assistance program described starting at page 218), but he also works in a recycling center designed to employ disabled workers. His earnings from his job are low enough that they do not interfere with his disability status.

When Hal's mother Carol retires at age 62, she is asked if she has any minor or disabled children. Because Hal is Carol's child and has been disabled since before age 22, he is entitled to child's benefits on Carol's work record. Hal's payment starts the same month as Carol's retirement payment, without a 5-month waiting period. He is paid $600, exactly 50% of Carol's $1,200 full FRA payment amount. (Carol receives $900, or 75% of her full payment amount, at age 62.)

Hal's $600 Social Security payment is not quite high enough to replace his SSI. Because the Social Security counts as income, Hal's SSI is reduced by the amount of the Social Security. In a way, Hal hasn't come out ahead yet—he still must deal with all of the paperwork required by SSI, since SSI is a public assistance or welfare program.

Next year, though, Hal's father George retires at age 65. Hal then qualifies for payments as George's disabled child. He switches from Carol's record to George's and receives 50% of George's full payment amount. George's full payment is $2000, based on his higher lifetime earnings, so Hal receives $1,000. This will stop the SSI permanently and leave Hal with higher income. He will also have far less bureaucracy to deal with, since Social Security is an insurance program, not public assistance like SSI.

To summarize:

- Disability payments are available to disabled individuals who are workers, widows or widowers of a worker, or adult children of a worker.

- A worker is paid as if he or she were a Full Retirement Age retiree (100% of the full payment amount). The full payment amount is based on average earnings up to the date of disability onset.

- A disabled widow(er) age 50 to 59 is paid like a 60-year-old widow(er) (71.5% of the worker's full payment amount).

- A disabled adult child is paid like a minor child (50% of the worker's full payment amount if the worker is living, 75% if the worker is deceased).

- In addition to monthly cash payments, disabled individuals are given Medicare medical coverage two years after their entitlement begins.

- If a disabled individual returns to work, special rules delay the termination of the Social Security payments to ease the transition toward being self-supporting.

In the next chapter, we will examine Medicare—who is eligible, what benefits are provided, and how to deal with medical bills not covered by Medicare.

FOR MORE INFORMATION...

"Disability Benefits"
www.ssa.gov/pubs/10029.html

"Disability Evaluation Under Social Security" (The Blue Book)
www.ssa.gov/disability/professionals/bluebook/

"Working While Disabled—How We Can Help"
www.ssa.gov/pubs/10095.html

"Incentives To Help You Return To Work"
www.ssa.gov/pubs/10060.html

"Red Book (Summary Guide to Employment Supports for Persons With Disabilities)"
www.ssa.gov/redbook/eng/main.htm

"Choose Work" (SSA videos on work incentives)
www.youtube.com/user/choosework

Choose to Work webinars
www.choosework.net/wise

★ CHAPTER SIX ★

MEDICARE

BACKGROUND INFORMATION ON MEDICARE

Medicare provides basic health insurance protection when you are over 65, disabled, or a patient with chronic kidney disease. Its function is virtually identical to private health insurance available from insurance companies, but it is specially tailored and financed for its unique beneficiary pool.

Enacted in July of 1965, Medicare has a huge job:

- As one of the largest health insurance programs in the United States, it supplies hospital and medical insurance for about 40 million people age 65 and over, plus 8 million disabled people under 65.

- It streamlines operations and minimizes overhead by making the claims process faster and cheaper, while at the same time simplifying the claims process for the consumer.

- It needs to crack down on insurance fraud by meticulously examining Medicare claims.

- Finally, it must lead the way in controlling the runaway rise of health care costs.

Despite the breadth and complexity of Medicare's many tasks, it is successful. Medicare functions without fault for most eligible Americans, paying health claims accurately and timely. For health providers such as hospitals, clinics, and doctors, Medicare is no harder to deal with than any other insurance program.

Features

Medicare's benefits are divided into four separate programs, or "parts":

- Part A is called "Hospital Insurance" and covers hospital room and board, plus other services.

- Part B is called "Supplemental Medical Insurance," or simply "medical insurance," and covers medical bills inside or outside the hospital, such as visits to your physician's office or (some) inpatient doctor care.

- Part C consists of "Medicare Advantage" plans. These are private insurance plans that replace Parts A and B's services and may offer additional services. Many Part C plans provide prescription drug coverage.

- Part D is Medicare drug coverage, available from private companies. It partially covers costs of prescription medicines.

☆ **Reform note:** The Affordable Care Act—the health insurance reform of 2010—added two new taxes on high income taxpayers to fund Medicare, both effective with tax year 2013.

First, the "Additional Medicare Tax" applies to wages and self-employment income. A new 0.9% Medicare tax is levied on earnings over $200,000 for individuals or $250,000 for married couples filing jointly. See www.irs.gov/Businesses/Small-Businesses-&-Self-Employed/Questions-and-Answers-for-the-Additional-Medicare-Tax.

Second, the "Net Investment Income Tax" applies to investment income. The new 3.8% tax applies to taxpayers with investment income and with Modified AGI over $200,000 for individuals or $250,000 for married couples filing jointly. Investment income includes interest, dividends, capital gains, and more. See www.irs.gov/uac/Newsroom/Net-Investment-Income-Tax-FAQs.

Revenue from both taxes fund the Medicare Part A trust fund.

Parts A and B comprise the core of Medicare. Together, they're called *Original Medicare* and provide basic hospital and medical coverage. They're both run by the federal government. Virtually all retired people over 65 are on Parts A and B. (There are a few exceptions such as older workers with health insurance from current work.) By contrast, Parts C and D are private alternatives or supplements to Original Medicare, and assume you have enrolled in A and B.

Other features of Medicare include:

- *Paperwork.* Doctors and other healthcare providers file all payment claims directly with Medicare, rather than billing you. This saves you paperwork and increases the efficiency of the system.

- *Fee cap.* Doctors' charges for Medicare services are capped. The cap is 115% of the Medicare approved charge; no higher charges are allowed for any doctor accepting Medicare. The cap is a direct approach to combating the rise in health-care costs for retirees. Most providers do not charge more than the approved charge (see pages 147 and 149).

- *Guaranteed Medigap enrollment.* You are guaranteed a 6-month open enrollment period in "Medigap" insurance coverage with no refusal due to a pre-existing condition. (Medigap insurance is private insurance that supplements Medicare's coverage; see page 151.) The 6-month period applies to those 65 and over and begins when you enroll in Medicare Part B. In addition, restrictions on Medigap coverage for pre-existing conditions are limited to the first six months following enrollment (see page 157). This enrollment guarantee greatly broadens the availability of supplemental insurance. Note that it also applies to disabled individuals already on Medicare, allowing them to obtain Medigap coverage upon turning 65.

- *Medigap standardization.* All "Medigap" insurance policies are standardized into ten varieties of coverage, designated by letters (A, B, C, etc.). In addition, selling duplicate policies is illegal. The standardization simplifies what had been an extremely complex selection process for new retirees (see pages 152-154).

- *Other options.* Medicare offers many ways to receive your covered services through a private company in the Medicare Part C/Medicare Advantage program. Advantage Plans can be Health Maintenance Organizations (HMOs), Preferred Provider Organizations (PPOs, similar to traditional fee-for-service insurance), or other arrangements (page 158).

Medicare is an important benefit for retired and disabled Americans. Without Medicare, health insurance would be inaccessible for millions of Americans. Furthermore, Medicare covers those individuals who tend to have the highest health care costs—older and disabled citizens. Finding substitute coverage would be a costly problem even for those able to afford private insurance. For many people, the loss of Medicare would mean choosing between having no health coverage or turning to *Medicaid*, the public assistance health care program for the needy. By comparison, Medicaid is more complex, more expensive, accepted by fewer health-care providers, and preserves less personal dignity than Medicare.

In this chapter, you will learn who is eligible for Medicare, what Medicare costs, and what it covers. Most importantly, you will learn what Medicare does *not* cover and how to fill these coverage gaps.

ELIGIBILITY FOR MEDICARE

Medicare's four components, Parts A, B, C, and D, will be explained in the next section. First, let's find out who is eligible for Original Medicare—the core programs, Parts A and B—and how to apply.

General requirements for Medicare eligibility

First, you must be a US citizen or legal resident. Then there are three ways to become eligible for Medicare:

- *Age.* You gain Medicare eligibility when you turn 65.

- *Disability before age 65.* You are eligible if you are disabled and entitled to Social Security disability benefits for at least two years.

- *Chronic kidney disease.* If you have End Stage Renal Disease (ESRD) and require treatment by transplant or regular dialysis, you qualify for Medicare if you are *currently insured* (meaning you have 6 work credits in the past 3 years).

Sam retired at age 63. When he turns 65, he is eligible for Medicare.

Sheila became disabled at age 42. She is eligible for Medicare two years after her disability payment eligibility.

Edward is 30 and requires kidney dialysis. He is currently insured. His Medicare pays for the treatments.

Most people gain Medicare eligibility because of age. If that is the case for you, you will be eligible for Medicare insurance coverage beginning the first of the month in which you *attain* age 65. Remember, you attain age 65 the day *before* your birthday, so if you were born on the first of the month you are actually eligible one month early (see page 38).

Sam turns 65 on March 14. His Medicare coverage begins March 1.

Henny turns 65 on August 1. That means she attains age 65 on July 31. Her Medicare coverage begins July 1.

Additional requirements for Medicare eligibility

In addition to the age, disability, or ESRD requirements, you must either meet certain work requirements or pay a premium to gain Medicare eligibility.

Work requirement

Your work record can qualify you for *premium-free* Medicare Part A (explained below) if:

- You are eligible for retirement or disability payments from SSA, or

- You are eligible for a pension from the Railroad Retirement Board, or

- You paid Medicare taxes on your non-covered government work, sufficient for eligibility in private-sector work.

In these cases, your work automatically makes you, your qualifying spouse, and your qualifying former spouse eligible for Medicare, including free Part A.

Henny has over 40 work credits on her Social Security work record. Therefore, she is eligible for Social Security retirement payments at age 62, and she is eligible for Medicare at age 65. Her husband is also eligible through Henny's work.

Chip's career was with the railroad under the Railroad Retirement Board. Since he qualifies for RRB retirement benefits, he also qualifies for Medicare at age 65. His wife will also qualify when she is 65.

Jane is a federal government retiree. She is eligible for Medicare because of her government work.

What about an older spouse married to a younger worker? A special provision allows a non-insured spouse over 65 to get Medicare once the working spouse attains age 62. Neither spouse needs to apply for Social Security payments. This allows a "bridge" to Medicare eligibility 3 years early for the non-insured older spouse.

Note that in order to qualify for premium-free Part A, you must be *eligible* for Social Security payments. However, you do not need to apply for Social Security to get your Medicare.

For example, suppose you are reaching age 65 but continuing your work. You can decide not to apply for Social Security payments until later, when you retire, but you could enroll in Medicare immediately at age 65—even though you have not filed for Social Security (see restrictions below).

Mike is turning 65 and still working. He has not applied for Social Security, but he does have enough work to qualify. He could enroll in Medicare at age 65, if he chooses to do so.

For *Medicare based on ESRD,* the work requirements are not as stringent as those for Medicare based on age or disability. To qualify, you must meet *one* of these standards:

- Meet *fully insured status* on your own work record (defined the same as Figure 4.2, page 85), or

- Meet *currently insured status* on your own work record (defined as 6 work credits earned in the past 13 quarters), or

- Be the spouse, former spouse or widow(er) of a worker who is or was fully or currently insured, or

- Be the dependent child of a worker who is or was fully or currently insured.

If you are filing on another's record, he or she does not have to be receiving benefits for you to become eligible.

Because of the many ways to become eligible for ESRD Medicare, it is highly likely that you will meet the work requirement. Anyone with chronic kidney disease should contact Social Security promptly to enroll.

Premium requirement

Part A is normally premium-free if you or your spouse meet the work requirement above. Otherwise, you can purchase Medicare Part A coverage for a premium.

To purchase "premium Part A," you need to meet these conditions:

- If 65 or over, you must be enrolled in Medicare Part B, and either be a citizen or be a legal resident for at least 5 years.

- If disabled and under 65, your free Part A must have ended because you returned to work (see page 114).

The premium varies with the number of Work Credits (see page 39) on your or your spouse's work record. Here are the premium requirements for 2014:

Work Credits	Monthly Part A Premium (2014)
40+	$0 (free)
30-39	$234
Under 30	$426

Bob does not qualify for free Medicare Part A but he wants the health coverage. When he turns 65, he enrolls for premium Part A and pays for his Medicare coverage.

Part B has a monthly premium starting at $104.90 in 2014, but it can be higher for retirees with high income (Figure 6.1). The increased premiums are called Income-Related Monthly Adjustment Amount (IRMAA).

The income used to determine if you pay the increased Part B premium is your Modified Adjusted Gross Income (MAGI) from two years prior. Your MAGI is your Adjusted Gross Income plus tax-fee interest income. IRS supplies the figure to SSA automatically. If your income has declined—for example, through retirement—contact SSA to use a more recent tax year.

There is no work requirement for Part B. Anyone who is eligible for Part A may enroll in Part B. Normally, you must purchase Part B by paying the premium (unlike Part A, which is usually free).

2012 Yearly Income			2014 Part B Monthly Premium
Single Individual	Married, Filing Joint Tax Return	Married, Filing Individual Tax Return	
$85,000 or less	$170,000 or less	$85,000 or less	$104.90[1]
$85,001 - $107,000	$170,001 - $214,000	Not Applicable	$146.90[1]
$107,001 - $160,000	$214,001 - $320,000	Not Applicable	$209.80[1]
$160,001 - $214,000	$320,001 - $428,000	$85,001 - $129,000	$272.70[1]
Above $214,000	Above $428,000	Above $129,000	$335.70[1]
[1]Does not include late penalties, if applicable. See text, page 136.			

Figure 6.1. Your 2014 Medicare Part B monthly premium depends on your 2012 income level.

Because it costs money, Part B is optional. However, it is also an outstanding insurance value, since the basic premium is only about 1/4 of the cost of the program. The federal government pays the remaining 3/4 from general revenues (not Social Security or Medicare taxes).

Henny enrolls in Part A and B at the same time. Since she is eligible for free Part A, she gets full Original Medicare coverage by paying only the Part B premium, $104.90 per month.

While enrolling in Premium Part A, Bob also enrolls in Part B. He receives full Original Medicare coverage even though he does not meet the work *requirement. His Part A and Part B premiums total $530.90 per month ($426 for Part A and $104.90 for Part B).*

Certain low-income individuals and families may qualify for state programs that pay the premium, resulting in free Part B coverage. These are called "Medicare Savings Programs." In addition to paying all premiums, these programs might also pay Medicare deductibles and coinsurance. Your local public assistance office can give you more information about the savings programs, or see www.medicare.gov/Publications/Pubs/pdf/10126.pdf.

Bob investigates the Medicare Savings Programs to see if his state will pay his Medicare premiums. His public assistance office tells him that he does not meet the income and asset guidelines because of his savings, but that he might qualify next year since his savings are declining.

Most American citizens and legal residents, then, are eligible for Original Medicare—Parts A and B—if they are age 65 or disabled, and eligible for Social Security, Civil Service, or Railroad benefits.

APPLYING FOR MEDICARE

In addition to the requirements mentioned above, you must actually *enroll* to gain your Medicare coverage. Some enrollments are automatic, and some require filing an application. The following guidelines explain when and how to enroll in Medicare.

When to enroll

There are three opportunities to enroll in Medicare:

- The *Initial Enrollment Period*
  —if you retire at or before age 65
  —enroll on or close to your 65th birthday
  —enrollment is automatic if you already get Social Security, federal retirement, or railroad benefits

- The *Special Enrollment Period*
  —if you or your spouse work past age 65 and have health coverage from the workplace
  —enroll on or close to your retirement date, or when your health coverage stops

- The *General Enrollment Period*
  —for late enrollment
  —penalties apply for late enrollment in Part B
  —coverage is delayed

Each of these enrollment opportunities is detailed below, but a simple rule of thumb appears in Figure 6.2.

If you are already drawing Social Security at 65, you will *automatically* be enrolled in Medicare. The same is true if you get a federal or railroad pension. You do not need to file a separate application. Your automatic enrollment will include both Part A and Part B, with an option to drop Part B if you wish (Parts A and B are explained below).

Sam started drawing Social Security at age 63. Therefore his Medicare enrollment is automatic. He automatically receives his Medicare card, good for Parts A and B, three months before his 65th birthday, along with an option to refuse Part B enrollment. Medicare also sends him a **Medicare and You** *handbook describing the program.*

Applying for Medicare

- If you receive Social Security, U.S. Civil Service, or Railroad Retirement payments at age 65, Medicare enrollment is automatic.

- Otherwise, contact Social Security 3 months before age 65 to discuss your options.

Figure 6.2. Summary of Medicare enrollment rules.

If you are not drawing Social Security or federal or railroad pension at 65, you may enroll during the Initial, Special, or General Enrollment Periods. In short, you can either apply for Medicare at 65 or have two opportunities later on.

Initial Enrollment Period: For Medicare at 65

Most people should apply at 65. To do so, you must file within 7 specific months: the month you attain 65, the 3 months before, and the 3 months after (see Figure 6.3).

If you enroll during the first 3 months, your Medicare coverage starts with the month you attain 65. If you enroll during the last 4 months, your Part B coverage will start 1 to 3 months after you sign up. In other words, for coverage to begin promptly when you turn 65, you *must* apply 1 to 3 months early.

Note that like other Social Security benefits, you attain age 65 the *day before* your birthday (page 38). Therefore if your birthday is on the first of the month, you are Medicare-eligible the *preceding* month.

Georgette turns 65 on June 15. She applies for Medicare in May. Her coverage begins June 1.

Rosemary turns 65 on January 10. She applies for Medicare in March. Her coverage begins June 1.

Initial Enrollment Period						
7 Months: Birth Month, 3 Months Before, and 3 Months After						
Month 1	Month 2	Month 3	Birth Month	Month 5	Month 6	Month 7
Coverage starts 1st day of Birth Month			Coverage starts 1st month after enrollment	Coverage starts 2nd month after enrollment	Coverage starts 3rd month after enrollment	

Figure 6.3. Summary of Medicare Initial Enrollment Period.

Special Enrollment Period: For Medicare after delayed retirement (past 65)

The Special Enrollment Period applies if you are over 65 and covered by an employer's health plan. Your health insurance must stem from your own work or your spouse's work. The work must be *current* work (i.e. insurance for active employees). COBRA or retiree insurance will not qualify you for a Special Enrollment Period.

If you are already covered by your employer or your spouse's, you may choose to *delay* enrolling in Medicare until the coverage from work ends.

Why would you delay enrollment? For three good reasons:

- *Little coverage.* If you are dually covered by an employment health plan and Medicare, Medicare becomes the *secondary payer*. Since Medicare is only *basic* health insurance, it may pay little or nothing after your employment plan pays.

- *Premium cost.* If you enroll in Part B, even accidentally, while still working, you will have to pay the Part B premium ($104.90 per month in 2014) even though you get no real benefit from the coverage—again, because Medicare will be the secondary payer.

- *Lost guarantee.* Finally, if you enroll in Part B prematurely, you may lose your Medigap enrollment guarantee—the six-month period for open enrollment in Medigap policies with no refusal due to poor health (see page 156 for more information). At your later retirement date, you may find that every Medigap company refuses to cover you. At that point, unfortunately, you would have no recourse, since your guaranteed enrollment period would have been used up back when you turned 65.

In short, if you have health coverage at work, enrolling in Medicare could cost you money, give you no extra coverage, and could deny you an important right.

To help you decide whether to delay enrollment, contact your employer's benefits office and Social Security (1-800-SSA-1213) to explore your options.

Most people with work-related health insurance delay Medicare enrollment, or apply for "Part A only" coverage—which is usually free—at 65, and delay filing for Part B of Medicare until later retirement. That's when the Special Enrollment Period comes into play.

Here are the rules for the Special Enrollment Period, summarized in Figure 6.4:

- You may enroll at any time while covered by the employer's health plan as an active employee, or

- You may enroll during the 8 month period beginning with the first full month employment or work health insurance has ended, *whichever comes first.*

- Enrollment after the month of termination delays coverage until the month after you enroll.

- You will need to prove that you were covered by the employer plan. A letter from your benefits office will serve.

Mike was still working when he turned age 65, and was covered under his health plan at work. He knew he could enroll in Medicare at 65, but he chose to postpone enrolling until his retirement.

*He retired at age 67 and signed up for Medicare A and B **then** with no penalties or delays in coverage. He still had the 6-month Medigap enrollment guarantee period, because he did not enroll in Part B earlier. He used the 6-month period to shop for a private Medigap policy with good coverage and a good price.*

William worked past age 65 and was covered by the health plan at work. He signed up for free "Part A only" coverage when he turned 65. He retired at age

*66 and enrolled in Part B **then**, without penalty or delay in coverage. That started his 6-month Medigap enrollment guarantee period, so he had plenty of time to shop for a Medigap policy.*

Special Enrollment Period							
8 Months: Work or Insurance Termination Month, and 7 Months Following							
Termi-nation Month	Month 2	Month 3	Month 4	Month 5	Month 6	Month 7	Month 8
Coverage starts 1st day of enroll-ment month	Coverage starts first day of the month after enrollment						

Figure 6.4. Summary of Medicare Special Enrollment Period. "Termination Month" is the first full month your health insurance from current work stops due to end of coverage or employment, whichever comes first.

General Enrollment Period: Medicare for late enrollees

The General Enrollment Period is for late enrollees who missed the Initial and Special Enrollment Periods. This is an "open enrollment" period each year in the months of January, February, and March. Penalties apply for late enrollment in Part B. Here are the facts, summarized in Figure 6.5:

- The General Enrollment Period is limited to Jan. 1 - Mar. 31 of each year.

- Coverage begins July 1 of the year you enroll.

- Premiums are permanently increased 10% for each year of delay.

James retired at 64, but waited until he was 67 to apply for Medicare. He learns in April that he could enroll only during the next General Enrollment Period (January to March the following year). His coverage would not begin until the following July. He did not want to be uninsured for 15 months, but there was no recourse.

Since he applied 2 years late, his Part B premium was permanently raised 20% over the usual premium.

Notice the *three penalties* for delaying your enrollment: limited enrollment dates, delayed coverage, and increased premiums.

General Enrollment Period January-March each year. Coverage effective the following July 1.						
January	February	March	April	May	June	Eff. Date: July 1

Figure 6.5. Summary of Medicare General Enrollment Period.

Note also that you can find yourself trapped between a rock and a hard place, with penalties for enrolling too *late* or too *early*. Because of the complexity of the decision, *Social Security strongly urges everyone approaching 65 to contact Social Security to discuss Medicare.* This is a wise course—it is extremely important to enroll at the proper time, and an SSA representative can give you expert, personalized advice.

To summarize: You are eligible for Medicare if you are 65 or disabled, and have the required coverage from work performed by you, your spouse, your former spouse, or in certain cases, your parent. If you are getting Social Security you will be enrolled in Medicare automatically. Otherwise you must apply through SSA. Always contact SSA before your 65th birthday to explore your best application date.

Once enrolled, you'll get a Medicare card (Figure 6.6). Show the card to most doctors and hospitals and Medicare will pay part of the bill, based on Medicare's benefits, described in the next section.

MEDICARE BENEFITS

Medicare provides *basic* health insurance coverage. It is not the Cadillac of health insurance policies, but Medicare does give good coverage for most people's needs. Government cost-sharing keeps the price low.

Medicare's benefits are divided into four separate programs, or "parts." Parts A and B comprise *Original Medicare.* Parts C and D are optional approaches to fill the gaps in traditional Medicare. We'll focus first on Original Medicare.

Part A is called "Hospital Insurance," and covers you when you are hospitalized. Part B is called "Supplemental Medical Insurance," or simply "medical insurance," and covers medical bills inside and outside the hospital, such as visits to your physician's office.

In the following sections, we will examine what Medicare covers, its costs, and the gaps in coverage that can cost you extra money. For more detail on what medical services Medicare does and does not cover, request the free *Medicare and You* handbook from Social Security by calling 1-800-SSA-1213, or download it from the Medicare website at www.medicare.gov/Publications/ Pubs/pdf/10050.pdf. See also the list of additional resources at the end of this chapter.

Figure 6.6. Typical "A-B" Medicare card showing the claim number and eligibility for both Parts A and B.

Part A Hospital Insurance

Medicare Part A helps pay for inpatient hospital care, inpatient care in a "skilled nursing facility" (described below, and not to be confused with "nursing home" care), home health care, and hospice care (see Figure 6.7). There are limits to the number of days of care under each category.

Part A Hospital Benefits

When you are an inpatient in a hospital, Medicare Part A covers 100% of the hospital room and board, plus medications, for the first 60 days, after you pay a deductible. In 2014 the deductible is $1,216 *per benefit period*. A benefit period starts when you enter a hospital or skilled nursing facility, and ends when you haven't received any inpatient care for 60 days in a row. If you are re-admitted after the benefit period ends, you will have to pay a new deductible.

Sam is hospitalized on February 1. He pays the hospital deductible. He is released on February 6.
On March 20, he is readmitted for 10 days. Since he is in the same benefit period, he does not pay another deductible.
On June 24—over 60 days after his last discharge—Sam is again hospitalized. He must pay the deductible again.

Medicare Part A Summary
Coverage:
•   Inpatient hospital care
•   Skilled nursing care after hospitalization
•   Home health care
•   Hospice care
Cost:
•   Coverage is normally **premium-free**

Figure 6.7. Summary of major Part A benefits and cost.

What if you are hospitalized for over 60 consecutive days? For the 61st to the 90th day of hospitalization in 2014, you must pay $304 per day. After 90 days, you can choose to pay $608 per day for up to 60 "lifetime reserve" days, or to pay the full charges (see Figure 6.8). Once the lifetime reserve days are used, you may never use them again—you will have to pay full hospital charges from day 90 on. In other words, the longer you are hospitalized, the less of the daily bill Medicare covers.

Both the deductible amount and the daily care charges increase annually with inflation.

Days 1-60	Days 61-90	Days 91-150	Days 151 & Up
$1,216 deductible (Once per 60-day benefit period)	**$304 per day**	**$608 per day** (Using 60 one-time "Lifetime Reserve" days)	**You pay all charges**

Figure 6.8. Hospital charges you must pay under Medicare (2014 amounts shown).

Coverage includes:

- semi-private room
- meals
- nursing care
- medications, and
- other supplies and services while you are an inpatient.

Medicare does not cover private rooms, private nurses, or personal convenience items you request such as a telephone or television in your room.

Also note that most *doctor's services* are not covered under hospital insurance, even if you receive them in a hospital. Rather, they are covered under Medicare Part B medical insurance. Part B is not as generous as Part A, as you'll see shortly.

In general, hospital coverage is good—as good as some private health insurance policies. But see the "Medicare's Gaps" section below to identify and fill the gaps in Part A (page 147).

For more on hospital care, see "Are You a Hospital Inpatient or Outpatient? If You Have Medicare—Ask!" at www.medicare.gov/Publications/Pubs/pdf/11435.pdf.

Part A Skilled Nursing Facility Benefits

Medicare Part A will help pay for the costs of care in a Skilled Nursing Facility (SNF). However, both the facility and your treatment plan must meet Medicare's extremely strict definition.

Don't confuse SNF care with nursing home care—SNF care is a higher level of care than the usual "custodial" care provided by a nursing home. Custodial care is help with eating, dressing, bathing, and other activities of daily living, usually provided by people with less medical training. Medicare does not cover custodial care. Skilled nursing care, on the other hand, means daily, continuous therapy provided by licensed professionals, such as physical therapy or intravenous injections requiring a doctor or registered nurse. This is a level of care very close to full hospitalization. In fact, Medicare will not pay for SNF care unless it follows a hospital stay of at least three days.

If your doctor orders such care, and the facility and level of care both qualify, Medicare will share the costs as follows:

- First 20 days: Medicare pays 100% of recognized charges.

- Days 21-100: Medicare shares the bill with you. Your payment is $152 per day (2014) during this period.

- Days 101 and up: you must pay the entire bill during that "benefit period."

- The benefit period is defined the same as the hospital benefit period—it ends when you have been discharged for 60 continuous days.

- Covered services are very similar to the services covered during hospitalization (see list above).

Under Medicare Advantage plans (described below), your costs can vary from these amounts, either higher or lower, depending on the plan.

For details, see "Medicare Coverage of Skilled Nursing Facility Care" at www.medicare.gov/Publications/Pubs/pdf/10153.pdf.

Part A Home Health Services Benefits

While you are confined at home, Part A home health benefits include:

- part-time or intermittent skilled nursing care or home health aides
- physical therapy
- speech therapy
- occupational therapy
- medical social services, and
- certain medical supplies and equipment.

Not covered are full-time nursing care at home, medications, meals, or homemaker services.

Care must be ordered by a doctor and provided by a certified home health agency.

Most home health services will be covered by Medicare as long as you need them. However, coverage for skilled nursing care and home health aides must be part-time or "intermittent." That means care must be needed or given on less than 7 days per week or less than 8 hours per day, over a period of 21 days or less.

Skilled nursing care and home health aide services combined cannot exceed 8 hours per day or 28 hours per week.

Services beyond these limits are approved in special cases. Otherwise, you will be responsible for paying for any further services.

Medicare pays the full approved cost of all covered home health visits and 80% of the cost of durable medical equipment.

Details can be found in Medicare's publication, "Medicare and Home Health Care" at www.medicare.gov/Publications/Pubs/pdf/10969.pdf.

Part A Hospice Care

Terminally ill individuals may choose to receive such services as pain relief, symptom management, and supportive services from an approved hospice organization rather than from a hospital or other standard providers. Medicare Part A will cover up to two 90-day periods of hospice care, followed by an unlimited number of additional 60-day periods, as long as your doctor continues to certify your eligibility. Virtually all services are covered, including nursing services, doctors' services, home health care, grief counseling, medications, and more. Not covered are a $5 copayment on medications, a 5% copayment on respite care for your usual caregiver, and room and board if you live in at home or in a facility like a nursing home.

For details, see "Medicare Hospice Benefits" at www.medicare.gov/Publications/Pubs/pdf/02154.pdf.

Other Part A Coverage

- Part A also covers inpatient mental health care in a hospital or specialty psychiatric hospital. Care in a specialized psychiatric hospital is limited to 190 days in your lifetime. Your share of the deductible and daily charges are the same as for hospital care, as shown in Figure 6.8. See "Medicare and Your Mental Health Benefits" at www.medicare.gov/Publications/Pubs/pdf/10184.pdf.

- Medicare will help pay for inpatient hospital and skilled nursing services in a certified Religious Non-Medical Health Care Institution, such as a Christian Science sanatorium.

- Medicare normally does not cover *foreign care*, except in a few restricted circumstances.

For more information on the special kinds of coverage, consult "Your Medicare Benefits" at www.medicare.gov/Publications/Pubs/pdf/10116.pdf.

Part B Medical Insurance

Medicare Part B medical insurance, the other half of Original Medicare, helps pay for health costs not covered by Medicare hospital insurance, including doctor's bills, outpatient hospital care, diagnostic tests, durable medical equipment, and ambulance services, plus new preventive care benefits.

There are limited covered services from chiropractors, podiatrists, dentists, and optometrists. Medicare *does not cover* routine dental and vision care. With few exceptions, prescriptions are not covered by Part B, but by optional Medicare Part D drug policies.

The Part B *payment schedule* is similar to private medical insurance.

You must pay a *deductible* of $147 per year (2014). That means you must pay the first $147 each year before Medicare begins its coverage.

After the deductible is met, Medicare pays 80% of all Medicare *approved charges*. You are responsible for:

- The other 20% of approved charges ("coinsurance"), *and*

- Any portion of medical charges that exceed the Medicare allowable amount ("excess charges").

Figure 6.11 illustrates the portion that Medicare pays and the portion you pay in the case of a $115 medical bill, assuming that the Medicare allowable fee for the procedure is $100. You would be responsible for up to $35.

Medicare Part B Summary

Coverage:

- Physician's and outpatient services

- Certain other medical items and services

Cost:

- Basic monthly premium: $104.90 per person (see Figure 6.1 for variations)

- After annual deductible of $147 per person, Medicare pays 80% of approved charges

---

Figure 6.9. Summary of Part B coverage and costs. (2014 amounts shown.)

If you are low income

Several programs can help with your medical bills if you are low-income:

- *Medicaid.* If you are very needy, *Medicaid* can cover virtually all your medical bills. Your Medicare premiums and deductibles will also be paid. You are automatically eligible for Medicaid if you get SSI (see Chapter 9), or you can apply on your own if you meet the stringent income and resource limits.

- *QMB (Qualified Medicare Beneficiary).* The QMB program (pronounced "quimbee") will pay your monthly Medicare Part B premium, deductibles, and coinsurance. To qualify, your income must be under 150% of the poverty level. That's $993 per month for an individual, or $1,331 for a couple (2014).

- *SLMB (Specified Low Income Medicare Beneficiary).* The SLMB Program (pronounced "slimbee") will pay your monthly Medicare Part B premium. To qualify, your income must be under 200% of the poverty level. That's $1,187 per month for an individual, or $1,593 for a couple (2014).

- *QI-1 and QI-2 (Qualifying Individual 1 and 2).* These programs can help you with part of your Medicare Part B premium if you have slightly higher income levels of $1,333 for an individual, or $1,790 for a couple (2014).

Each of these programs has income limits and resource limits. You might qualify if your resources are less than $7,160 for an individual or $10,750 for a couple (2014). Resources include money in bank accounts or other investments, but do not include your home, household items, and one car.

All of these programs are provided by your state, and work with your Medicare to help with your medical bills and premiums. For more information or to apply, contact your local public assistance office. For their number, call 1-800-MEDICARE (1-800-633-4227) and say "Medicaid." See also "Get Help with your Medicare Costs" at www.medicare.gov/Publications/Pubs/pdf/10126.pdf, and "Medicare Savings Programs" at www.medicare.gov/your-medicare-costs/help-paying-costs/medicare-savings-program/medicare-savings-programs.html.

To summarize: Original Medicare—Part A hospital insurance and Part B medical insurance—offers basic health coverage. Medicare includes major coverage for most hospitalizations and medical care, without providing 100% coverage. You must apply for Medicare on time when you turn 65, or when your health insurance from current work ends, whichever is later. Always contact SSA before your 65th birthday to be sure you apply properly and timely.

In the next section, you will learn more about the gaps in Medicare coverage and your various options for plugging these gaps.

SUPPLEMENTING MEDICARE

These are perhaps the most important questions you can ask as you approach Medicare eligibility:

- Where is Medicare coverage weak?

- What are my options for strengthening my health coverage in those areas?

In other words, what are Medicare's gaps and how can I fill them?

Medicare coverage is extremely valuable. It would be quite expensive to buy the same coverage privately.

Medicare's market value can be estimated from its premiums (2014):

Premium Part A:	$426 per month
Part B premium:	$104.90 per month

Part B government subsidy:	$315 per month
Total Medicare value:	$845.90 per month per person.

The same coverage offered by private companies might cost even more, after sales commissions and corporate profits were factored in.

Still, Medicare has always been intended as *basic* coverage, just as Social Security retirement is a basic pension program. Medicare doesn't cover 100% of health bills, just as Social Security isn't intended to cover 100% of your retirement costs. There are enough gaps in Medicare's coverage that your savings could easily be exhausted just paying *your portion* of medical bills.

Fortunately, there are many options to supplement Medicare coverage. A large number of the private insurance plans specialize in filling Medicare's gaps, and there are other strategies to reduce your medical bills.

First, let's take a look at the gap itself. Instead of looking at what Medicare covers, let's see what it doesn't cover.

Identifying Medicare's gaps

Pre-Medicare gap

The first Medicare gap is fairly obvious: you need health insurance before you are Medicare-eligible, especially if you retire early from a job with health benefits.

There are three pathways to help you get to age 65 or other Medicare eligibility, summarized in Figure 6.10 and explained here:

- *Retiree health plan.* You might be eligible for retiree coverage from an employer or union. This is similar to pension coverage, and usually comes from public employers, large companies, or unions, after some years of service. Remember to explore this option not just from your latest employer, but past ones as well. For example, you might have Tricare or VA coverage from military service years ago. To explore retiree health plans, contact benefits offices from your previous employer(s).

- *Employer group plan.* You might be able to get insurance from an employer group plan in one of three ways:
  - *COBRA.* Any time you leave employment at a larger company (with 20 or more employees), they must offer you COBRA coverage. Under COBRA, you can stay on your work health plan for 18 months after you leave employment. Contact your benefits office to learn more. Note that you could retire at age 63-1/2, have COBRA for 18 months, and then switch directly to Medicare with no gap in coverage.

- ○ *A job with benefits.* You could get health benefits by taking a job with benefits.
- ○ *Spouse's work.* If you have a working spouse or other relative, you might get benefits from that job.

- *Individual plan.* You could obtain individual coverage through insurance companies or your federal or state insurance exchange. For more information, contact individual companies, www.HealthCare.gov (or 1-800-318-2596), or your state's insurance commissioner. Find your state's commissioner at www.shiptalk.org.

One of the three pathways, or some combination of them, will get you to age 65 or other Medicare eligibility:

Bill was laid off at age 62. He received COBRA coverage for 18 months, until eligibility ended. He then obtained individual coverage through his state's insurance exchange. Three months before his 65th birthday, he applied for Medicare. His Medicare coverage was effective the first day of his birthday month, and he cancelled his individual plan.

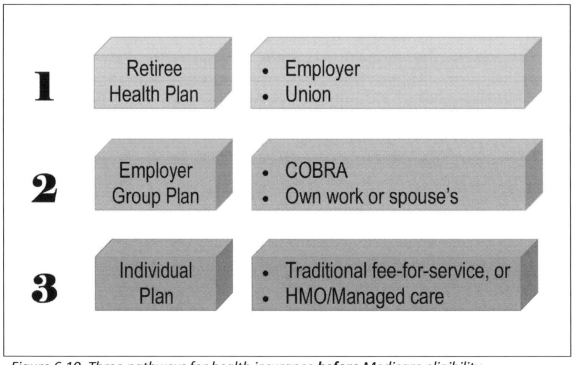

*Figure 6.10. Three pathways for health insurance **before** Medicare eligibility.*

Once you are on Medicare, there are still gaps to cover. Here are the largest Medicare gaps (2014 figures):

Gaps in Part A hospital insurance

- *The Part A deductible*. You must pay the $1,216 deductible per benefit period. The way benefit periods are defined, you could pay up to five deductibles per year, for total deductibles of $6,080 per year.

- *The phase-out period for long hospital stays*. If you are hospitalized for over 60 days you must pay $304 per day for days 61-90, and $608 per day for days 91-150. After that, you must pay all costs. For example, if you were hospitalized for 150 days (highly unlikely, but possible), you would pay a deductible of $1,216 plus daily fees of $45,600, for a total of $46,816.

- *Foreign care*. Medicare will not cover your health services while you travel or live outside the U.S.

- *Long-term care (LTC)*. Medicare currently pays a tiny fraction of the nation's long-term care bill. The only types of LTC that qualify are Skilled Nursing Care and home health care, and in both cases strict limits apply. That leaves you or your family exposed to huge long-term care bills. For example, nursing home median cost in 2013 was over $75,000, according to Genworth.

Gaps in Part B medical insurance

- *The deductible*. You must pay the $147 deductible per year.

- *Medical bills: 20% "coinsurance."* Even if your health-care provider charges only the Medicare allowable fee, you will still be responsible for the 20% remainder after Medicare pays its 80% share. The 20% you must pay is called the "coinsurance," represented by the middle block in Figure 6.11.

- *Medical bills: 15% "excess charges."* Your health provider can charge more than the Medicare allowable fee, up to 115% of the allowable fee. You would then be responsible for the 15% "excess" charges, represented by the top-most block in Figure 6.11.

- *Prescriptions*. There is almost no prescription drug coverage under Part B. Prescription charges can be a sizeable expense. Many people spend $1,000 to $2,000 per month on prescription medications.

- *Dental and vision care*. Medicare does not cover routine dental and vision services.

- *Foreign care.* Like Part A, Part B does not cover services you need while travelling or living outside the U.S.

Unlimited liability

Note that **Medicare has no out-of-pocket maximum, either annual or lifetime.** Your risk exposure is essentially unlimited.

Take another look at Figure 6.11 and imagine that the doctor bill is $230,000 for heart surgery, a year of chemotherapy, or other expensive procedure. Medicare's approved charge would be $200,000, of which Medicare would pay $160,000. Your responsibility would be $70,000.

You might need such procedures or therapies repeatedly in one year or for following years, and would have to pay your share over and over.

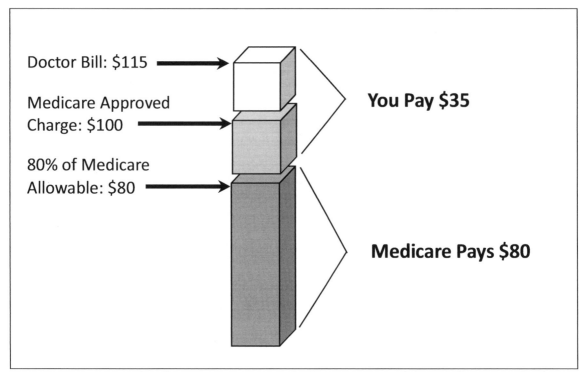

Doctor Bill: $115

Medicare Approved
Charge: $100

80% of Medicare
Allowable: $80

You Pay $35

Medicare Pays $80

Figure 6.11. Example of Part B coverage and patient responsibility in the case of a $115 medical charge (The 2014 yearly deductible of $147 is already paid).

How to Fill Medicare's gaps

There are three mainstream pathways to fill Medicare's gaps, plus some options to fill out your health coverage. Let's start with some background on self-pay and assignment pay, and then explore the three pathways.

If you are low-income see page 143 for help options.

Self-pay

One option is to pay your medical bills yourself, from income or savings.

Under any insurance plan, you will share some costs with the insurance company. However, if Medicare is your sole insurance, can you afford to pay for all health costs that Medicare doesn't cover? Remember that Medicare has *no maximum out-of-pocket payment,* either annual or life-time—costs are potentially unlimited.

Self-payment is an option, but is not recommended for retirement security or peace of mind. Remember: you exercise this option whether you actually *decide* that Medicare alone will be enough insurance, or you never pursue *another* option.

If you follow the self-pay course, you stand a good chance of financial hardship, particularly if you develop a chronic disease or require nursing home care. You could be exposed to hundreds of thousands of dollars per year in medical bills not covered by Medicare, for the rest of your life.

There are two variations on this option. One is that your *family* can help pay your bills. This is quite common in the case of nursing home stays.

Another variation is that you pay as much and for as long as you are able, until your funds are exhausted. At that time, you can apply for *Medicaid,* the public-assistance program that pays medical costs for low-income Americans. Medicaid is an aid program not connected with Social Security or Medicare.

Medicaid is a vital part of our social safety net, but most of us hope to avoid depending on it if possible.

Using doctors who accept assignment

You can save money if your doctor or other health-care provider agrees to accept the Medicare-approved charge as total payment for services. This is called "accepting assignment" on your health-care services. For example, in Figure 6.11, a doctor accepting assignment would charge no more than the $100 Medicare-approved amount.

You save with this option because you avoid the 15% "excess charges" doctors are allowed to charge. Your total responsibility will be only your 20% "coinsurance" (the middle block in Figure 6.11), once you pay the annual deductible.

Most doctors accept assignment on a case-by-case basis, because they would rather keep you as a satisfied patient than lose you because of a 15% extra charge. This could be particularly helpful if you are facing a single expensive procedure, such as outpatient surgery. In that case, the savings might be thousands of dollars.

There are also doctors called "participating physicians" who always accept assignment for every Medicare-covered service.

To find doctors or other providers who accept assignment, see www.medicare.gov/find-a-doctor/provider-search.aspx, or call Medicare at (800) MEDICARE (800-633-4227). Or simply ask your doctor.

Three Pathways

Now let's examine the three pathways for filling Medicare's gaps. The pathways are summarized in Figure 6.12 and detailed in the following sections.

Note that every pathway assumes you already have Medicare Parts A and B.

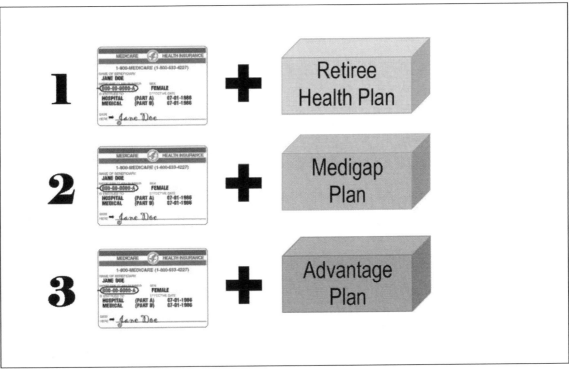

*Figure 6.12. Three pathways for health insurance **while on** Medicare.*

Pathway 1: Medicare plus Retiree Health Plan

You might be eligible for retiree health coverage from past work or affiliation with a union or tribe.

- *Employer or Union retiree insurance.* Your employer or union may offer retiree insurance. TRICARE, Federal Employee Health Benefits Program, RRB, and other government plans are examples, as are retiree plans from unions or large private employers. Generally you would enroll in Original Medicare and your retiree insurance. Medicare is then your primary insurance and your retiree coverage is secondary, so all medical bills would go to both programs. Check with your benefits office for details and advice. Most retiree plans also provide prescription drug coverage. If not (particularly if your retiree plan does not provide "creditable coverage" for drugs), you might want to also enroll in Medicare Part D drug coverage, described in its own section below (page 162).

- *COBRA.* Having COBRA coverage does not extend the deadline for filing for Medicare Part B (unlike insurance from *current* work), so don't delay filing for Part B even if you are eligible for COBRA. As soon as you enroll in Part B, you only have 6 months of guaranteed enrollment in a Medigap policy (page 156), and you might want to drop the COBRA then. The bottom line is that COBRA won't do you a lot of good when you're Medicare-eligible. However, if your COBRA has better prescription coverage than Medicare Part D ("creditable coverage"), you may want to keep your COBRA for drug coverage. When COBRA expires you'll get a special enrollment period for Part D enrollment with no late fees. Check with your state's SHIP (page 154) to learn whether your COBRA or Part D is the better route.

- *Veterans Administration.* Find out if you can get all your medical care through VA. If so you do not need to take Medicare Part B or buy additional coverage. Many veterans enroll in Part B anyway if they ever want to get medical care outside the VA system.

- *Indian Health Services, or tribal coverage.* Medical choices vary. Be sure to discuss your Medicare options with your coverage provider in order to get the best coverage for you and your family members.

Pathway 2: Medicare plus a Medicare Supplement plan ("Medigap")

Background. Medigap insurance, properly known as "Medicare Supplement" insurance, is private insurance designed to fill the gaps in Medicare. This is the most popular kind of insurance to fill Medicare's gaps. It works like traditional fee-for-service health insurance you may have in your pre-retirement years. It is time-proven, effective and affordable for most retirees.

Medigap policies are widely available from many major insurance companies. Policies that cover fewer gaps are less expensive, while those that cover more gaps are more expensive. Some insurance companies offer a number of policies at different prices so you can choose the right coverage for your needs.

Medigap eligibility. All of the Medigap plans assume you are already enrolled in Original Medicare, Parts A and B. Most Medigaps are for those over 65, but some policies cover disabled people eligible for Medicare before 65.

Types of Medigap plans. Medigap policies are standardized into ten policy types, lettered A, B, C, etc., as summarized in Figure 6.13. (*Note:* in Massachusetts, Minnesota, and Wisconsin, policies are standardized in a different way. See www.medicare.gov/Publications/Pubs/pdf/02110.pdf or contact your state's SHIP for details—see page 154.)

Every Medigap Plan A has the same defined coverage as every other Plan A, all Plan B's are the same, and so on. The only differences between several policies with the same letter designation are the premiums and the customer service you get from the companies.

Not counted as Medigap policies are:

- Medicare Advantage plans (Medicare Part C)

- Medicare Prescription Drug plans (Medicare Part D)

- Medicaid.

These will be covered separately below.

Note that neither original Medicare nor Medigaps cover long-term care (for example nursing home care), most outpatient prescriptions, vision or dental care, hearing aids, eyeglasses, or private nursing care.

New plan lineup. You might notice that some alphabetical labels are missing. On June 1, 2010, several changes to Medigap plans went into effect:

- Two new kinds of policies were offered, Plans M and N.

- Plans E, H, I, and J were no longer available to new subscribers. However, if you already owned a Plan E, H, I, or J as of June 1, 2010, you have the option of keeping that plan.

Basic Benefits						Plan				
	A	B	C	D	F*	G	K	L	M	N
Part A: Hospital coinsurance costs up to an additional 365 days after Medicare benefits end.	✓	✓	✓	✓	✓	✓	✓	✓	✓	✓
Part A: Hospice Care coinsurance or copay	✓	✓	✓	✓	✓	✓	50%	75%	✓	✓
Part B: Coinsurance or copay	✓	✓	✓	✓	✓	✓	50%	75%	✓	✓ ***
Parts A & B: Blood (first 3 pints)	✓	✓	✓	✓	✓	✓	50%	75%	✓	✓
Additional Benefits	A	B	C	D	F*	G	K	L	M	N
Skilled nursing facility care coinsurance			✓	✓	✓	✓	50%	75%	✓	✓
Part A deductible		✓	✓	✓	✓	✓	50%	75%	50%	✓
Part B deductible			✓		✓					
Part B excess charges					✓	✓				
Foreign travel emergency (up to plan limits)			✓	✓	✓	✓			✓	✓
Out-of-pocket yearly limit**							$4,940	$2,470		

*Plan F also offers a high-deductible plan. This means you pay for Medicare covered costs up to the deductible amount ($2,140 in 2014) before your Medigap plan pays anything.

**After you meet your out-of-pocket yearly limit and your yearly Part B deductible ($147 in 2014), the Medicare Supplement plan pays 100% of covered services for the rest of the calendar year. Out-of-pocket limit is the maximum amount you would pay for coinsurance and copays.

***Plan N pays 100% of the Part B coinsurance except up to $20 copays for office visits and up to $50 copays for emergency room visits (emergency room copay is waived if you are admitted to hospital).

Figure 6.13. The ten standard Medicare supplement benefit plans. See text for explanation of terms.

Definitions. Here are explanations of the terms used in Figure 6.13.

Basic Benefits, included in all plans, cover the following:

- *Part A hospital coinsurance.* This feature provides full coverage for long hospital stays. This includes your share for hospital days 61-90, your share for each of Medicare's 60 non-renewable lifetime reserve days, and all approved costs after Medicare is exhausted, to a total of 365 additional days.

- *Part A hospice care.* This covers the copayments or coinsurance costs of outpatient prescriptions and inpatient respite care while in hospice care. Plans K and L will cover the portion shown in Figure 6.13.

- *Part B coinsurance or copay.* This covers your 20% share of the Medicare approved charge for doctor bills—the middle cost block in Figure 6.11. Together with Medicare's coverage, 100% of the approved charges will be paid, not including the deductible or excess charges. Plans K and L cover the portion shown.

- *Part B coinsurance or copay.* This covers your 20% share of the Medicare approved charge for doctor bills—the middle cost block in Figure 6.11. Together with Medicare's coverage, 100% of the approved charges will be paid, not including the deductible or excess charges. Plans K and L cover the portion shown.

- *Blood.* Pays all charges not covered by Medicare for the first 3 pints of blood for transfusion. Plans K and L cover the portion shown.

Additional Benefits, available in some plans, may cover the following:

- *Skilled Nursing Facility coinsurance.* Pays your share of SNF bills for days 21-100 ($152 per day in 2014). Together with Medicare's payments, 100% of SNF bills for days 1-100 will be paid. Plans K and L cover the portion shown.

- *Part A deductible.* Covers your deductible for each hospital stay ($1,216 in 2014). Plans K, L, and M cover the portion shown.

- *Part B deductible.* Pays your annual deductible ($147 in 2014) for doctor bills.

- *Part B excess charges.* Covers the amount your doctor charges above the Medicare allowable fee, if the doctor does not accept assignment (page 147). This is the topmost block in Figure 6.11.

- *Foreign travel emergency.* Pays for medically necessary emergency care during the first 60 days of foreign travel. You pay the first $250 per calendar year of such care, then the Medigap covers 80% of costs, up to a lifetime maximum of $50,000.

Shopping for the right Medigap. It won't be hard to find insurance companies willing to sell you a Medigap policy. As you near 65, you will be showered with offers in your mail, on the TV, and by telephone.

You can organize your Medigap shopping by following these two steps: first, choose the type of coverage you want (A, B, C, etc.). Second, find an insurance company that can deliver the coverage you want at a reasonable price.

An easy way to find the right company is simply to check with your state insurance commissioner's office. All 50 insurance commissioners have a SHIP—a

Senior Health Insurance Program. They provide publications and individual help with insurance decisions, especially Medicare supplements. Many of them even list all insurance products sold in the state, along with their prices. To find your state's SHIP, check your state government phone listings, call 1-800-MEDICARE, or go to www.shiptalk.org.

Another "instant shopping" option is to use Medicare's online "Medigap Policy Search" at www.medicare.gov/find-a-plan/questions/medigap-home.aspx. Once you input your zip code, you'll get a chart of available Medigap policies with a monthly premium range, estimated annual out-of-pocket costs, and links to the companies selling those policies. You can contact the companies directly for more detail.

Joan is shopping for a Medicare supplement policy. She studied the ten policy types available and decided she wanted either type "C" or "D" coverage. Then she called four insurance companies and asked for prices on type C and D policies.

Just to be sure, she checked with her state's SHIP on the two lowest-priced policies, to make certain the companies were reputable.

Helen took an easier path. She started with Medicare's Medigap Policy Search online, and reviewed the chart of all policies sold in her area. She quickly narrowed the field to two choices, then called her SHIP office to check on the complaint record of those two companies.

Insurance companies selling Medigaps are required to offer at least Plan A, then may or may not offer other plans. Any company that sells other plans must offer at least either Plan C or Plan F. Each state's insurance commissioner has authority to accept or reject any policies offered, so selections will vary from state to state.

Multiple policies. Companies and agents are prohibited from selling you multiple Medigaps. Instead of buying multiple policies, buy one policy that gives you the coverage you need and can afford. *Exception:* you should consider Medicare Part D drug coverage (page 162) in addition to your Medigap policy. Part D policies do not count as Medigap policies.

More help. If you need further help making your selection, there are several excellent sources of information:

- See the free booklet *Choosing A Medigap Policy: A Guide to Health Insurance for People With Medicare* at www.medicare.gov/Publications/Pubs/pdf/02110.pdf. You can also obtain it by phoning (800) 633-4227. The booklet explains the gaps in Medicare and what insurance options can fill the gaps. It's also an excellent guide for those wishing to change policies.

- AARP has excellent online information on Medicare and Medigap policies. See www.aarp.org/health/medicare-insurance/.

- The Medicare Rights Center has good educational material. See www.medicareinteractive.org/index.php.

- Find a step-by-step guide to buying a Medigap at www.medicare.gov/Publications/Pubs/pdf/02110.pdf, pages 25-30.

With guides like these, you will have an easier time understanding and comparing the features of various insurance policies available to you.

As you shop, check to see if you can get a Medigap policy for free or at reduced cost from your work or your spouse's. Some employee benefits include this benefit for retired employees, and this could save you time and money.

Medicare and Medigap plans are individual-only—there are no family plans. If you and your spouse or partner are each Medicare-eligible, you'll each need to purchase your own Medigap policy. Your policies might be different plan types, and from different companies. The two of you might even be on different pathways—one with a Medigap policy and one with an Advantage plan, as shown in Figure 6.18 (page 169).

Medigap costs. Premiums for Medigap policies range from about $50 to about $250 per month, per person. Premiums depend on the insurance company and which Medigap plan you want. The policies assume you are enrolled in Medicare Part B, so to figure your total cost, you should add the Part B premium (Figure 6.1).

Joan found that her chosen Medigap policy would cost $150 per month. She will also pay $104.90 per month (in 2014) for her Medicare Part B premium. Her total health insurance bill will be $254.90 per month.

You'll also pay any medical bills not covered by Medicare and your Medigap. Find estimates of your total annual expenses at the Medigap Plan Finder at www.medicare.gov/find-a-plan/questions/medigap-home.aspx.

When to buy a Medigap. There are complex rules about when to buy your Medigap policy. The best time to buy is the Medigap *guaranteed enrollment period,* which lasts 6 months. This period starts when *both* of the following are true:

- You are at least age 65, and

- You are enrolled in Medicare Part B

For most people, that's the first 6 months after their 65th birthday. If you or your spouse work past 65 and have health insurance from that work, it would be when you stop work and file for Part B (see "Special Enrollment Period" on page 134).

During the Medigap guaranteed enrollment period, your Medigap insurance company cannot do any of the following:

- Refuse to sell you any policy it offers

- Delay the start of your coverage

- Charge you more because of a pre-existing condition.

Exception: If you have a pre-existing condition, the company can refuse to cover it for the first 6 months you're enrolled, or the first 6 months after diagnosis, whichever comes first. After that, you would be fully covered. Even during this "waiting period," Medicare would cover your pre-existing condition, and your Medigap would pay any covered costs not related to that condition. If you had health insurance coverage before your Medigap enrollment, the waiting period may be shortened or completely waived; check with the Medigap insurer.

Aside from the Medigap open enrollment, you also have a *guaranteed issue right* to buy a Medigap plan without restrictions if your previous insurance ends under certain circumstances. You have guaranteed Medigap issue if any of the following occurs:

- You are in a Medicare Advantage Plan that ends its service in your area, or you move out of its area.

- You enrolled in a Medicare Advantage or Medicare Select plan, but decide to switch to Original Medicare within the first year.

- You have an employer or union plan that is secondary to Medicare, including COBRA coverage and retiree coverage, which ends your coverage.

- You are on a Medicare Select plan and move out of the service area.

- Your Medigap company goes out of business, or otherwise ends your coverage through no fault of your own.

Your rights to enroll in a Medigap plan are protected in these situations. Outside of these cases you may be unable to buy a Medigap policy.

Changing Medigap policies. Choose your Medigap carefully. After your 6-month guaranteed enrollment period, it can be hard to change policies, either within an insurance company or to a different company. There's no federal law to allow changing policies, but some states allow periodic changes. Learn the rules in your state by contacting your SHIP (p. 154).

How to enroll in a Medigap. You enroll through the insurance company offering the policy you choose.

Pathway 3: Medicare plus a Medicare Advantage plan ("Medicare Part C")

Background. The third pathway to fill the Medigap is to enroll in Medicare plus a Medicare Advantage Plan, also called MedAdvantage, MA, Medicare Part C or a Medicare Health Plan. In effect you would replace your Medicare coverage with a private plan that gives you comprehensive coverage in one package.

These plans are offered by private companies and must provide all the services of Original Medicare (Medicare Parts A and B), plus additional benefits. They don't cover hospice care, but Original Medicare will still cover your hospice care while you are enrolled in an Advantage Plan.

Many Advantage Plans include prescription drug coverage. Additional benefits can include vision, hearing, dental, or preventive care.

Advantage Plans have a geographical service area, such as a county or state, where care is covered. There may not be an Advantage Plan in your area, so check availability early in your shopping. Outside the service area, care is usually limited to urgent care or emergency care only.

Advantage Plans usually have a network of doctors, hospitals, and other medical providers. Make sure their network meets your needs.

Advantage Plans are not considered Medigap plans, but a substitute or alternative way to pay for and receive all your Medicare services. You need a Medigap or an Advantage Plan, but not both.

Eligibility. To be eligible for an Advantage Plan, you must enroll in Medicare Parts A and B, including paying your Part B premium (Figure 6.1). In addition, you may have to pay a premium for the Advantage Plan, although some Advantage Plans have a zero premium.

Types of Advantage Plans. It used to be that Advantage plans were all HMOs. Now there are several different types:

- Health maintenance organizations (HMOs)

- Preferred Provider Organizations (PPOs)

- Private Fee For Service (PFFSs)

- Medical Savings Account (MSAs)

- Special Needs Plans (SNPs)

- Point of Service (POSs)

- Physician Service Organizations (PSOs)

The types available to you depend on your geographical area. Each arrangement works with you and your medical providers in different ways:

HMOs are the health-care networks of doctors, clinics, and hospitals which offer you comprehensive health care for a single monthly fee plus co-pays. You must get all your medical care in-network, with few exceptions. Generally, you name a Primary Care Physician (PCP) who directs all of your care. A referral from your PCP is usually needed to see a specialist.

PPOs are like traditional, fee-for-service insurance. You can see any doctor, even out of network, but you will pay more for out-of-network care. You do not need to name a PCP, and you don't need a referral to see a specialist.

PFFSs are networks of doctors, clinics, and hospitals that agree to treat you according to the terms of the plan. Like PPOs, you might pay more for out-of-network care. You do not need to name a PCP, and you don't need a referral to see a specialist. Care providers like doctors or hospitals can decide on a case-by-case basis whether to accept your plan's payment, so you need to confirm with the provider what you will pay to avoid surprises.

MSA Plans are similar to the Health Savings Account plans available to some workers, but for Medicare beneficiaries instead. You enroll in a high-deductible insurance plan, plus you establish a Medical Savings Account. The plan may make a deposit to start the account. You pay for all care up to the deductible, and share in costs up to the annual out-of-pocket maximum. Once the maximum is reached, the plan pays all covered expenses. Any money left in your MSA at the end of the year can be carried over to future years. You can go to any doctor, but some plans feature lower prices in-network. You do not need to name a PCP, and you don't need a referral to see a specialist. MSA plans do not cover prescriptions.

SNPs are limited plans for special populations, such as people living in institutions, on Medicaid, or with particular medical conditions like diabetes or HIV/AIDS.

POSs are similar to HMO plans, but you may be able to get out-of-network care for additional cost.

PSOs are plans run by a care provider or a small group of providers. You would get all care from the providers who enrolled in the plan.

Shopping for an Advantage Plan. As you approach age 65, offers for Medigaps, Advantage Plans, and Part D policies will stuff your mailbox. Your two best resources for sorting out the offers are your state's Senior Health Insurance Program ("SHIP," see p. 154) and Medicare itself.

Probably your most powerful resource for comparing Advantage Plans is Medicare's online "Plan Finder" at www.medicare.gov/find-a-plan/questions/

home.aspx. Input your zip code to get a list of all Advantage Plans in your area, their premiums, estimated annual costs, quality rating, coverage, and more. You can choose to input additional search criteria, like the prescriptions you take and the pharmacies you prefer. You can even enroll in a plan right from the Plan Finder.

Bill is searching for a Medicare Advantage plan. He goes to the Plan Finder and inputs his zip code and the two prescription drugs he takes. He narrows his search to plans with prescription drug coverage.

The Plan Finder lists four plans available. Bill reviews their coverage, premiums, estimated annual costs, out-of-pocket maximums, and quality rating. He narrows his choice to one, and clicks "Enroll" on the Plan Finder.

Your state's SHIP (see p. 154) can give you individual help with your shopping. Check to see if you can meet a volunteer.

Mary has narrowed her search for a Medicare Advantage plan using the Medicare Plan Finder. She can't decide between three possibilities. She calls her state's SHIP to discuss the three plans. When she has a clear choice she enrolls through the Medicare Plan Finder.

In urban areas you'll find many Advantage Plans to choose from. In rural areas there are fewer or no choices.

Like Medigaps, Advantage Plans are individual-only—there are no family plans. If you and your spouse or partner are each Medicare-eligible, you'll each need to purchase your own policy. Your choices might be quite different; you may choose an Advantage Plan, and your partner might choose a Medigap.

Advantage Plan costs. If you enroll in an Advantage Plan, you will pay Medicare for your Part B premium, and you will usually pay a premium to the plan as well. Once enrolled, all your health bills and claims will be handled by your plan. You will not be billed by Medicare for any covered services you receive.

All Advantage plans have an annual *out-of-pocket maximum* for Medicare-covered services to limit your expenses.
benefits office.

☆ ***Reform note:*** The Affordable Care Act—the health insurance reform bill of 2010—reduced the amount that Medicare pays Advantage Plans starting in 2012. Government subsidies averaged 114% of average Medicare billing from 2003 to 2010, and 120% in some cases. In other words, the government was paying more for medical care through Advantage Plans than they paid for care through Original Medicare. As these "overpayments" are phased out, Advantage Plans are expected to raise premiums and/or cut benefits, and might become harder to find.

Advantage Plan premiums range from $0 up to about $250 per month, per person, in addition to your Part B premium. Costs vary with the breadth of services covered, but typically you receive full hospitalization and additional skilled nursing coverage, full medical care, and possibly other services such as dental and vision coverage and Part D drug coverage.

How can some Advantage plans be *premium-free* while providing all Medicare services and additional services? Because Medicare pays the Advantage plan directly for every person enrolled.

Like Medigap insurance, your Advantage Plan premiums might be subsidized by your former employer or your spouse's. Be sure to check with your employee benefits office.

When to buy an Advantage Plan. You can join an Advantage Plan at these times:

- When you first become eligible for Medicare.

- During the annual Open Enrollment, October 15-December 7.

- If you move from your plan's service area, or if your plan leaves the Medicare program.

- You can change *at any time* to a plan that receives a 5-star quality rating from Medicare, once per year. See the quality ratings on the Medicare Plan Finder (page 159).

Once enrolled, you are generally enrolled throughout the calendar year.

Changing Advantage Plans. You can switch Advantage Plans at any of the "when to buy" times listed above.

Note that the annual Open Enrollment allows you to switch Advantage plans each year. One strategy is to take a less expensive plan early in retirement when you're younger and healthier, and switch to a more expensive plan if your medical needs change.

In addition, if you're enrolled in an Advantage Plan, you can drop it and return to Original Medicare in a special period, January 1 to February 14. You will also have an option to enroll in a Medicare Prescription (Part D) Drug Plan at that time. Note that there is no guaranteed enrollment in a Medigap plan, so make sure you can get Medigap coverage before you drop your Advantage Plan.

How to enroll in an Advantage Plan. You can enroll in two ways: through the plan or through the Medicare Plan Finder at www.medicare.gov/find-a-plan/questions/home.aspx. You can also enroll by calling Medicare toll-free at (800) 633-4227.

To learn more about Medicare Advantage Plans and the options open to you, see "Medicare and You" at www.medicare.gov/Publications/Pubs/pdf/10050.pdf, or contact your state's SHIP (page 154).

How to add prescription coverage: Medicare Part D

Background. You can add prescription coverage to any of the three pathways with optional Medicare Part D prescription drug coverage. Coverage is provided through private companies that are approved by Medicare. A Medicare Part D policy can help pay the costs of prescription drugs, lowering your cost of medications.

Here's how Part D works with the three pathways:

- *Retiree health care* usually includes drug coverage that's comparable to Part D coverage (technically called *creditable coverage).* If it doesn't, you can add a stand-alone Part D policy.

- *Medigap policies* don't cover prescriptions. You should consider enrolling in a stand-alone Part D plan to get drug coverage.

- *Advantage Plans* often include Part D drug coverage as part of their insurance package. If not, you can add a stand-alone Part D policy.

Don't buy more than you need. In particular, if you enroll in a stand-alone Part D plan when you're in an Advantage Plan that already includes Part D coverage, you'll be disenrolled from your Advantage Plan and put back on Original Medicare. In addition, if your Advantage Plan's insurance company offers a policy that includes Part D coverage, you must sign up for the "in-house" plan rather than an outside stand-alone plan.

Bottom line: if you have a retiree health plan from employment, make sure it includes prescription coverage comparable to Part D. If you're enrolling in a Medigap plan, be sure to consider a Part D policy in addition. If you're enrolling in a Medicare Advantage (Part C) plan, consider a plan that includes Part D coverage.

You should enroll promptly, since there are late fees for late enrollment; details appear below (page 165). You should enroll even if your prescriptions aren't currently expensive, since drug costs can escalate as we age. Many older people face drug costs of $1,000 to $2,000 a month, or more—costs that could largely be covered by insurance.

Part D eligibility. To be eligible for Part D, you must have Medicare Part A and/or Part B. To get drug coverage through a Medicare Advantage plan, you must have *both* Parts A and B. You must also live in the service area of the Part D plan you're considering.

Types of Part D plans. Part D plans can either be standard or enhanced. All plans have to meet at least the standard design. Enhanced plans may offer different additional coverage, such as a lower deductible or better donut hole coverage (defined below).

As noted above, Part D plans can be stand-alone (mainly to supplement Medigaps) or can be included in an Advantage Plan.

Shopping for Part D. Selecting and securing your Part D plan is a complex process, but computers make it easy. By following a few steps, you'll find the right plan for you. Be sure to enroll timely to avoid late fees (see below).

In most areas, there are many plans to choose from. In my urban county, for example, there are 33 stand-alone Part D plans, plus another 27 Part C plans that include drug coverage.

Part D plans are not created equal. Each plan covers different drugs differently, has different pharmacy outlets, and different costs.

The Medicare website is a great shopping tool. Collect your prescription drugs from your medicine cabinet and go to the online Plan Finder www.medicare.gov/find-a-plan/questions/home.aspx. Input your zip code and the names of the drugs you need, and your favorite pharmacies. Medicare will tell you which plans cover your drugs, monthly premiums, estimated annual costs, and quality ratings. Alternatively, call Medicare at (800) MEDICARE (800-633-4227) or your state's SHIP (see page 154).

Here's a tip: your pharmacy already knows which prescriptions you fill. Their computer might know which Part D plans work best for you, so you might start there.

You'll want to consider three "C's" and a "Q": Coverage, cost, convenience, and quality:

- *Coverage.* Be sure to consider the plans that cover your prescriptions best.

- *Cost.* Review the plans with the right coverage with an eye to costs. Remember, in addition to premiums you'll pay deductibles, copayments, and more. See if there's a zero deductible, donut hole coverage, or other "enhanced" features. The Plan Finder provides an estimate of your total annual costs for each plan.

- *Convenience.* Some plans fill prescriptions only through mail order or only through "in-network" pharmacies. Find the plans that offer pharmacy choices that are convenient for you.

- *Quality.* Medicare gives each plan a quality rating, from one to five stars, based on claims data and patient complaints. You can also check for quality with your state's SHIP (page 154).

Part D costs. Costs begin with the monthly premium, and can include an income adjustment and/or late fees:

- *Monthly premium.* Premiums vary from plan to plan. In my state, for example, 2014 monthly premiums for stand-alone Part D plans vary from $13 to $143, with many around $30-$60 per month. Premiums for Part C plans that include prescription coverage range from $0 to $328 in my county, with many in the $0 to $100 range. Depending on your plan, premiums can be paid by check, or be deducted from your bank account, charge card, or even your Social Security payment.

- *Income adjustment.* You may have to pay a higher premium for your Part D plan if you are a higher-income retiree, similar to the higher premium you pay for Medicare Part B. You would pay your Part D premium plus an income-related adjustment amount. See Figure 6.14 for details; the amount in the last column would be added to your regular policy premium. The income used, from two years previous, is the same MAGI used to determine your Part B premium (see page 131). Note that the income-related adjustment would also apply to Part C plans with prescription coverage.

2012 Yearly Income			2014 Part D Income-Related Monthly Adjustment Amount
Single Individual	Married, Filing Joint Tax Return	Married, Filing Individual Tax Return	
$85,000 or less	$170,000 or less	$85,000 or less	$0.00*
$85,001 - $107,000	$170,001 - $214,000	Not Applicable	$12.10*
$107,001 - $160,000	$214,001 - $320,000	Not Applicable	$31.10*
$160,001 - $214,000	$320,001 - $428,000	$85,001 - $129,000	$50.20*
Above $214,000	Above $428,000	Above $129,000	$69.30*
*This amount is added to your regular policy premium. Does not include late penalties. See text, page 165.			

Figure 6.14. Your Medicare Part D monthly premium may be adjusted upward based on your income level. The income used and the income brackets are the same as those for Medicare Part B premiums—see Figure 6.1 on page 131. (2014 amounts shown.)

- *Late Fees.* If you have a period of 63 days when you were eligible for Part D but did not have Part D, late fees will apply unless you had creditable coverage elsewhere, like from your employer. Late fees in 2014 are $0.32 for each month you could have had Part D or creditable drug coverage but didn't. That amount is added to your monthly Part D premium forever. The late penalty is recomputed each year, so expect your late penalty to grow in future years.

Part D coverage. Your prescription costs will be shared between you and your Part D plan. The costs are split differently as you pass through four stages in every calendar year: the deductible period, the initial coverage period, the coverage gap ("donut hole"), and the catastrophic period.

- *Deductible period.* As the year starts, you pay 100% of drug costs up to the deductible. The maximum allowable deductible is $310 (2014) for *Standard* plans. *Enhanced* plans can have deductibles as low as $0.

- *Initial coverage period.* Once your deductible is met, you enter the initial coverage period. Here your plan will share costs with you. The portion of each prescription that you must pay is your *copayment* or *coinsurance*— typically 25% of covered costs.

- *Coverage gap ("donut hole").* Once you reach total shared expenses of $2,850 (in 2014), including the deductible, you enter a *coverage gap* where you must pay more of prescription costs. This is commonly called the *donut hole,* because it's a gap or "hole" in your drug coverage. Standard Part D plans have a donut hole; Enhanced plans may partially fill it but charge higher premiums. In 2014, you'll pay no more than 47.5% of the plan's cost of brand-name drugs in the donut hole, and no more than 72% for generic drugs. (See "Reform Note" below.)

- *Catastrophic period.* You continue to pay higher prescription costs until total shared costs reach the catastrophic maximum, $4,550 (in 2014). Then you enter the catastrophic period, when your plan will pay most or all of your prescription costs for the rest of the calendar year. Expect to pay about 5% of your drug costs in the catastrophic period.

Costs for "standard" Part D plans are illustrated in Figure 6.15.

Help with costs. If paying these costs is a problem, there's help available. Programs called "Extra Help" can help pay Part D premiums, deductibles, and co-

---

☆ **Reform note:** The Affordable Care Act—the health insurance reform bill of 2010—phases out the donut hole by 2020. The phase-out is on schedule.

payments. In 2012, the resource limits are $12,640 (individual) or $25,260 (couple). Annual income limits are $16,335 (individual) or $22,065 (couple), with less help possible even for higher income. To apply for Extra Help, contact Social Security at their offices, https://secure.ssa.gov/i1020/start, or (800) 772-1213.

When to buy a Part D plan. You can and should enroll when you're first eligible for Medicare to avoid late fees (page 165).

After you enroll, you can change your plan annually during Open Enrollment, which occurs from October 15 through December 7.

Your enrollment is effective for the calendar year. In limited circumstances, you can change plans mid-year (for example, if you move out of your plan's service area). In addition, *at any time* you can change to a plan that earns a 5-star quality rating from Medicare, once per year.

When changing plans, whether at open enrollment or mid-year, you don't need to cancel or notify your old plan. When your new plan starts, your old plan automatically stops.

How to enroll in Part D. You can enroll in three ways: through the plan, through the Medicare Plan Finder at www.medicare.gov/find-a-plan/questions/home.aspx, or by calling Medicare toll-free at (800) 633-4227.

Deductible Period First $310	Initial Coverage Period $310-$2850	Coverage Gap ("Donut Hole") $2850-$4550	Catastrophic Period Over $4550
You pay 100%	You pay 25%	You pay 47.5% (brand name) or 72% (generics)	You pay ~5%

Figure 6.15. Typical Part D drug costs. You pay monthly premiums throughout the year, in addition to the drug costs shown. 2014 "standard" amounts shown.

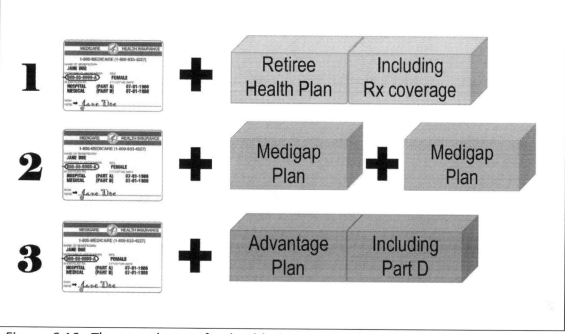

*Figure 6.16. Three pathways for health insurance **while on Medicare**, with added prescription coverage. Retiree and Advantage plans usually include prescription coverage. Medigaps require an added Part D plan.*

Sorting your options

With dozens of insurance options for most people, how can you decide which pathway is best for you?

If you have access to a retiree health plan, be sure to check it out. It has been pre-screened by your employer or union and might be your best option.

Otherwise the one big decision you need to make is if you prefer the Medigap pathway or the Advantage pathway. Once you make that decision the other decisions, like which policy to buy and whether you need a Part D plan, flow easier.

Learn the options in your area. After all, if there are only one or two Advantage plans and they're not attractive, you know you'll be on the Medigap pathway.

Figure 6.17 gives general guidelines to compare pros and cons of the Medigap and Advantage pathways.

Remember that there are no family plans under Medicare, so every plan is individual. If you are married, you and your spouse may not only have different supplemental insurance plans, you may even be on different pathways. See Figure 6.18 for an example.

Medigap Plans	Medicare Advantage Plans
Plans are designed to supplement Medicare by filling specified gaps.	Plans are designed to replace Medicare with comprehensive, all-in-one coverage.
Available in all 50 states.	Availability varies with zip code
Accepted by any provider who accepts Medicare.	Network of providers, with limited coverage or higher charges out-of-network.
No geographical service area; good throughout the U.S.	Defined service area with limited coverage out of area.
Guaranteed enrollment only in first 6 months of Medicare Part B eligibility; after that enrollment can be refused, especially with pre-existing conditions.	Open enrollment every Oct. 15-Dec. 7. No pre-existing condition limitations.
Switching plans after enrollment is limited; not guaranteed by law (but some states allow switching).	Able to switch plans annually during Open Enrollment. Able to enroll in a 5-star quality-rated plan anytime, once per year.
Can be difficult or impossible to switch from Advantage pathway to the Medigap pathway; such switching is guaranteed by law only in a few instances—see page 157 (but some state laws allow such switching).	No restrictions on switching to an Advantage plan from a Medigap plan.
No outpatient drug coverage; must purchase separate Part D plan.	Many plans include integrated Part D coverage.
Claims and appeals must be submitted separately through Medicare, Medigap plan, and possibly Part D plan.	All claims and appeals processed by the Advantage plan (including prescriptions if plan includes Part D coverage).
Premiums are paid through separate billing.	Premiums can be deducted from Social Security payments.

Figure 6.17. Comparing general characteristics of Medigaps vs. Advantage plans.

Other ways to get Medicare and gap coverage

- *Medicare Cost Plans.* Medicare cost plans are a type of HMO. The difference is that you can obtain care out-of-network through Original Medicare, although you must then pay all deductibles, coinsurance, and other non-covered costs. This option is only available in some areas.

- *Demonstrations/Pilot programs.* Occasionally, research studies are conducted to test improvements in Medicare. Enrollment is usually restricted to a particular population in a limited region.

- *Programs for All-Inclusive Care for the Elderly (PACE).* These programs provide intensive medical, social, and long-term-care services for frail people who would otherwise need to live in a nursing home.

"John" Older than "Marsha"	Both under 65	John turns 65	Marsha turns 65
John	Individual Plan	Medicare + Medigap + Part D Plan	Medicare + Medigap + Part D Plan
Marsha	Individual Plan	Individual Plan	Medicare + Part C Plan (Includes Part D)

Figure 6.18. All Medicare plans are individual-only, with no family plans. John turns 65 first and chooses the Medigap pathway. Marsha turns 65 later and chooses a totally different company and pathway.

Long-Term Care Insurance

A final way to fill Medicare's gaps is with Long-Term Care (LTC) insurance.

LTC is often thought of as *nursing home care* or equivalent *home health care,* provided over an extended period of time. However, there are other LTC options, including adult family homes, assisted living, adult day-care facilities, respite care, and hospice care.

Medicare does not cover most long-term care. Its Skilled Nursing Facility (SNF) coverage helps with medical care but offers no coverage for typical personal care ("custodial care") that many need (see page 140). Many people feel this is Medicare's largest gap, and the one most likely to cause financial strain.

Today, many LTC costs are borne by individuals or their family members. Medicaid (an aid program for the needy, *not* Medicare) pays most of the country's LTC bills. Private LTC insurance is assuming a small but growing role in paying these costs.

Many large insurance companies offer LTC insurance. It's also offered by some employee benefits plans. It is available in a broad range of prices and covered services. Some of the key options are:

- *Type of care.* Some policies cover only nursing home or only home health care, for example; others cover more or all types of care.

- *Benefit triggers.* These determine when benefits are payable. They can include which Activities of Daily Living (ADLs) are needed, whether a period of hospitalization is required, whether cognitive impairments are covered, and whether a doctor's certification is required.

- *Elimination period.* This is a period of time that must elapse before your benefits begin, varying from zero days to 100 days or more. During the elimination period, you are responsible for paying your entire LTC costs.

- *Length of coverage.* Some policies limit benefit payments to, say, three years; others range up to your entire lifetime. Most modern policies simply give you a *maximum benefit limit* that can be paid. Then your length of coverage would vary depending on the type of care received. For example, limited home care might be less expensive than assisted living care, so you would be insured for more months of home care before the policy is exhausted.

- *Daily payment amount.* You can specify how much per day you want the policy to provide. If you can pay two-thirds of your LTC costs, for example, you may need to buy only a $50 per day LTC policy. This is implicit if the policy specifies a maximum benefit limit (above).

- *Inflation protection.* You can also choose to purchase inflation protection for your benefit, so that the $50 policy you buy today retains its buying power ten years from now, when you may need it. Inflation may be stated as a simple added percentage, or—better—a compounding percentage.

- *Tax advantages.* Some policies, called Tax-Qualified LTC Insurance Contracts, can have tax advantages for premiums and/or benefits.

- *Other insurance benefits.* Some LTC policies include a life insurance component or other add-ons.

Costs of LTC insurance vary depending on how much coverage you buy, whether benefits are adjusted for inflation, how old you are when you purchase, and, in most cases, your current health. The less expensive policies have fewer covered services, no inflation protection, and are sold to younger individuals, e.g. in their 40s or 50s. Average premiums in 2010 were $2,261 per year for 55- to 64-

year-olds and \$2,781 per year for 65- to 69-year-olds, according to the AARP Public Policy Institute LTCI Fact Sheet 2012 Update.

Reasons for purchasing LTC insurance include:

- *Maintaining independence.* By financing your own care, you avoid dependence on family members or public assistance programs.

- *Estate planning.* You will protect your estate to the erosion of long term health bills—a frequent cause of poverty, even among financially comfortable families.

- *Broader care choices.* You will not be limited to facilities accepting public assistance cases. Your choices will include home care or higher-cost nursing home options.

In addition to private LTC insurance, you might have options like VA or other programs. Explore your options at www.longtermcare.gov.

A great resource for learning about LTC insurance is "A Shopper's Guide To Long-Term Care Insurance," published by the National Association of Insurance Commissioners. A free copy can be ordered at https://eapps.naic.org/forms/ipsd/Consumer_info.jsp. You can also learn from insurance companies, your state Insurance Commissioner, or AARP.

☆ **Reform note:** You may have heard that a new LTC option would be available in late 2012. The Affordable Care Act—the health insurance reform bill of 2010—created the Community Living Assistance Services and Support (CLASS) program to provide LTC coverage for workers. In October 2011 the Health and Human Services Secretary suspended the program, citing cost concerns. At press time the future of CLASS is dim.

To summarize, you must enroll in Medicare promptly when eligible; contact SSA to determine your best enrollment date. Medicare will cover the bulk of your medical bills once you enroll. You are expected to obtain additional insurance to fill Medicare's gaps.

You can and should obtain supplemental insurance when you enroll in Medicare. All supplement options assume you already have Original Medicare— Parts A and B. Wise supplement choices are summarized in Figure 6.16 and here:

- Enroll in retiree insurance from an employer or union, if available to you, or

- Purchase a Medigap policy plus a Part D drug plan, or

- Join a Medicare Advantage "Part C" plan that includes Part D drug coverage, if available in your area.

Finally, long-term-care insurance is growing in popularity and is also worth investigating.

FOR MORE INFORMATION...

"Medicare"
www.ssa.gov/pubs/10043.html

"A Quick Look at Medicare"
www.medicare.gov/Pubs/pdf/11514.pdf

"Medicare and You" (handbook for beneficiaries)
www.medicare.gov/Publications/Pubs/pdf/10050.pdf

"Your Medicare Benefits"
www.medicare.gov/Publications/Pubs/pdf/10116.pdf

"Are You a Hospital Inpatient or Outpatient? If You Have Medicare—Ask!"
www.medicare.gov/Publications/Pubs/pdf/11435.pdf.

"Medicare Coverage of Skilled Nursing Facility Care"
www.medicare.gov/Publications/Pubs/pdf/10153.pdf

"Medicare and Home Health Care"
www.medicare.gov/Publications/Pubs/pdf/10969.pdf

"Medicare Hospice Benefits"
www.medicare.gov/Publications/Pubs/pdf/02154.pdf

"Medicare and Your Mental Health Benefits"
www.medicare.gov/Publications/Pubs/pdf/10184.pdf

"Choosing a Medigap Policy"
www.medicare.gov/Publications/Pubs/pdf/02110.pdf

"Things to Think About When You Compare Medicare Drug Coverage"
www.medicare.gov/publications/pubs/pdf/11163.pdf

AARP's website on Medicare and other insurance:
www.aarp.org/health/medicare-insurance/

"A Shopper's Guide to Long-Term Care Insurance" free order form at
https://eapps.naic.org/forms/ipsd/Consumer_info.jsp

CHAPTER SEVEN

LEARN WHERE YOU STAND

"MY SOCIAL SECURITY" ACCOUNT AND STATEMENT

Remember the Social Security Statement?

You used to get a personalized annual statement from Social Security that showed where you stood with the program. Statements were suspended in the spring of 2011, saving millions of dollars in printing and postage costs, then reinstated in 2012 on a limited basis. Now statements are mailed once to workers turning 24, and annually to those over 60 until they file for Social Security. SSA is considering resuming mailings every five years, at 25, 30, 35, etc.

But there's a better way.

Just as your bank statements and investment accounts are accessible online, so is your Social Security information. Go to www.ssa.gov/myaccount and set up your own "My Social Security" account. Once you establish your identity and create a username and password, you can log in anytime.

Before you get Social Security you can review:

- Your earnings history for accuracy

- Estimates of your retirement, survivors, and disability benefits

- The amount of Social Security and Medicare taxes you've paid

In addition, you can generate the traditional Social Security Statement. It's provided in PDF format so you can save it, print it, or email it to your financial advisor as part of your financial planning.

If you are already getting Social Security, you'll still want a My Social Security account so you can:

- Get an official benefit verification statement to prove your income, for example to loan officers or public benefits officials

- Review your earnings record and benefit payments

- Change your address

- Change your direct deposit information

In short, everyone should have a My Social Security account to keep tabs on their status with SSA.

SOCIAL SECURITY CALCULATORS

Social Security offers both online and downloadable calculators to help you learn where you stand.

Quick Calculator

For a quick online estimate, go to www.ssa.gov/planners/benefitcalculators.htm and click on "Quick Calculator." You simply input your date of birth, this year's earnings, and your expected retirement date. The output is a rough estimate of your retirement, disability, and survivor benefits.

The calculator simply projects your current earnings backwards and forwards to perform the estimate. That would be accurate only if you've had steady earnings for your whole life. But you can fine-tune the earnings amounts.

From the estimate page, click on "See the earnings we used" for a chance to input your actual earnings rather than the projected amounts. The resulting estimate will be closer to your actual future benefits.

You can find your actual past earnings from any previous Social Security Statement you might have saved, from your tax records like W-2s, or by calling Social Security at (800) SSA-1213 and requesting your earnings record.

There's a better way. See "Online Retirement Estimator" below.

Online Calculator

For a much more accurate estimate, go to www.ssa.gov/planners/benefitcalculators.htm and click on "Online Calculator." You input your date of birth, estimated future earnings, and expected retirement date. The catch is that you must input all your past earnings, year by year. See the paragraph above for ways to find your past earnings, or the next section to automate the task.

Online Retirement Estimator

This program is much easier to use than the Online Calculator because it already knows your past earnings. Online, see the *Retirement Estimator* at www.ssa.gov/estimator/. You can use it if you have enough work credits to be eligible and if you're not already on Social Security. Click the "Estimate Your Retirement Benefits" button.

Once you fill in your request, you'll get an estimate based on actual past earnings and the future earnings you can post.

To model additional scenarios, click the "Add a New Estimate" button. You can change your stop-work age and future earnings estimates. You can view these estimates online or print them out for your records.

The Estimator cannot take into account railroad pensions, WEP, or GPO. Also, it can only estimate retirement benefits, not survivor or disability benefits. If WEP or GPO applies to you, see the next two sections, "AnyPia calculator" and "More calculators."

There are detailed instructions on using the Estimator at www.ssa.gov/pubs/10511.html. There's additional background on the Estimator at www.ssa.gov/pubs/10510.html.

AnyPIA calculator

For even more forecasting ability, download the AnyPIA calculator. Go to www.ssa.gov/planners/benefitcalculators.htm and click on "Detailed Calculator." If you're a Mac user, note the link to the Mac version.

Once downloaded, AnyPIA can compute retirement, disability, or survivor benefits for any earnings history you input. It also can perform WEP calculations (see page 55). Furthermore, it provides the numbers behind these calculations in detail. AnyPIA was used to generate the sample computation in Appendix A. In short, it's the ultimate wonky calculator.

The only caveat is that the user interface is, well, kludgy. It helps if you have a background in Social Security computations.

More calculators

Finally, you'll find a variety of additional charts and calculators at www.ssa.gov/planners/benefitcalculators.htm. Select the tab "Charts and More Calculators." Included are calculators for earnings limits while you get Social Security, payments at various retirement ages, life expectancy, WEP and GPO, and more.

Paper and pencil

If you are at least 62 and prefer the time-tested tools of paper and pencil, there are manual forms you can use to calculate your benefit. Go to www.ssa.gov/pubs/index.html, select "Retirement" under Topics, and page down to "Your Retirement Benefit: How It Is Figured." Select the proper birth year in the drop-down box, and you'll get a form and instructions to manually compute your benefit. It's a great way to get a "behind-the-scenes" feel for how benefits are computed. Sharpen your pencil and have a go.

RETIREMENT PLANNING WITH ONLINE CALCULATORS

The SSA calculators are valuable planning tools. With them, you will know what your Social Security income will be in retirement. In addition, if you have a pension plan and a similar pension statement, you can quickly calculate your total cash income in retirement. At that point, it will be easy to figure out what you will need from savings to support your retirement lifestyle.

These tools are even more powerful if you request two (or three, or more) estimates. You can use multiple estimates to compare several different retirement options such as early vs. late retirement, or part-time vs. full-time work until retirement. This section suggests some uses of the online calculators. Your imagination can add to the uses here.

Will I draw on my own record or my spouse's?

Getting the answer from SSA is fairly easy—just get an online estimate for yourself, and have your spouse do the same. With the estimates in hand, check to see if your own benefit is less than the payment you could get as a spouse (currently 35% to 50% of your spouse's full retirement benefit, as explained in Chapter 3).

If you are widowed, divorced, or separated, call Social Security (1-800-SSA-1213) and explain that you might be eligible on your spouse's record and need an estimate. In many cases, the SSA representative can give you an estimate over the phone.

There is a related question: *Should I keep working to try to get a higher benefit on **my own** record? Or am I going to draw a **spouse** payment anyway?*

If your own benefit is very close to what you would receive as a spouse, you may wonder if there's much incentive to work for a higher benefit on your own record.

To determine where you stand, try this:

- Get one estimate showing little or no future work.

- Get another estimate showing your current wages continuing.

Reviewing the estimates, see if stopping work keeps your benefit below what you would receive as a spouse. Also, see if continuing work boosts your payment above what you would receive as a spouse. Consider whether postponing your own payment to age 70 would make a difference. If your spousal payment will always exceed your own payment, continuing to work will not raise your Social Security. Together with other financial factors (pension, savings, etc.) and your personal preferences, this information can help you decide whether to continue working.

When should I retire?

This is one of the most frequently asked questions. A variation of the question is *"I want to retire early, at age 58 (or 55, or 60), but how much will my Social Security be reduced because of early retirement?"*

The SSA calculators can give you the answer:

- Get one estimate assuming a late retirement date, say age 66.

- Get a second estimate assuming an early retirement date, say age 58.

With the estimates in hand, compare the Social Security amounts. How big is your "penalty" for early retirement? Can your personal finances afford the difference? These considerations will help you determine your best retirement date, especially if you consult with a financial planner.

What about part-time, "phased" retirement?

Phased retirement is becoming a very attractive option for many. In phased retirement, you reduce your work to part-time to "ease into" retirement during your last few years at work, thus splitting the difference between working steadily to age 65 and retiring early. A similar strategy is to change work to something that pays less but you love more. The question then becomes, "How much will my Social Security be reduced because of lower earnings in the last few years before retirement?"

To answer this, get two estimates:

- On one, show your projected retirement age and show your *current full-time earnings* as your future earnings.

- On the other, show the same retirement date, but make your future earnings about half (or 1/3, or 2/3, etc.) of your current earnings.

Reviewing the estimates, you can quickly compare your future Social Security payments under each option.

Don't overlook more exotic claiming strategies like File and Suspend or Spousal-Only payments. See Chapter 10, "Maximizing Your Social Security."

To summarize: The My Social Security account and the online calculators are informative, flexible tools. They provide personalized information about your projected Social Security payments. By requesting multiple estimates, you can even answer "what if" questions about a number of retirement options.

In the next chapter, we will get to the nuts-and-bolts level of dealing with SSA: How to file your claim.

FOR MORE INFORMATION...

SSA "Benefits Planner":
www.ssa.gov/planners/

"Plan Your Retirement"
www.ssa.gov/retire2/

CHAPTER EIGHT

FILING YOUR CLAIM

GENERAL INFORMATION ON FILING YOUR CLAIM

The big day has finally come. You are ready to start drawing your Social Security payments or enrolling in Medicare. Now—how to apply?

This chapter examines how to file your Social Security or Medicare application. You will learn when and how to claim your benefits, what documentation may be needed, and what to expect when talking with a Social Security representative.

The purpose of the claims process is two-part: to make sure you meet the requirements for payments, and to establish a computer record which will pay you properly.

Your role in filing your claim

Your role in filing your claim is to initiate the claim, to provide accurate information to SSA, and to provide proper documentation, each in a timely manner.

If you start the claim on time, the other tasks are not difficult since a Social Security representative will be providing verbal or written instructions or requests every step of the way. For the typical retirement claim, filing for Social Security can be easier than renewing your driver's license. A more involved claim, especially a disability claim, will be more difficult.

The process can be easier than you think for two reasons:

- First, by reading this book, you have become an informed claimant with a strong background in SSA policies and practices. You are in a much better position to understand your rights and benefits than the average claimant, and to confidently navigate the claims process.

- Second, the typical Social Security representative will handle your claim with expertise and sensitivity. The staff at SSA consistently receives top ratings in surveys of public service delivery.

The role of your Social Security representative

Your Social Security representative has a unique role. She (or he) is the liaison between you and the government, and acts as a translator and "go-between." She works for SSA and must represent the agency to you. On the other hand, she must also represent your interests in your claim to the government. Her job is very different from the old stereotype of government workers "out to get you."

Her many roles include:

- Assisting you in any way possible to file your claim,

- Helping you obtain necessary documentation,

- Explaining the program so you know where you stand,

- Explaining any options you have and the short-term and long-term effects of each decision you make,

- Processing your claim as efficiently as possible, and

- *Paying you as much as possible.*

That last line is correct. If a representative fails to explore every possible avenue or option that could result in a higher payment for you, she hasn't done her job properly. Her performance would be chargeable as an error and could lead to a low evaluation or worse.

The point is, your representative is trained in the technicalities of SSA. Her job is to pay you the proper amount at the proper time—not too much or too little, and not too early or too late.

Are Social Security representatives perfect? Of course not. They're human, have good days and bad, and make inadvertent mistakes. But because of the background you have gained from reading this book, you will be in a better position to spot errors before they become problems.

HOW AND WHEN TO CONTACT SSA

When to file your claim

Call Social Security *early* to file your claim. The following guidelines will give you a good idea of when to contact SSA:

- For a *retirement or Medicare* claim or a claim for *family benefits,* file three months before you want your payments or eligibility to begin. That would be three months before your retirement date, your 62nd birthday, your 65th birthday, or other key date as appropriate.

Sam wants his retirement payment to begin in April. He could contact SSA as early as January to start the claim.

Marsha will turn 62 in August. She wants to file for spouse benefits as early as possible. She should contact SSA in May.

- For a *survivor* claim, file in the month of death if you are immediately eligible, and definitely within 6 months to avoid loss of benefits. (This is an appropriate chore for a friend or family member who asks "Is there anything I can do to help?") For later eligibility (for example, as you approach age 60 or your retirement date), follow the suggestions under retirement claims in the paragraph immediately above.

Harold died in November at age 28. His widow Hannah needed to contact Social Security to file for survivor benefits for herself and the children. Her brother called SSA in November to start the claims process.

Fran will turn 60 in June. She can apply for her widow's payment in March.

- For a *disability* claim, contact SSA as soon as possible after the onset of disability—definitely within 18 months. Your onset is generally the date your impairment makes you unable to work.

Sheila stopped work due to disability on January 10. She should apply as soon as possible for Social Security—definitely within 18 months to avoid a loss of benefits.

The reason for filing as soon as possible is to avoid any loss of benefits. One of the changes in the 1983 overhaul of Social Security was to severely limit retroactivity of claims. Most claims are now effective with the month of filing, so if you file late, you are losing valuable payments. Retirement claims are filed early to allow time for normal processing (usually only a few days) and for unforeseen delays such as problems obtaining proof of your age.

Three ways to file

There are three different ways to file your claim:

1. *In the office.* You can visit any Social Security office to file your claim in person.

2. *By phone.* You can call SSA and file over the phone, completing the claim by mail.

3. *Online.* You can complete an online application, completing the claim by mail.

1. Filing in the SSA office

You can file your claim the old-fashioned way, face-to-face in an SSA office. It can be the best bet for a complex claim, especially for exotic options like File and Suspend (see page 232). In-office is actually the least popular and most inconvenient way to file. However, a few steps will streamline the process:

- *Find your local office.* There are SSA offices in most towns and cities. Offices are assigned to geographic areas by zip code. Go to www.ssa.gov/locator/ and input your zip code. Or just call (800) SSA-1213 and ask for your office location. See the tips in the next section to avoid a busy signal on SSA's phone line.

- *Make an appointment.* You don't need an appointment to file, but it will shorten your wait at the office and smooth your visit. Call the 800 line (above) a week or two before you want to file. Don't be surprised if you're offered a telephone application instead, right on the spot. See below, "Filing by phone," to see if you'd prefer the phone route.

- *Take your proofs.* For a typical retirement claim, you'll always need proof of age, possibly your latest W-2, and possibly your DD-214 military discharge form, if applicable. Don't delay filing just to locate proofs. For more on proofs, see "Documenting your claim" below.

- *Be patient.* You might have a wait, so a magazine or other pastime could be helpful.

Once at the office, things should go smoothly. A retirement application usually takes less than 20 minutes and you'll be on your way. A disability claim takes about an hour. For details, see "The Claims Process, Step By Step" below.

2. Filing by phone: SSA's national telephone number

Your entire claim can be completed over the phone. This is currently the most popular way to file. To start the application process, call Social Security at their national toll-free number: 1-800-SSA-1213.

The good news is that through this miracle of modern technology, you can call any time of day from anywhere in the country. The bad news is that when you do, you might get a busy signal. Here are the details and some strategies for avoiding that busy signal.

The SSA phone lines are staffed from 7 am to 7 pm every workday, no matter what time zone you call from. (At night and on weekends, you can call and leave a recorded message. SSA is committed to call-backs for every message on the next business day.) Average wait time was only 4.9 minutes in 2012.

Unfortunately, many of SSA's calls come during the middle of the day, from about 10 am to 3 pm. Even though SSA doubles its shifts during those hours, backups are inevitable.

To avoid the backups, try these ideas:

- Avoid the core hours of 10 am to 3 pm. Call during non-core hours, e.g. at breakfast or dinner time.

- Call at night and leave a message.

- Avoid calling at the beginning of the month. Most payments are delivered on the first of the month (SSI payments) or the third (regular Social Security payments). Any delivery problems turn into phone calls to SSA during the first week of the month.

You'll find that by using these strategies, you will reach an SSA representative quickly almost every time. Still, it is always a good idea to have a magazine or other pastime handy when you call, just in case of delay.

Once you're connected, tell the representative that you want to file a claim.

A typical retirement claim takes under 20 minutes to complete on the phone. Disability can take an hour. For details, see "The Claims Process, Step By Step" below.

The rest of the application, including proofs, will be handled by mail.

3. Filing online

Filing online is becoming more and more popular. 41% of retirement claims were filed online in 2011 and the percentage was rising. One benefit to online filing is that you can do it quickly and easily any time it's convenient for you. You also can save a partially-completed application and finish it later.

Online filing is available during these hours (Eastern Time):

Monday-Friday:	5 a.m. until 1 a.m.
Saturday:	5 a.m. until 11 p.m.
Sunday:	8 a.m. until 10 p.m.
Holidays:	5 a.m. until 11 p.m.

☆ **THE INSIDE STORY** ☆

Who am I talking to?

When you call Social Security's toll-free number, you reach a *Service Representative* (called an "SR" inside the agency) or more specifically a *TeleService Representative* ("TSR"—an SR specializing in telephone assignments).

SRs and TSRs are trained to provide a variety of front-line client services, such as answering general inquiries and scheduling appointments. They are also expert at solving problems with Social Security payment records and handling Medicare issues. TSRs work in TeleService Centers, handling thousands of calls per day. SRs work in Social Security field offices, meeting face-to-face with hundreds of visitors per day.

The person who takes and processes your claim is called a *Claims Representative* (or "CR"). CRs also provide front-line client services, but of a more complex and technical nature. Examples include processing claims, writing appeals determinations, and troubleshooting stubborn computer problems.

The CR may have more in-depth training than the SR and rises to a higher pay grade, but make no mistake: when it comes to understanding certain Social Security payment records or complex Medicare problems, a CR will typically seek out an SR for expert help.

To start, go to www.ssa.gov/applyonline/ and click on the type of claim you'd like to file. Then follow the on-screen instructions.

For guidance, there are general instructions at www.ssa.gov/info/isba/retirement/ and www.ssa.gov/pubs/EN-05-10523.pdf, and a brief video at www.ssa.gov/hlp/video/ iclaim_r01.htm, with more information nearby on each webpage.

Once you complete the online application, the rest of your claim will be handled by phone and mail.

THE CLAIMS PROCESS, STEP BY STEP

The process of filing your application will follow certain identifiable steps. Let's walk through the typical process for filing a retirement application by phone.

Your initial call to Social Security

The day you've been waiting for has arrived. It is three months before your scheduled retirement date, so you pick up the phone to call SSA's toll-free number, (800) SSA-1213. Because you follow the calling guidelines above (under "Filing by phone"), you reach a Social Security Service Representative in a few moments. You tell him that you want to file for retirement benefits.

He asks whether you would rather go into a Social Security office or file the entire application by phone. Like 80% of people filing non-internet claims, you decide to avoid the trip and ask for a phone interview. You'll probably be routed directly to a teleclaims unit. If not, the representative obtains identifying information from you, makes an appointment for the claims interview, and says that a Claims Representative will call you at that time.

You can skip this step if you file online.

The claims interview

At the appointed time, your phone rings. It is your Claims Representative, ready to complete your retirement application. She starts by introducing herself. Then, she checks your identifying information and asks some general background questions about your work and planned retirement. Once this preliminary information is clear, your Claims Representative starts completing your application.

The application is a series of questions about you, including:

- *Identification*—your name and Social Security number, along with any other names or numbers you may have used. Your name and Social Security number are needed to confirm your identity and to associate your SSA records properly.

- *Age*—your date of birth, place of birth, and whether there is a civil or religious record of your birth made at an early age. These questions provide information about your age and how to prove it.

- *Work history*—where you worked this year and last, how much you earned, and an estimate of future earnings if you continue working. Your recent work will be manually added to your earnings record and may increase your payment. Your earnings will also be assessed to see whether they will affect your Social Security payments.

- *Special factors*—information about railroad work, Civil Service employment, foreign work, military service, and any pensions related to such work. Your railroad or government work history allows SSA to take such work into account in computing your payment, whether the effect is to limit your payment or increase it.

- *Family data*—your family members, including your current and former spouses and your children, if any. These questions explore whether someone may be eligible for a payment on your work record, or whether you may be eligible for a payment on someone else's record.

- *Payment information*—where you would like your payments sent. SSA no longer issues paper checks. The default is direct deposit into your bank or credit union. If you have no bank account, your benefits can be loaded onto a prepaid Direct Express Debit MasterCard. For details on Direct Express, see www.usdirectexpress.com/. SSA has switched to direct deposit and Direct Express because of the much lower loss and error rate. Electronic payment saves the government about $120 million per year in printing, postage, and processing lost checks.

Completion of your retirement application will typically take 10 to 20 minutes. As mentioned above, more complex applications—survivor or disability claims or complex retirement claims—will take longer.

If you file online, you'll input all of this information yourself, with on-screen instructions. You'll get an application number for follow-up and a receipt for your claim. There's a great preview of the online retirement process at www.ssa.gov/pubs/EN-05-10523.pdf.

Documenting your claim

After the application is completed, your Claims Representative will send the application to you for your signature. She will also ask for certain documentation, or "proofs," of particular facts on the application.

The documents you supply should always be original documents, not photocopies of originals. *Certified copies*, identified by the stamp, seal, or signature of the official record-keeper, are always acceptable. Notarizing is not needed.

Here are some kinds of documentation that might be requested:

- **Proof of age.** Proof of age is usually required for retirement claims and most other Social Security business, since every computation is based on your exact age. Preferred proof is a civil or religious record of birth made before you were age 5 (such as your birth certificate or baptismal certificate). If one of these is at all available, SSA will require you to produce it. Social Security representatives in any office and at the toll-free phone service can help you obtain your birth certificate from any state and from most countries in the world. If such proof is absolutely unavailable, secondary proofs such as census records, U.S. entry records, school records, etc. will be accepted.

Your Claims Representative will help you establish your age in the simplest acceptable way, and help you obtain the documentation.

- **Last year's wages.** You may be asked to provide last year's W-2 (for employees) or tax return (for self-employed individuals) to prove your recent earnings. Manually posting these earnings to your earnings record could boost your payment if last year has not yet been posted automatically. (If you are unable to provide this proof, your payments will automatically be recomputed anyway, when your earnings record is updated every year).

- **Military service.** If it will help your computation, you will have to prove your 1951-1967 military service (see page 211). Your DD-214 discharge form is the usual documentation.

- **Marriage.** If you will draw benefits on a former spouse's record, you will need to prove you were married for at least ten years. Your marriage certificate and divorce decree are the usual proofs requested. Proof of marriage for spouses filing together might not be requested.

- **Death.** If you are applying for survivor benefits, you may have to supply the death certificate of the worker.

- **Other public pensions.** If your public-employment or military pension affects your computation, you may be asked to provide detailed award letters from the issuing agency, so that their exact effects can be assessed.

Other proofs are sometimes needed, but the ones described above are the most common.

Documentation requirements are usually quite modest. When you apply for retirement, you will probably be asked for no more than your birth certificate and *perhaps* last year's W-2.

Your Claims Representative will mail your application to you with a written request to mail in the signed application and required proofs. But what if you don't want to send your original documents away in the mail?

Your documents will be returned to you. It's extremely rare to lose a document in the mail. Still, rather than risk a loss, you can take the application and the proofs to your local Social Security office in person—delivering valuable papers is a very common reason for visiting an office. In that case, the receptionist will probably move you to the head of the line so you can submit your papers. It can help if you call ahead for an appointment; your Claims Representative's telephone number is included with your application.

What is your Claims Representative doing when she takes your documents for a few minutes? She is *photocopying them,* after she told you not to do so! Actually, she has examined your original document to be sure it is authentic (this sometimes involves screening with ultraviolet light, for example), and she must certify the photocopy by affirming that she examined the original and that the copy

Applicant, Claimant, Beneficiary, Appellant

Depending on your precise status with Social Security, staffers will refer to you in different terms.

Before you file a claim for Social Security, you are called a *Number Holder*. This means that you are the person who was issued your Social Security number.

When you file a claim you are referred to as a *claimant.*

When the claim is approved, you become a *beneficiary* (or "bene," pronounced "bennie," for short).

If you file an appeal, you are called an *appellant.*

In some cases, the person filing the claim is not the claimant. For example, you may file and sign a claim for your minor child, who legally cannot sign his own claim. In that case, your child is the *claimant* and you are called the *applicant.*

matches the original. In other words, she is *creating a certified copy* of your original.

After examination, your original documents will be returned to you either in person or by mail.

There is only one step remaining in your claims process: posting a payment decision to your computer record. The computer record was established by your Service Representative back when you first called about applying for payments. It has been expanded as you answered the application questions and supplied the necessary documentation. Now your Claims Representative examines the entire claim—your application, documents, and earnings record—and decides whether or not you meet all "eligibility factors" required for payment.

If you do meet all requirements, an allowance is posted to your computer record and your first payment is triggered. You will receive an *award letter* describing when and how much you will be paid, including any back pay due. (You'll get to know these computer-generated Social Security letters well. They're sometimes a bit difficult to understand, but they mean well. Save them all.)

Payments will continue at the same level every month until a change is posted. For example, you might call in to change your address or report a new job; then, the new facts would be posted to the computer and appropriate changes made in your payment. In addition, the computer will *automatically* detect certain changes that could affect your payments. For example, an annual cost-of-living-adjustment (COLA) could be posted to all Social Security records, increasing your payment. Or new earnings could be detected on your earnings record, which could increase or decrease your payment.

If (1) your claim shows that you do not meet all requirements for payment, or (2) *if it fails to show either way that you do or do not meet the requirements,* your claim must be denied. An example of the first would be a birth certificate that shows you are not yet old enough for retirement payments. An example of the second would be if you failed to submit proof of age altogether. In other words, the burden of proof of eligibility is yours.

If your claim is denied for any reason, you will be sent a *denial letter* explaining why the claim was denied. The denial letter also informs you that you have the right to file an *appeal* of the denial. The appeals process is described in the next section.

THE APPEALS PROCESS, STEP BY STEP

Sheila's disability claim has been denied. The letter explaining the denial says there is no medical evidence to establish her disability.

Sheila believes this denial is wrong. Where does she turn to reverse the denial?

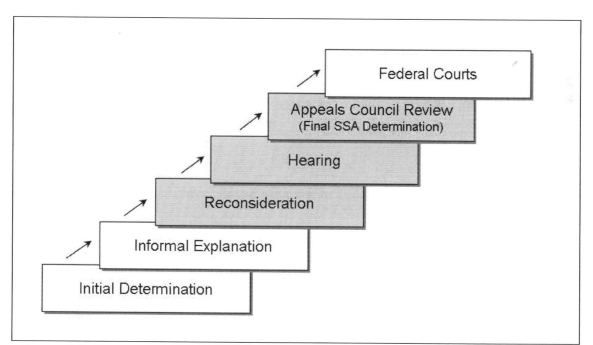

Figure 8.1. The appeals "ladder." Shaded boxes are part of the formal administrative appeals process.

Social Security is dedicated to making decisions and payments that are fair, timely, and accurate. But to err is human, and since Social Security is a human enterprise, error is possible.

The appeals process recognizes the possibility of errors and offers a way to correct them as quickly and inexpensively as possible. The process is built like a ladder, with lower, simpler levels of appeal to correct simple error, and higher, more complex levels of appeal available if needed (see Figure 8.1).

In a nutshell, the idea behind the appeals process is that if you are dissatisfied with a decision that SSA makes, you can request a new decision by a different person or persons.

The adverse initial determination

The seed of the appeals process is the *adverse initial determination.* This is the "bad news" you get from Social Security which sparks your disagreement. An *initial determination* is a decision about your payments made by Social Security which is subject to the appeals process. An *adverse* initial determination is one which in some way harms you or is not fully favorable to you.

Some examples of initial determinations which could be adverse:

- Entitlement or continuing entitlement to benefits. Your claim might be denied or your continuing payments stopped.

- The amount you are paid. Your payments could be reduced.

- Revision of your earnings record. Posted earnings could be reduced or deleted.

- Deductions from your benefits because of work. Your payments could be reduced because you returned to work.

- Termination of your benefits. Your payments could be stopped.

- Whether your impairment meets the definition of disability. Your disability claim could be denied because your impairment is not serious enough.

- Adjustment or recovery of an overpayment you received. Your payments may be stopped because you were previously paid too much.

In cases like these, you may initiate an appeal to get a new determination on the issue.

However, there are Social Security decisions which are *not* initial determinations and are *not* subject to the appeals process. Some examples:

- The amount of fee payable to an attorney representing you before SSA. By law, only SSA can determine the attorney's fee.

- Withholding part of your monthly payment to recover an overpayment you received. SSA is empowered to reduce your payments if previous payments were too high. SSA has the final decision on how much to withhold.

- Extending or not extending the time to file a report of earnings. SSA's deadlines are firm.

- Disqualifying a person from representing you before SSA. SSA may decide that your chosen representative is not capable of doing so.

In decisions like these, there is no appeal possible. SSA's decision is final.

When SSA makes an initial determination, you are notified in writing. The notice tells you about the determination and informs you of your *appeal rights*. The determination becomes *final* 60 days after you receive the notice (assumed to be 5 days after the notice date). Once a determination is final, you cannot appeal it, although Social Security will "reopen" the decision if a mistake is discovered within a specified time period, usually within a year.

In other words, if you are dissatisfied with a decision made by Social Security, you have 60 days to request a formal appeal. After that, it is too late.

When you are dissatisfied: the first step

The first step in handling an adverse determination is to simply contact your Social Security representative and ask for an explanation. Call the toll-free number (1-800-SSA-1213) or visit the office and say you got a letter that you need explained. Perhaps you will be satisfied by the explanation, or perhaps your Social Security representative will readily see the mistake and correct it on the spot.

At this stage, a confrontational attitude is rarely productive. Whether the problem is a lack of understanding, a simple error, or a major disagreement between you and SSA, there are procedures to handle the situation. By *working with* your SSA representative, you may solve the problem immediately without escalating it unnecessarily.

Sheila calls SSA to ask about the denial of her disability claim. She learns that the decision was actually proper because Dr. Smith, her cardiologist, did not supply two important test results.

No one suggests that you relinquish your rights at this stage. If you are not satisfied by this first step of explanation and discussion, you should request an appeal. At this point, the appeal is called a *reconsideration*.

The reconsideration level

The first level of appeal is called a *reconsideration* (or "recon" in SSA-speak). It handles only *initial determinations* with which you are dissatisfied.

Exception: if the issue is the waiver of an overpayment, the first level of appeal is a hearing, described below.

A reconsideration is a new decision on your case made by a new person. You will have an opportunity to review your file and present new evidence or point out important features of evidence already submitted.

Issues addressed by the reconsideration are not limited to the point of disagreement. Occasionally, a reconsideration opens a whole new can of worms—it could reveal another error in your case which must then be corrected. In rare occasions, you may win a higher payment on the point of disagreement, but end up with a lower overall payment because of the other adjustment.

You must request the reconsideration *in writing*. Initiating the request is as simple as calling SSA and asking for the form—a very brief, one-page form requesting the new decision with space for you to explain the disagreement. Remember, the request must be *signed and submitted to* SSA within 60 days of the initial determination, or it is too late (a postmark before the deadline is acceptable).

Exception: If the issue is a medical denial of a disability claim, you may file an *iAppeal,* an online alternative to the written request for reconsideration. Your denial letter will give you the internet link if an iAppeal is an option for you.

The time frame for a reconsideration, from request to decision, is usually between one and eight weeks.

Sheila files for a reconsideration and makes sure Dr. Smith provides the needed tests. A new decision is made by a different evaluation team, taking the new information into account.

After the review or the conference, the new decision-maker writes a fresh determination on your case. You will receive written notice of the new decision. The *reconsidered determination* becomes final 60 days after the date of the notice (plus five days for mail time).

If you are still not satisfied with the decision, you or your appointed representative can request a *hearing* on the decision. Remember, you must request the hearing within 60 days of the date of the reconsideration decision. This keeps your appeal open and raises it to the next level.

The hearing level

Sheila's reconsideration decision arrives. It says that her claim must be denied even though the new test results were considered. What is Sheila's next step?

The second level of appeal is called a *hearing.*

Exception: if a decision has been rendered at the reconsideration level or above, and you wish to challenge the constitutionality of the law governing the decision, you may request the *Expedited Appeals Process* (EAP). If SSA agrees, under the EAP you would skip any further SSA administrative appeals and go straight to federal court, described below.

You must request a hearing *in writing* within 60 days of the reconsidered determination. Like a reconsideration, the paperwork is straightforward; SSA supplies a one-page form for requesting the hearing with space to state your disagreement. (If the issue is a medical denial of a disability claim, you will be offered an online *iAppeal,* described above under "Reconsideration.")

The hearing is conducted almost like a legal proceeding, although it is less formal. The typical site is a hearing room in a federal courthouse, or by video connection. Presiding is an Administrative Law Judge (ALJ) assigned to your case.

The ALJ is not a "regular" judge; he or she works for SSA and makes decisions only on Social Security cases. The ALJ's background is impressive: a minimum of 7 years' experience as a trial lawyer, plus years of specialized training in Social Security law and in making medical determinations.

The judge will thoroughly review your case file and consider any additional evidence you wish to present. During the hearing, she may ask you questions about your side of the story. An expert may attend to offer expert opinion. (For instance, at each hearing I attended where the issue was disability, the judge asked a vocational expert to attend, to talk about possible jobs the appellant might hold despite the impairment.) You will also have a chance to have witnesses support your side of the story.

*Sheila's impairment is a combination of three impairments: heart disease, breathing difficulty, and arthritis. She points out to the judge that although no **one** of the impairments would be disabling by itself, in combination they are disabling.*

The judge asks Sheila for examples of her work limitations and consults with a vocational expert about Sheila's abilities and limitations.

After the hearing, the judge will write a determination on your case. It may be partly or wholly favorable to you, or it may be adverse. Another course is that the judge can send the case back to a lower level for a new decision because the earlier procedure was flawed.

The time frame for a hearing, from request to decision, is anywhere from two months to over a year.

The ALJ writes a decision favorable to Sheila, allowing her claim of disability. Sheila's award letter arrives one month after the hearing date. Because she filed timely requests for the reconsideration and hearing, her claim has been considered active since her first application date. She is awarded disability payments with full back payments.

The hearing decision becomes final 60 days after you receive the written notice, unless you appeal to the next higher level, the Appeals Council.

Appeals Council Review

If you disagree with the hearing determination, you may request a review by the Appeals Council. This is a panel of three ALJs in Washington, D.C. who review hearing decisions. There is no provision for your attending the review, but you can provide evidence in writing. Time frame from request to decision is about 6 months to a year.

The only possible issue at "AC Review" is whether the hearing followed proper procedures.

If a flaw is found, the AC will send the case back to the hearing judge for further consideration. The hearing judge might then find in your favor, but occasionally, the procedural flaw is corrected and the decision remains adverse to you.

If the AC upholds the hearing decision, it becomes the *final* decision of the Social Security Administration. At this point, the *administrative* appeals process is exhausted. However, you still have a way to appeal the decision outside the administrative process, by using the court system.

Suing in Federal court

Once all administrative avenues of appeal have been completed, you can still bring civil suit against the Social Security Administration in federal district court.

Your suit must be filed within 60 days from the date you receive notice of the Appeals Council decision. The court may make a decision on your case or "remand" (return) the case to Social Security for further development.

If you are dissatisfied with the district court decision, you could appeal to higher courts like the Appellate Court and, eventually, the Supreme Court.

Interestingly, many of the changes in Social Security law and practices come not from the Administration or Congress, but from the court system. An example was a 1992 district court decision that SSA needed to simplify the procedure for workers to correct erroneous earnings records. SSA agreed to simplify evidence requirements and improve communication links with IRS, the source of earnings information.

The point is, don't believe the old saw that "you can't fight city hall." You can, and you could win, leading to better conditions for all.

Let's move now from the "ladder of appeal" to a question raised by many Social Security claimants: should a representative handle the appeal and other Social Security business?

Should an attorney handle the appeal?

You are welcome to have a friend, family member, or professional representative (such as an attorney) handle any Social Security business you may have, including your appeal. The representative you appoint must be an individual, not a corporation or other organization, and must be qualified to represent you.

The decision to appoint a representative is a personal one. Social Security is not in the business of "putting one over" on you. SSA employees normally extend to you every courtesy to help you make proper choices, and they should make fair decisions on your case. However, Social Security can be intimidating, especially at the appeals level. At the very least, I would recommend that you have a friend or family member accompany you to a hearing or other conference. Many appellants have told me that having a friend along helps calm jittery nerves on the day of the hearing.

Hiring a professional representative can be a reasonable option to consider, depending on the complexity of the case and your ability to present your side clearly and convincingly. It's especially reasonable at the hearing level and above. If you are not represented, the ALJ will go the extra mile to understand your situation and make a fair decision, but having representation puts a knowledgeable professional on your side.

Any time you are dealing with the federal courts, it is strongly advisable to have legal representation.

If you choose to appoint a representative, try to find someone who has experience handling Social Security appeals. In many cities, retired ALJs or SSA attorneys have started private practices which specialize in SSA appeals. There are also other attorneys who specialize in Social Security. If fees are a problem, consider getting free or low-cost legal help from your local Legal Aid Society; Social Security is a familiar part of their practice. A call to your local bar association should produce several possible representatives. Or check your Yellow Pages under "Attorneys—Social Security."

Speaking of fees, your representative cannot charge a fee without written approval from SSA. In many cases, a professional representative will serve in return for a portion of any back pay you receive from a favorable decision. SSA limits such fees to 25% of the back payment, and commonly arranges direct payment for the representative by withholding a portion of your back payment.

To summarize:

- You should file your Social Security claim as early as possible—up to three months before your payments should begin.

- You can file in person, by phone, or online.

- You will be asked to provide certain documents to establish your eligibility.

- The appeals process is a mechanism for reconsidering decisions and correcting errors. Most Social Security decisions become final only after a period of 60 days, which allows you to question or appeal the decision. You may request an appeal of an initial decision. If the appeal decision is again unfavorable, you may appeal to a higher level.

- At your option, you may appoint a representative to handle your Social Security business, including an appeal.

FOR MORE INFORMATION...

"Boldly Go To www.socialsecurity.gov"
www.ssa.gov/pubs/10032.html

"How To Apply Online For Retirement Benefits" with screen shots
www.ssa.gov/pubs/10523.html

"How to Apply Online For Just Medicare"
www.ssa.gov/medicareonly/

"How To Apply Online For Medicare Only" with screen shots
www.ssa.gov/pubs/10531.html

"The Appeals Process"
www.ssa.gov/pubs/10041.html

"Your Right To Question The Decision Made On Your Claim"
www.ssa.gov/pubs/10058.html

"Your Right To Representation"
www.ssa.gov/pubs/10075.html

CHAPTER NINE

ASSORTED TOPICS

WORK IN RETIREMENT

I want to pursue my dream of starting a small business in my retirement. My husband has his eye on his ideal part-time job for his retirement. Can a person work and still receive Social Security retirement payments?

The answer is a *qualified yes*.

Social Security retirement payments are intended for retirement. Because they are meant to help finance retirement, SSA needs some way to determine whether an individual is fully retired. The solution is an earnings limit which applies to anyone who works and receives Social Security retirement, family, or survivor payments.

With two exceptions, everyone—retired workers, spouses, survivors, even children—is subject to the work limits detailed here. The two exceptions: first, there are no earnings limits if you are Full Retirement Age (FRA) and above, and second, there are special rules for disabled persons who work (see page 111).

The annual limit

How the earnings limits work

Each year two earnings limits are set, one for individuals under FRA, and another for those turning FRA, for the months prior to their actual birthday. In 2014, the earnings limits are:

Under FRA	$15,480 per year
Turning FRA	$41,400 (for months prior to birth month only)
Over FRA	No penalty

If your earnings are under your limit, your Social Security benefits are not reduced in any way. For example, if you are 64 and receiving Social Security, and you earn $11,600 this year, your monthly Social Security payment will not be reduced. In fact, the additional earnings, when posted to your earnings record, may increase the amount of your Social Security payment.

If you earn more than the annual earnings limit

Higher earnings may reduce, but not necessarily stop, your payments, according to the following formula:

- Under FRA: $1 is deducted from your Social Security payments for every $2 you earn above the limit (one-half of your "excess earnings").

- The year your attain FRA: $1 is deducted for every $3 you earn above the limit (one-third of your "excess earnings"), for months before your birth month *only*.

- Month of FRA and above: No effect, no penalty.

The amount deducted is called your "work deductions" for the year. Examples appear below.

Income that counts toward the earnings limits

There are only two types of income which count toward your limit: gross wages from your employment, or net earnings from your self-employment. (Included in your wages are bonuses, commissions, fees, vacation pay, cash tips of $20 or more a month, severance pay, and noncash compensation such as meals or living quarters.)

Other income does not count. So if you have investment income, interest, Veterans or other government payments, rental income (unless that is your business activity), or an inheritance, such non-work earnings will not affect your Social Security and you do not have to report them as income to SSA. Basically, then, SSA is interested *if you return to work,* in either employment or self-employment. If you do return to work after you begin to receive Social Security benefits, you must promptly report such work to SSA. Remember these points:

- SSA counts total yearly earnings, including all wages and self-employment income. Exception: in the year you turn 65, only earnings before your birthday month count.

- SSA counts gross wages, not take-home pay.

- SSA counts wages from a job even if you don't pay Social Security taxes.

- You will still have to pay Social Security taxes if they apply to your job. Your new wages will be credited to your earnings record and may increase your monthly Social Security payment.

If you're self-employed

Special rules apply if you are self-employed or a corporate officer. SSA may investigate your work to see if your stated earnings accurately reflect the true worth of your work. Again, the aim is to determine if you are actually "retired."

For more information on self-employment, see the SSA publications listed on page 204.

Examples of work in retirement

Some examples will make these rules clearer.

Example 1: Age 63, earning $19,480 in 2014.

Earnings	$19,480
Less your limit (under FRA)	—15,480
Excess Earnings	$4,000
x 1/2	x 1/2
Deduction amount	= $2,000

Therefore, $2,000 will be withheld from this year's Social Security payments. (The manner of deduction is discussed just after Example 3 below.)

Example 2: Turning FRA, earning $60,000 in 2014 ($44,730 before birthday month).

Earnings before birthday month	$44,730
Less your FRA limit	—41,400
Excess Earnings	$3,330
x 1/3	x 1/3
Deduction amount	= $1,110

Here, $1,110 will be withheld from this year's Social Security payments. Earnings in or after your birthday month will not count.

Example 3: Age 68, earning $75,000 in 2014.

There is no limit for those FRA and above, so there is no effect on Social Security payments.

How deductions are made

Impact on the worker's benefit

If work deductions apply, some or all of your Social Security payments will be withheld. In Example 1 above, the $2,000 would have to be deducted from this year's Social Security payments. This is done by stopping your payments until the full $2,000 has been held back. If your monthly benefit is $1,200, your entire January and February payments would be withheld. You would receive full payments every month for the rest of the year.

In Example 2, you would have your January payment withheld, then receive full payments for the rest of the year.

Impact on family benefits

In addition to your own payment, any *spouse benefits* or *child benefits* payable on your record can be reduced because of your work. Spreading out the deductions to these other payments will more quickly "pay off" your excess earnings.

There can be unpleasant effects when your work causes an interruption in payments to your spouse and children. Be especially aware that deductions can be imposed on your children being raised by a former spouse. (An exception: your *former* spouse's payments will not be withheld because of your earnings. Page 65 explains the reason for this exception.)

Impact if a family member works

Earnings of other family members will affect only their own Social Security payments. An exception would be if other family members are receiving Social Security on your spouse's work record.

You can work and draw Social Security at the same time

The bottom line is that you can work and draw Social Security at the same time. Too many people think that if they earn one dollar over their limit, all their Social Security payments will be immediately halted. But as you can see, you would have to earn quite a bit to completely stop your payment. If you are 64 and receiving

$1,500 per month from SSA, you would have to earn $51,480 to stop all 12 of your Social Security payments.

And anyone reaching their FRA, working or not, should consider filing, since there are no work penalties after your birthday.

The monthly limit

Starting Social Security mid-year

Mary wants to retire at 62 in July and then start her Social Security. But her earnings in the first 6 months exceed the annual earnings limit. Will her pre-retirement earnings decrease her Social Security after retirement?

For situations like this, a special rule applies. Under this rule, you can receive a full Social Security payment for any month you are "retired," regardless of your yearly earnings. This rule usually applies only during your first year of retirement, and you must be under your Full Retirement Age (page 51).

To meet this requirement, your earnings in any particular month must be under a *monthly limit*. The monthly limit is always 1/12 of the annual limit, so in 2014, the limit is $1,290 per month, or $3,450 per month in the year you attain FRA.

If you retire on July 1, then, you will be eligible for Social Security in July and every month through December—no matter what your earnings in the first half of the year were—so long as your earnings for each of those months are under the monthly limit.

Returning to temporary work

Let's change the example a bit. Suppose after you retire on July 1, your employer asks you to come back on a temporary basis. In September and October you earn over your monthly limit, then your earnings drop back to zero.

In that case you would be eligible for full Social Security in every month after June *except* September and October.

The monthly limit and self-employment

It is very difficult to compute monthly earnings for self-employed individuals, so the monthly limit measures your *hours of work* rather than your earnings. There are two important thresholds:

- Working over 45 hours in a month is generally considered "substantial services" and bars your Social Security for that month.

- Working under 15 hours in a month is not considered substantial.
- Work between 15 and 45 hours is judged on the individual characteristics of your case.

If you perform professional work in your business like marketing, bookkeeping, or providing professional services, only the 15-hour limit applies.

Applying the proper limit

In your first year of retirement, SSA will compute your payments using both the annual limits and the monthly limits. You will be paid using whichever method is best for you.

Credit back for stopped payments: The ARF

If any of your Social Security payments is stopped *due to work,* you get credit back for every missing month, and a raise in your future payments. It's called the Adjustment to the Reduction Factor (ARF), and happens automatically when you reach FRA.

Here's how it works: Let's say your FRA is 66 and you start your Social Security at 62. You get a 75% payment because you're 48 months early; SSA believes you will receive 48 early payments. The 25% cut is called your *Reduction Factor.*

Now suppose you get a great job 8 months later, and you earn enough that all the rest of your Social Security payments are stopped, all the way to your FRA.

When you reach 66, SSA looks back and sees that you actually received only 8 early payments, not the 48 early payments expected. SSA will perform an *Adjustment to the Reduction Factor (ARF)* and adjust your payments accordingly. Instead of a 25% reduction for 48 early payments, you'll have a 4.4% reduction for 8 early payments. In other words, you'll get a raise from a 75% payment to a 95.6% payment.

The ARF is automatic. If you forfeited some payments because of work, all you have to do is survive to your FRA to get credit back.

More information on working while retired

"How Work Affects Your Benefits"
www.ssa.gov/pubs/10069.html

"If You Are Self-Employed"
www.ssa.gov/pubs/10022.html

INCOME TAX ON SOCIAL SECURITY BENEFITS

General information about taxation of Social Security payments

Part of your Social Security benefits may be included in your taxable income. In general, lower-income retirees do not pay taxes on their Social Security, while higher-income people do, on a sliding scale.

No more than 85% of your Social Security is taxable; so at least 15% of your Social Security is always tax-free. Though your benefits are not completely tax-free, they are "tax-advantaged."

The tax money collected is reimbursed to the Social Security system.

Taxation of your Social Security is triggered when certain countable income exceeds a specified limit called the "Base Amount." Your IRS Form 1040 instructions will walk you through your individual computation, but here is a preview.

The computation

Determining if taxation applies

To see if your Social Security payment is taxable, follow these two steps:

(1)   Find the sum of these three amounts (your *combined income)*:

Your gross income
+

Your non-taxable interest income (e.g. from municipal bonds)
+

Your "countable" Social Security (1/2 of your yearly Social Security)

(2)   Compare to the IRS Base Amount:

Individual: $25,000
Couple: $32,000

If the result of Step 1 exceeds the IRS Base Amount, part of your Social Security is taxable.

The taxable amount

The amount that is taxable could be anywhere from 0 to 85% of your Social Security. To determine the exact amount, see "More information on taxation of benefits" just below.

The bottom line is that if you are single and your combined income is $25,000 to $34,000, you may have to pay taxes on up to 50% of your Social Security. If your combined income is over $34,000 you may have to pay taxes on up to 85% of your Social Security.

If you file jointly and your combined income is $32,000 to $44,000, up to 50% of your Social Security may be taxable. With combined income over $44,000, up to 85% of Social Security could be taxable.

Note that Social Security continues to be tax-advantaged: under the formula, *at least 15%* of your Social Security is always tax-free.

More information on taxation of benefits

IRS 1040 online instructions
www.irs.gov/pub/irs-pdf/i1040.pdf

Appendix D of this book (page 273)

YOUR SOCIAL SECURITY (FICA) TAXES

What "FICA" means

FICA stands for Federal Insurance Contributions Act, the law which authorizes collection of the tax.

What FICA does

Your FICA payroll deduction pays for your Social Security coverage. Just as Social Security is the foundation of most retirement income, the FICA Social Security tax is the foundation of Social Security.

When you are employed, the tax is deducted from your pay. Your employer matches your contribution, and the combined contribution is credited to the Social Security trust funds (by way of IRS, which collects the tax).

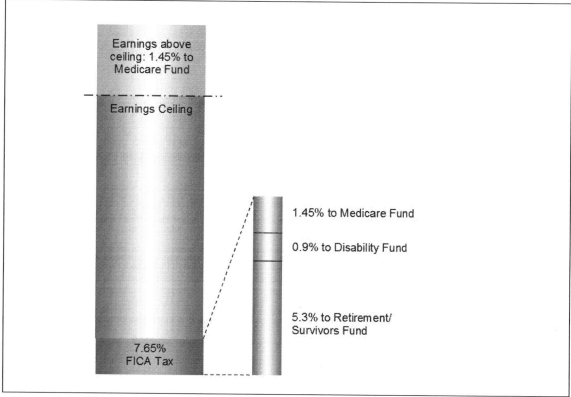

Figure 9.1. FICA taxes and their allocation.

The amount of the deduction

The tax is currently 7.65% from you and 7.65% from your employer. If you are self-employed, you pay *both* portions, or a total of 15.3%, on your net earnings from self-employment. In this case, it is called "Self-Employment Tax" rather than "FICA contributions."

The 7.65% is quite a bit higher than the 1% tax rate originally enacted in 1937. However, the original Act provided for automatic rate increases leading to 3% in 1949. Since then, the coverage you "buy" with your contributions has expanded many-fold to include more comprehensive spouse and survivor protection, disability benefits, and the Medicare program.

The taxable earnings ceiling

The tax is collected on all earnings up to a specified ceiling, or maximum. This is called the "taxable earnings base." In 2014, for example, you pay the full 7.65% on all earnings up to $117,000 (for each worker). Above that level, you pay only the 1.45% tax allocated to Medicare. Earlier ceilings are listed year-by-year in

Appendix A, Column 2. Like the tax rate, the taxable earnings base has increased, starting from $3,000 in 1937. Currently it is increased annually to account for inflation.

Where the money goes

The 7.65% is not invested in a lump sum. It is allocated among the three Social Security trust funds. 5.3% is deposited in the Old Age and Survivor Insurance Trust Fund for retirement and survivor payments, 0.9% is allocated to the Disability Insurance Trust Fund, and 1.45% goes to the Health Insurance Trust Fund for Medicare.

These allocations are summarized in Figure 9.1.

YOUR SOCIAL SECURITY NUMBER

The reason behind the number

The Social Security Number (SSN) was originally devised to keep an accurate record of each individual's earnings.

The number was needed to distinguish your earnings record from all other records. A glance at birth records will show that using traditional identifiers such as your name, birthdate, birth place, and even your parents' names would not always result in a *unique* identifier. Your SSN is not only one-of-a-kind, it is also certainly easier to use than a more traditional handle such as "Andrew, son of John and Elaine, born of Philadelphia."

The three sections

Take a look at the typical SSN. It looks like this, and each section has a name as shown:

987-65-4320
Area—Group—Serial

Each section carries particular information and has a specific job. To understand why this structure was adopted, we need to remember that the numbering system was devised in the 1930's. With modern computers, any 9-digit number will do, but with 1930's office technology, the number needed to "talk" to staff members. As you will see, this gives the SSN a human dimension, and about as much "charm" as a number can have.

The first three digits—area. These numbers were originally a geographical indicator. Before 1972, the area number specified the Social Security office which issued your Social Security card. From 1972-2011, they were issued centrally, but continued to specify the state where you applied for your SSN. With some exceptions, the "0" group—those numbers starting with zero—were from the far northeast (from Maine to Connecticut), the "100" group, from slightly farther south (New York, New Jersey, and Pennsylvania), and so on up to the 500 group in the far west.

Effective June 25, 2011, SSN "randomization" removed the geographical significance of the area number for new SSNs.

In addition to indicating where your number was requested, the first three digits determine which *Program Service Center* (PSC) will process your payments. Six PSCs handle the record-keeping and payment operations for the six regions of the country reflected in the various SSN area numbers. Two additional Program Service Centers are devoted to international operations and disability operations.

Some 600- and 700-series SSNs are being issued to specific groups of new U.S. residents. And many 700-series SSNs are reserved for railroad workers. That is because they are covered by the Railroad Retirement Board (RRB) rather than Social Security and, in the 1930's, a quick way was needed to recognize them so the proper agency would handle their retirement.

The reason for the geographic code, as best I can determine, is that some way was needed to distribute Social Security *cards* and the Social Security *workload* across the country in the 1930's. Remember, the cards were actual pieces of paper onto which your name would be hand-typed. They needed to be distributed in a systematic way to workers in every city in the nation in 1936. In 1937, the wage reports started coming in and each report needed to be associated with the proper file—by hand. And once the claims started coming in 1940, each claim had to be associated with the same file and the meticulous payment records kept in that file. To break all this work down to manageable-sized jobs, the Social Security Board divided the country, and the cards, and all the associated record-keeping tasks, into five areas (now six). In addition, staffers could trace backwards from a person's SSN to the exact office which issued the SSN—a permanent "paper trail" that was easy to trace if necessary.

The middle two digits—group. These are a "bundling" tool allowing early staffers to store and issue Social Security cards in convenient quantities.

There is also a special sequence code embedded in the group number. As numbers are assigned, the middle two digits advance following a special pattern, but not a straight numerical order. First, the odd group numbers from 01-09 are issued, then even numbers 10-98, then even numbers 02-08, and finally odd numbers 11-99. Then, on to a new number in the first three digits, where a similar pattern would be followed.

Why not simply follow numerical order: 01, 02, 03 and so on? Because the middle two digits are a 1930's *security measure*. By scrambling the order, it would be easy to spot counterfeit SSNs. A counterfeiter printing Social Security cards in the 987 series (our fictitious example number above) would print his 64's, then his 65's, then his 67's. But unknown to him, the "odd sixties" might be the *last* 987 numbers to be issued, not due for issue until years from now. His fraud would be quickly detected by anyone who knew the proper sequence.

The last four digits are simply a serial number. They start at 0001 and advance in numerical order until 9999. Then the "middle two" digits advance one step in their scrambled sequence, and the "last 4" start over at 0001.

Incidentally, the 9 digits allow a billion possible SSNs. Since 1936, about 450 million have been used, so we still have quite a bit of breathing space.

Today, the various sections of the SSN are not as critical, except that it is much easier to remember an SSN broken into its component sections than if it came all at once! When you apply for an SSN for the first time these days (generally at birth), your application is typed into a computer, the number is automatically assigned, and the card is mailed to you (usually within 7 days). The computer retains the order the numbers are issued and establishes a wage record for you automatically. Also retained is a "paper trail," including the office which processed your application, the person who helped you, and the person who typed the application into the computer. In other words, the geographic codes and security scrambling are little needed today. Personally, though, I'm glad the number was invented in the 30's and not today—somehow, the old area, group, and serial portions of the number give it a human touch.

By the way, there are still some security measures embedded in the SSN which we haven't discussed here. Counterfeiters beware.

For the complete story of the Social Security Number and the SS Card, see www.ssa.gov/policy/docs/ssb/v69n2/v69n2p55.html.

How to get a replacement card

Obtain a form SS-5 from SSA at (800) SSA-1213, any SSA office, or www.ssa.gov/online/ss-5.html. The form has instructions for completion and filing. Be sure to pay close attention to the documentation requirements, especially your identification.

MILITARY SERVICE AND YOUR SOCIAL SECURITY

Your military service affects your Social Security in several ways, some favorable and some not. Here is a summary of the major provisions related to your military service.

Your military service: 1940 through 1956

Manual earnings posting

You did not pay Social Security taxes for military service during this period, because military pay was not subject to FICA taxes until January 1, 1957. That means your military service in those years does not appear on your Social Security earnings record.

However, you certainly deserve recognition for your military service in those years. To do so, SSA manually posts a special $160 wage credit to your earnings record for every month you were in active duty (or active duty for training) between September 16, 1940, and December 31, 1956. This is extra credit on your Social Security record which could increase your Social Security payment. The following conditions apply:

- You must have been honorably discharged after 90 or more days of service, or released because of a disability or injury received in the line of duty, or

- You must still be on active duty, or

- If you are applying for survivor benefits, the veteran must have died while on active duty.

How to get the credits

To receive the manually-posted credits, you must prove the exact months of your military service. Your military discharge form (DD-214) is the usual proof. If you have trouble locating your DD-214, Social Security will help you obtain another from the military.

You might not be asked for proof of military service if adding the $160 monthly military credit does not raise your Social Security payment. After all, the $160-a-month credit is not large, and your military years may not be among your best 35 years even with the additional credit. In that case, there is no point to having you prove your military service, and no proof is requested.

Your military service: 1957 through 1977

Manual extra credit

Beginning January 1, 1957, your military pay was subject to FICA taxes just like most other jobs. Therefore, your military service automatically appears on your Social Security earnings record and will be used to compute your payment.

You are also credited with $300 in additional earnings for each calendar quarter in which you received active duty basic pay. These extra earnings may help you qualify for Social Security or increase the amount of your Social Security payment.

This *deemed credit* of $300 per quarter does not automatically appear on your earnings record for years before 1968. Therefore, in order for you to receive this deemed credit for your military service prior to 1968, you will need to submit proof of your service dates—usually your DD-214 discharge form.

Your military service: 1978 and later

More extra credit

Again, your military pay is subject to FICA taxes, appears on your Social Security earnings record, and influences your Social Security payment computation.

You are also credited with $100 in additional earnings for every $300 in active duty basic pay you received, up to a maximum of $1,200 a year in additional earnings. However, if you enlisted after September 7, 1980, and did not complete at least 24 months of active duty or your full tour, you may not be able to receive the additional earnings.

Your military pension and Social Security

You can receive both Social Security benefits and military retirement. Normally, your Social Security benefits are not reduced because of your military retirement. But watch for these effects:

Veterans Administration payments called "pension" are considered aid payments—other income you receive will reduce the amount of your VA pension payment. Therefore, your Social Security payment could affect your VA pension payment. Other VA payments such as "compensation" are not affected by Social Security payments.

If you receive military *retirement*, note that SSA's special wage credits for 1951 through 1956 cannot be granted to you unless you have active duty after 1956.

If you receive a military *disability* pension and apply for Social Security disability payments, your total compensation from these programs *plus workers' compensation* is limited to 80% of your average current earnings before you became disabled.

To summarize: In most cases, your military service is beneficial to your Social Security payment computation. In a few isolated instances, you may not qualify for the usual advantages or may have limits on your payments because of your military service.

More information on military service

"Military Service and Social Security"
www.ssa.gov/pubs/10017.html

GETTING SOCIAL SECURITY PAYMENTS OVERSEAS

Citizens of the U.S. and allies

In most cases, there is no problem receiving your Social Security overseas. If you are a citizen of the U.S. or a qualifying country friendly with the U.S., your payments can usually be sent directly to you for as long as you are eligible.

Any Social Security business that comes up can be handled at the nearest U.S. Embassy or consulate, or directly with SSA's headquarters in Baltimore.

You can even have your U.S. Social Security directly deposited to a foreign bank, in many friendly countries. And, in many cases, your Social Security payment will have much more purchasing power overseas.

Other citizenship

If you are not a citizen of the U.S. or other qualifying countries, your payments will stop after you have been outside the U.S. for 6 full calendar months. (There are many exceptions to this rule—for example if you are in the U.S. military or if you reside in a country with special treaty privileges.) If the exceptions do not apply, your payments will stop after you have been outside the U.S. for 6 months, and cannot be started again until you are again in the U.S. for one full calendar month.

Where payment is barred

There are a few countries where you cannot receive Social Security. U.S. Treasury regulations require your payments to be withheld while you are in Cuba or North Korea. If you are a U.S. citizen, your withheld payments are issued to you when you leave those countries. If you are not a U.S. citizen, you *forfeit* your Social Security payments while you live in Cuba or North Korea.

Social Security regulations prohibit payments while you are in Cambodia, Vietnam, and many of the former members of the USSR. There are exceptions, for example if you receive your payments at the U.S. embassy in person.

Working overseas

Special work rules apply when you are overseas. If you are under Full Retirement Age and outside the U.S., your monthly Social Security benefit is withheld for each month you work more than 45 hours. This applies whether you work in employment or self-employment. Furthermore, if other people receive payments on your work record, *their* payments will stop when your payment stops.

The foreign work rule is very strict, but is understandable when you consider how difficult it would be to establish individual earnings limits for each foreign nation.

An exception applies if you are a U.S. citizen or resident, and your foreign work is covered by the U.S. Social Security program. In that case, you are subject to the same annual earnings limits that apply to people in the U.S. (see page 199).

Income tax on Social Security while overseas

Your Social Security payments continue to be taxable while you are outside the U.S. If you are a U.S. citizen or resident, you are subject to the same tax rules as people inside the U.S. (see page 205). If you are not a U.S. citizen or resident, Federal income taxes will be withheld from your Social Security. The withholding is 30% of 85% of your payment amount. In addition, many foreign governments tax U.S. Social Security payments. You should contact the embassy of your foreign host country for information.

Medicare while overseas

Your Medicare covers medical treatment only in the U.S.

Working with Social Security while outside the country

Because of the special rules while you are outside the U.S., you are required to notify Social Security promptly if you move overseas, work overseas, or experience other changes that could affect your eligibility. While you are outside the U.S., you will periodically receive a questionnaire to fill out and return to the U.S. Embassy, consulate, or SSA. Based on your answers, SSA will determine whether your eligibility continues.

Brief foreign trips are normally not a problem. When in doubt, contact Social Security.

To summarize: you can usually receive Social Security when you travel overseas or even live overseas. You Medicare does not cover foreign medical treatment. Many special rules apply to foreign travel, residence, and work.

More information on eligibility overseas

"Your Payments While Your Are Outside The United States"
www.ssa.gov/pubs/10137.html

REPRESENTATIVE PAYMENT

Amy's 6-year-old daughter will be eligible for Social Security. Amy wonders how the payments will be issued—in the name of a child?

Fred's mother is in a nursing home and has Alzheimer's. She is not aware of her Social Security payments or other financial arrangements for her care. Fred wonders if the payments should continue to be sent directly to his mother.

Situations like these call for *representative payment.* Representative payment means that a *representative payee* other than the beneficiary receives the Social Security or SSI payments and uses the money for the beneficiary. (The SSI program is described on page 218.)

When a representative payee is needed

A representative payee is needed when a beneficiary is not capable of managing or directing the management of his or her own funds in his or her own best interest.

This does not mean that the beneficiary is *physically unable* to pay bills or go to the bank; it means that the person is unable to properly manage or direct the use of Social Security funds. For example, an individual may be bedridden but able to direct family members to properly handle financial affairs. In that case, no representative payee would be needed. However, a physical impairment can be so severe that the individual cannot manage funds.

Indications of inability to manage funds include confusion about financial matters, mishandling or losing Social Security payments, inability to care for oneself, unconsciousness (e.g. coma), or other signs of financial difficulty.

How Social Security determines capability or incapability

There are three different determinations for three different situations:

- Minor children generally need representative payees, since they are not legally competent. An exception is made if the child is over 15, has no legal guardian, and is independent (e.g. self-supporting, serving in the military, a head of household, etc.).

- An adult beneficiary who has been legally determined to be *incompetent* is considered incapable of managing funds. Incompetence can be determined only by a court of law.

- A legally competent adult can be determined by SSA to be incapable of managing funds. The SSA determination of incapability is normally based on a physician's written opinion. (Exception: the law requires that a medically determined drug addict or alcoholic *must* have a representative payee to handle funds.)

Choosing a representative payee

SSA guidelines indicate that the best payee is one who will best represent the beneficiary's interests.

This usually means the payee should be a close and trusted family member. The parent is the usual choice for a minor child.

If no family member is able to serve, a friend or institution may be named as the payee. For example, a nursing home may receive payments for a resident who cannot manage funds.

Safeguards

Representative payment is a serious matter. As noted above, a physician or court must determine that representative payment is in the individual's best interest.

Before representative payment is started, the beneficiary and family members are notified of the proposed change. Any party to the decision may file an appeal of the change. The beneficiary may apply for direct payment at any time.

A representative payee must account for the money entrusted to him or her. Mishandling Social Security or SSI funds is a federal offense.

If capability returns (as after treatment for a serious illness), then *direct payment* to the beneficiary is reinstated.

How payments are issued

The payment legend shows the representative payee's name *for* the beneficiary. For example, if Mary Jones is the payee for John Smith, the payment would show:

Mary Jones for
John Smith
(Mary's address)
(Mary's city, state, zip)

Only Mary Jones could cash or deposit the payment.

Duties of the representative payee

- The representative payee acts as a substitute for the beneficiary in all Social Security business.

- The payee is responsible for all reports to SSA, and for signing all SSA documents.

- The payee receives all notices and payments from SSA (copies of notices are also sent to the beneficiary).

- The payee is responsible for managing the Social Security funds in the best interest of the beneficiary. This usually means opening a separate bank account to receive, hold and disburse the Social Security funds.

- Finally, the payee must make periodic reports on the use of the benefits and, if requested by SSA, the payee may have to provide a detailed accounting.

More information on representative payment

"A Guide for Representative Payees"
www.ssa.gov/pubs/10076.html

SUPPLEMENTAL SECURITY INCOME (SSI)

General questions about SSI

If you have low income and resources, the SSI program may be able to help.

Many people become disabled or retired only to discover that they are eligible for no payments from Social Security or other pension programs, or are eligible for such a small amount that they could not survive. SSI was created with these people in mind.

SSI basics

SSI's full name is Supplemental Security Income for the Aged, Blind, and Disabled. It is part of the "safety net" of public assistance or welfare programs for the needy.

The purpose of SSI is to provide a subsistence level of income to aged or disabled people in need, together with incentives to develop other sources of income such as wages. SSI establishes a "floor level" of income, below which aged or disabled people will not drop. In addition, everyone receiving SSI is also eligible for Medicaid medical assistance.

SSI's funding

Since SSI is part of the public assistance program, its funding is totally separate from Social Security funding.

Many people mistakenly believe that part of their Social Security taxes are used to fund "welfare." Actually, Social Security payroll taxes fund only the Social Security insurance programs—the retirement, family, survivor, disability, and Medicare programs. SSI is funded from federal *general revenues* provided by federal income taxes, excise taxes, etc. Some states also contribute state monies to augment SSI's payments. Nothing in the SSI program, not even the overhead such as payroll and office space, is funded by Social Security FICA taxes.

SSI federal payments totaled $51.7 billion a year in 2012. Administrative costs were $3.9 billion, or 7.5%. The total cost was 0.33% of GDP.

SSI's history

SSI was created and brought under SSA's umbrella in 1974. Before 1974, similar assistance had been provided by three separate programs, one providing aid for aged individuals, one for blind individuals, and one for disabled individuals.

The three pre-1974 programs were administered by local public assistance offices, just as the Food Stamp program, Medicaid, and other aid programs are administered today.

In 1973, Congress merged the three programs into one, and simultaneously transferred administration of the new SSI program to the Social Security Administration.

The merger made good sense, since many of the rules of the three separate programs were identical. The transfer to SSA also made sense because most income programs for aged, blind, and disabled individuals could be housed in one office. After all, SSA was already providing Social Security services for most of the same people who were included in the SSI program (though certainly not all SSA recipients were also on SSI).

The transfer made SSI the first—and still only—federally-administered public assistance program. Part of SSI's success results from its close ties to the Social Security program. For example, the SSI and Social Security computers are linked so that changes in Social Security income are automatically incorporated in SSI payment computations. And proof of age or disability for Social Security constitutes proof for SSI as well, eliminating duplicated efforts. Today SSI provides supplemental payments to over 8.1 million individuals, 2.6% of the U.S. population.

Who qualifies for SSI

To be eligible for SSI you must meet all of the following:

•   Be a U.S. citizen or legal permanent resident

•   Be aged, blind, or disabled

•   Have low income

•   Have low resources

"Aged" means that you have attained age 65. There is no provision for "early retirement," unlike regular Social Security payments.

"Blind" is defined just as it is for Social Security disability insurance: either visual acuity no sharper than 20-200 *corrected* vision, or a visual field no wider than 20° (tunnel vision).

Similarly, *"disabled"* is defined the same as for Social Security disability.

SSI for children

Children can receive SSI, even a newborn, if disabled. If the child lives with the parents, part of the parents' income and resources are counted in determining eligibility and payment amount.

Once the child reaches age 18, the parents' income and resources are no longer counted. Only assets in the child's own name count.

Income: definition and impact

Income refers to money coming into your ownership during a month. Examples include cash gifts, Veterans payments, wages, and even Social Security payments. Income can also include non-cash items such as free or reduced rent, free food, or free clothing you receive during a month.

To oversimplify a bit, you are considered *low income* if your total income is lower than these standards (2014):

- For a *single individual:* $721 per month

- For a *couple:* $1,082 per month

In some states, standards are higher because the state subsidizes the SSI program with state funds. Also, *earned income from work* is largely exempted, allowing higher income for workers.

Again, to oversimplify, your SSI payment is determined by subtracting your income from these standards. In effect, SSI supplements you up to the income standard—thus the name *Supplemental* Security Income.

In actual practice, part of your outside income is not counted—there are *deductions* and *disregards* from your income. Because of these deductions, your total income, including your SSI payment, can be slightly higher than the payment standard—typically $20 higher. In the particular case of *earned income* such as wages, the discounts are significantly higher, creating a substantial raise if you work. This serves as a work incentive, with higher and higher total income as the reward for successful work attempts.

Resources: definition and impact

Your *resources* are composed of all the things of value that you own on the first of the month (as opposed to income, which you obtain *during* the month). Examples include cash on hand, bank accounts, and non-cash items such as your car or house—basically anything you could convert to cash to live on.

To be eligible for SSI, your *countable* resources cannot exceed $2,000 (for an individual) or $3,000 (for a couple). Countable resources include all cash and liquid resources. Not counted are your residence, one vehicle of reasonable value, and some other assets. If your resources exceed these standards on the first of the month, you are ineligible for SSI throughout the month. The idea is simple: if you own resources above the standard you should live on the resources that month instead of SSI.

To summarize: SSI has two roles. It guarantees a living income to aged, blind, and disabled people, so it serves as an important safety net for needy individuals. In addition, with its efficient operation, it is a model for effectively administering other aid programs.

If Social Security is the foundation of income security for retirees, survivors, and disabled individuals, SSI is the bedrock that underlies the foundation.

More information on SSI

"Supplemental Security Income (SSI)"
www.ssa.gov/pubs/11000.html

"Benefits for Children With Disabilities"
www.ssa.gov/pubs/10026.html

"Supplemental Security Income (SSI) for Noncitizens"
www.ssa.gov/pubs/11051.html

CHAPTER TEN

MAXIMIZE YOUR SOCIAL SECURITY

BACKGROUND

For most people, Social Security is simple. When they retire (or when they reach 62, if already retired), they file for retirement. If married, their spouse also files at retirement. They receive payments every month for life, with annual Cost-of-Living Adjustments (COLAs).

But Social Security is like a new smartphone or computer: there's a lot more to it than just turning it on. There are numerous "hidden" features to make it do more for you, to personalize it.

For some people, it's important to maximize their lifetime Social Security payments. This may be for financial reasons—needing to pay the bills—or it may be for philosophical reasons such as simply wanting to get the most from the system they paid into for so many years.

In this chapter, we will explore a number of different approaches to optimize your Social Security, from the simple to the exotic.

MAXIMIZE YOUR EARNINGS

The Social Security system rewards higher lifetime average earnings, as measured by your best 35 years of earnings. If you increase your lifetime average earnings, you get more Social Security.

There are two ways to do this: increase your earnings per year (earn more), or increase the number of years you work (work longer).

The first makes sense only if you have a choice between higher earnings and lower earnings in a given year. If Social Security is your only criterion, (doubtful!) take the higher earnings.

The second approach is more practical. If you have less than 35 years of earnings, every extra year of work will increase your Social Security. The new earnings will replace a "zero" year from the past, increasing your lifetime average.

More work years can help even if you already have 35 years of work. New work might replace a previous "low" year, i.e. when you were in high school or just starting out.

This works even if you have 35 years of substantial earnings, like a long career of steady high earnings. That's because recent earnings are weighted slightly heavier in the computation, even after earlier years are indexed for inflation. The index used is the *increase in average earnings.* That increase has been lower than either Consumer Price Index (CPI) increases or increases in high earnings in the overall economy.

For example, maximum taxable earnings in 1980 were $25,900. Even after indexing for a 2014 age-62 application date, only $91,686 will be used in the computation. That's quite a bit less than the $117,000 maximum in 2014. Thus, new high earnings in 2014 would replace high earnings in 1980, increasing the Social Security computation.

Bottom line: continuing to work generally increases your Social Security, at least modestly. That's generally true for your own retirement or disability claim and also for your family or survivor benefits. To quantify the effect of additional work, use the online calculators at SSA's website (page 176).

Work and the ARF

You can even draw Social Security payments while you maximize earnings.

You may recall that if you return to work before Full Retirement Age, some of your Social Security payments may be stopped (page 199). Recall also that you will get credit back for the missing payments when you reach FRA, in a process called *Adjustment to the Reduction Factor (ARF)* (page 204).

The ARF allows you to draw early Social Security, continue working, and reduce the lifetime reduction for early filing. It provides a safety net for the early filer who wants to return to work. This is especially helpful if job loss forces you to file for Social Security:

Fred was laid off at 61 and was unsuccessful in finding a new job. He had always intended to file for Social Security at FRA but now he needed income. He reluctantly applied at 62 for a 75% payment. Fred was thankful for the Social Security—a lot of his younger friends had it harder—but he regretted the steep "permanent" reduction in his payments.

6 months later, Fred landed a great job. His Social Security stopped due to his earnings. At 66, his Social Security automatically restarted because Fred's current work no longer affected his payments. Because of the ARF Fred's payments were raised from 75% (48 months' reduction) to 96.7% (6 months' reduction). His steep reduction for early filing wasn't so permanent after all. Fred's payments got a second boost: his new earnings increased his 35-year computation a small amount.

The bottom line here is that if you're temporarily unemployed and seeking work, you can tap into your Social Security early with little permanent damage, as long as you return to work. You'll get an ARF for every month payments are stopped, plus a new payment computation every year you pay FICA taxes.

THE DELAY STRATEGY

Quite simply, the later you apply for retirement payments, up to age 70, the higher they'll be for the rest of your life. You'll get a higher payout if you live at least to average life expectancy. And the higher payments can continue for *two* lifetimes, for you or your spouse after one of you passes away—it's the gift that keeps on giving. Perhaps the simplest strategy for maximizing your Social Security is to postpone filing until age 70, or at least until your FRA. Call it the *Delay Strategy.*

Break-even points for the Delay Strategy

If your FRA is 66, there are a couple of "break-even" points you need to know about: age 78 and age 82-1/2.

Obviously, filing at 62 gives you the earliest retirement benefit but also the lowest monthly payment for the rest of your life. Filing later gives a higher monthly payment but fewer payments.

Using simple dollars (no inflation, no COLAs, no taxation of benefits, no additional work, and no return on invested money), filing at 62 instead of 66 puts you "money ahead" until age 78. Those four years of early payments pay off for a good number of years. But at age 78, the age-66 filer has caught up, and from then on is ahead, with higher monthly payments for the rest of his or her life. The bottom line is that if you just want the most dollars from SSA and expect to live past age 78, file at 66, not 62.

Again, using simple dollars, filing at 66 instead of 70 puts you money ahead until age 82-1/2. After that, the age-70 filer is ahead for the rest of his or her life.

Mabel's full payment amount at her FRA of 66 is $1,000 per month. Therefore, if she files at 62, she would get $750 per month; filing at 70, she would get $1,320 per month—an increase of 76%. Mabel wants to know which choice yields the highest lifetime payments.

First, Mabel compares filing at 62 vs. 66. If she files at 62, by the time she is 66, she has gotten $750 per month x 48 months = $36,000, a great head-start.

However, if she filed at 66 she would get $250 per month more ($1,000 vs. $750). At $250 per month, it will take $36,000/$250 = 144 months or 12 years to *recoup the head start. That's age 78. After that, she will be $250 ahead every month for the rest of her life because she waited until age 66.*

To check the break-even point, Mable considers that, at age 78, she will have received either $750 per month x 192 months (16 years) = $144,000. Or she will have received $1,000 per month x 144 months (12 years) = $144,000. This calculation confirms the age 78 break-even point.

Next, Mable compares filing at 66 vs. 70. Her head-start is $1,000 per month x 48 months = $48,000 by age 70.

However, if she files at age 70, she gets $320 per month more. That would recoup the head-start in $48,000/$320 = 150 months (12.5 years), at age 82-1/2. After that, her $320 raise is hers to keep forever.

To check the break-even point, Mabel calculates that at 82-1/2 she will have received either $1,000 x 198 months (16.5 years) = $198,000. Or she will have received $1,320 x 150 months (12.5 years) = $198,000, confirming the age 82-1/2 break-even point.

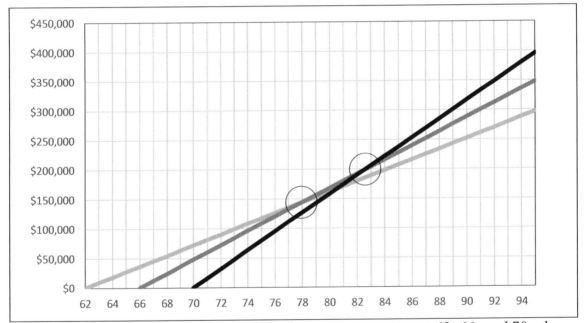

Figure 10.1. Lifetime payouts to age 95 with payments starting at 62, 66, and 70, along with break-even points (circles). FRA is 66, with payment amount of $1,000/month at 66.

The same break-even points hold true regardless of the full payment amount. The bottom line: if you expect to live a shorter life, file early. If you expect to live longer, file later.

My friend and colleague Steve Vernon, President of Rest-of-Life Communications, has wonderfully clear analyses to pick the right application date based on simple dollars. To read his article "When Should You Start Social Security Benefits? Do the Math!" and others, go to http://moneywatch.bnet.com/ and search for "when should you start Social Security." (You'll also find another Vernon article on the qualitative effects of later Social Security for a better life.) Vernon concludes that you should file at 62 if you expect to live only to age 70; file at 66 if you expect to live to 80; and file at 70 if you expect to live to 90. In general, Vernon is a great supporter of the Delay Strategy.

Life expectancy and the Delay Strategy

Clearly, the question of when to file depends on your life expectancy. If you know your death date you know exactly when to file to maximize your Social Security. Since we don't know that date, we need to rely on averages.

Your can view your average life expectancy at www.ssa.gov/planners/benefitcalculators.htm, and click "Life Expectancy Calculator." For a broader view, an excellent table of average life expectancy for all ages from birth to 119(!) can be found at www.ssa.gov/OACT/STATS/table4c6.html. (Note that web URLs are case-specific; use capital letters as shown.)

Life expectancy tables show median age of death—the age when one-half of a given group will have died; the other half lives longer. Thus, you have a 50% chance of out-living the table age, and an even better chance if you're in good health.

If you are a member of a couple, you should know that *joint* life expectancy—the median age at the *second* death—is longer than individual life expectancy. For example, IRS estimates 21 remaining years of life for a 65-year-old individual, but 26.2 years for a 65-year-old couple. That's age 91 for the longer-living spouse. And remember, if you are married, your spouse may receive widow's benefits after you pass away, for the rest of his or her life.

These long life expectancies argue for taking Social Security as late as you possibly can. Since SSA uses average life expectancies and the above break-even points, your SSA representative may recommend filing late, just as Steve Vernon does.

All of this is based on *average* life expectancy. Be sure to take other factors into account, like your family longevity and personal health.

Present-Value and the Delay Strategy

The complete story is not as straightforward as simple dollars and life expectancy. Remember the old saying, a bird in the hand is worth two in the bush? The same is true with money. Money today is worth more than money tomorrow. Money today has today's dollar value; tomorrow's money may be inflated and worth less. Money today could be invested and earn interest; money tomorrow cannot be invested now.

To account for the time value of money, financial planners perform a *present-value* computation, taking into account inflation, taxes, and interest on savings or potential investment gains. When present-value is used instead of simple dollars, drawing Social Security *earlier* can be wiser than drawing later, especially if the alternative is to draw from your tax-deferred retirement savings like a traditional IRA. Consider the factors in Figure 10.2.

Item	Drawing Social Security	Drawing from tax-deferred savings
Inflation	Annual COLAs make Social Security inflation-proof. No disadvantage for drawing early.	Need to draw more each year to keep up with inflation. Increasing loss to savings.
Tax rates	Always tax-advantaged. At least 15% will be tax-free.	100% taxable when withdrawn from tax-deferred accounts.
Savings growth rates	Savings stay relatively intact, allowing further compounding (preferably tax-deferred). Or part of Social Security payments can be saved and earn interest.	Withdrawals deny compounding power of each dollar withdrawn.

Figure 10.2. Financial implications of drawing living expenses from Social Security vs. from tax-deferred savings (e.g. traditional IRA, 401(k)).

Because of these advantages, many financial planners recommend drawing Social Security as *early* as possible after retirement and postponing or minimizing savings withdrawals. (This assumes, of course, that you're already retired. You'll normally be money ahead by staying on the job.)

Check www.analyzenow.com under "Computer Programs" for a private spreadsheet to help inform your decision.

"Bridges" to later filing

Say you want to delay filing until FRA or age 70. The problem is what to live on while you delay Social Security. You need a "bridge" to help you get to a later filing age. Here are some ideas:

Work strategy. The classic bridge to later Social Security. By working you have some income to pay your bills. You're probably paying FICA or Self-Employment taxes on your ongoing work, possibly increasing your future payment. You may also be building pension eligibility or retiree medical coverage. Even part-time work can allow you to delay Social Security.

Draw-down strategy. Blessed with some retirement savings? It can be worth it to draw down savings to postpone Social Security. Think about it. Delaying Social Security from age 62 to 70 yields a 76% increase, above the inflation rate, with lifetime cost-of-living adjustments and tax benefits, all guaranteed by the government. Which of your investments will perform that well, guaranteed?

A problem with the draw-down strategy is that it's so psychologically difficult to use savings to pay current bills when the income stream from Social Security is already available. Here's an exercise that might help: compute how much it would cost to use your savings to replace your Social Security payments.

Say you're 62 and eligible for $1600 per month at 66, $1200 at 62 (75% of $1600), or $2112 at 70 (132% of $1600). To get from 62 to 66 would cost you $57,600 ($1200 x 48 months). To get from 62 to 70 would cost $115,200 ($1200 x 96 months).

That's a lot of money, but if you can afford the "investment," it pays huge dividends in the long run—an extra $912 per month for the rest of your life (and possibly your spouse's life too.) It helps, at least psychologically, to set aside the dollars, earmarked for Social Security replacement.

Be sure to discuss your draw-down strategy with a financial professional.

File and Suspend strategy. If you have a spouse, you could File and Suspend at FRA, and your spouse could draw spousal payments to act as a bridge from your FRA to age 70. See the description of File and Suspend below.

Spousal-Only payment strategy. If you are potentially eligible for Social Security spousal payments from your current or former spouse, you could draw *only* the spouse payments from FRA to age 70, then switch to your own payments at 70 at the 132% level. The spousal payments act as your bridge, giving you smaller income in the first four years so you can higher income after age 70.

There are restrictions. See the description of Spousal-Only payments below.

THE "UNDO"

When you make a mistake on your computer, you hit the "undo" key. It reverses the process and puts you back where you were before. Guess what: Social Security has an undo key also.

The "Undo" offers another way to draw early Social Security without a permanent reduction. It's a way to have your cake and eat it too, since you get the benefit of early Social Security payments *plus* higher payments later in life, as if you delayed filing. Anyone can take advantage of the Undo if they recently took Social Security any time before age 70, but there are some limitations:

- You have to have some savings available to make it work
- Effective December 2010, you can only use the Undo in the first 12 months you are eligible for Social Security
- Also effective December 2010, you can execute the Undo only one time in your life

Officially, the Undo is called *application withdrawal and refiling*. The first step is to *withdraw* your earlier Social Security claim. You can withdraw at any SSA office using Form SSA-521, Request for Withdrawal of Application.

The catch is that when you withdraw your application, it's like you never filed for Social Security. That means every dollar you received is an overpayment and must be repaid. This is where your savings come in, or rather, go out. You will have to pay SSA thousands of dollars in a lump sum.

Why would you do that? Because once your withdrawal is approved, you refile for Social Security. Now that you're up to a year older, you will get a higher monthly payment. You've "undone" your claim and restarted your Social Security with new Reduction Factors or Delayed Retirement Credits.

The procedure goes like this:

1. File for early Social Security, and draw the reduced payments for up to 12 months.

2. Withdraw your former claim. Dependents will also have to approve the withdrawal. This could be fine with your spouse, but maybe not with your former spouse.

3. Repay all benefits received, including dependents' payments. No interest is charged. Again, your former spouse might balk.

4. Refile for Social Security. Your new claim will be based on your current age, and will yield a higher benefit.

SSA's description of the Undo can be found at www.ssa.gov/retire2/withdrawal.htm.

George's FRA is 66. His full payment amount is $1,000. He starts his Social Security at 62, getting $750 monthly payments.

At 63, George withdraws his application. At that point he has received $750 x 12 months = $9,000 (ignoring COLAs for this example).

He draws $9,000 from his retirement savings and repays it to SSA. He does not have to pay interest on the $9,000.

Then, George refiles for Social Security. Since he is now 63, he gets an 80% payment, or $800, for the rest of his life.

George sees that his $9,000 "investment" in Social Security results in a raise of $50 per month, (from his previous monthly benefit of $750 to his new amount of $800), or $600 per year. He calculates that this is a government-guaranteed 6.7% return on investment, with a payback period of only 15 years. He also discovers that he gets a tax credit for that year since he received "negative" Social Security. In addition, he has secured a higher widow's payment for his wife if he dies before her.

Mary's FRA is 66. She starts Social Security at 66 to get her full payment amount of $1,000 a month.

At 67, Mary withdraws her application. At that point she has received $1,000 x 12 months = $12,000 (ignoring COLAs). She repays the $12,000 to SSA without interest.

Then Mary refiles for Social Security. Now 67, she gets a 108% payment, or $1,080, for the rest of her life.

Mary's $12,000 "investment" yields a raise of $80 per month, or $960 per year. That's an 8% return, guaranteed for life by the government, with a payback period of 12.5 years, plus a possible tax credit.

Note that you don't pay interest when you repay SSA. Some call the early Social Security payments a free loan.

Normally claims are withdrawn only to undo a mistake. For example, you file on your own record at 66, and then discover that you could draw benefits instead on your former spouse's record, then switch to your own at 70 for a higher payment. You would withdraw the first claim to make way for the second.

But the undo can also be a strategy for those who want early payments from Social Security but also want the higher payments of later filing—a tactic to maximize their lifetime payments.

The undo is often framed as "withdraw and refile," as if you would immediately refile. In fact, you might not refile for years.

Ken filed for Social Security at 62 because he was desperate for income after he lost his job. Eight months later he got a great job. He understood about work offsets and the ARF (see page 204), but he still wished he had never drawn the first 8 Social Security payments.

Ken withdrew his claim, repaid the eight payments, and did not refile until he was age 70 for a full 132% payment.

Remember, the big catch is that you must repay SSA. All payments must be repaid, including dependents' payments, and dependents must approve the withdrawal. And you can only do it once, in the first 12 months of your Social Security.

Be sure to check all of this with SSA. You might drop this reference from their internal Program Operations Manual System: POMS GN 00206 ff, particularly POMS GN 00206.001 B, Example 3.

There are risks involved:

- SSA may eliminate the provision before you exercise it.

- You may die before completing the Undo, locking your survivor into your original lower payments.

- You may not have the money to repay when needed, again locking you and your survivor into the original lower payments.

- You may die before the payback period elapses, reducing or negating the benefits of the Undo.

FILE AND SUSPEND

File and Suspend is an incredibly powerful tool for maximizing Social Security. The general idea is to file for your own Social Security but suspend your payments. SSA calls this *voluntary suspension of benefits.*

Suspending gives you three benefits:

- *Increased payment.* Your suspended payments are gaining Delayed Retirement Credits (DRCs, see page 53) for every month they are suspended, and so are growing in the background at the rate of 8% per year. Your payments could rise to as much as 132% at age 70. The increased payment could be passed on to your surviving spouse as a widow's payment.

- *Spousal payments.* Your spouse can file for spousal payments on your record while your payments are suspended.

- *Contingency fund.* You can voluntarily "unsuspend" your payments at any time. Furthermore, you can unsuspend *retroactively* back to the month of suspension. SSA would immediately pay you every payment you suspended, up to 4 years' worth. In effect your suspended payments have created a contingency or hedge fund. (More details below.)

It applies for these people:

- Workers who are between FRA and age 70.

- Married couples who want to delay Social Security after FRA but want a spousal payment in the meantime.

- Anyone who took Social Security early and wants to erase part of the payment reduction for early filing.

- Anyone who wants to delay Social Security after FRA but wants the security of the contingency fund.

Note that for married couples, the highest payments result if both spouses are FRA or over. Also note that File and Suspend works whether you and your spouse are working or retired, once you reach FRA, because current work does not reduce Social Security payments after FRA.

File and Suspend procedure

The procedure is as follows, assuming *you* are the primary worker:

1. At FRA (or more), you file for your own retirement benefit. However, you request that benefits be suspended (held back). *Note:* you can also suspend existing Social Security payments. For example, you could file at 62, draw payments from 62 to FRA, then suspend payments for some or all months from FRA to age 70.

2. If married and eligible, your spouse files for up to 50% spouse payments on your suspended record.

3. At 70 your payments automatically resume. Or any month before 70 you can voluntarily re-start your payments.
   a. Your payment could be up to 132% for you (at age 70) plus up to 50% for your spouse, for a total payment of 182%.
   b. Flexibility and contingency fund: You may specify any start-payment date all the way back to suspension date, with resulting immediate back payment.

4. The long-term effect is that the 182% payments continue until the first death. After that, the survivor will get a 132% payment for life no matter who dies first, so the augmented payment will continue for the joint life of the couple.

SSA's description of File and Suspend is here: www.ssa.gov/retire2/suspend.htm.

File and Suspend example 1

Bill and Barb are both turning 66, their FRA. Barb is not eligible for Social Security on her own. Bill is eligible for $1,000 a month at FRA. They have long life expectancies, have additional funds to live on, and want to maximize lifetime Social Security.

At 66, Bill files for Social Security retirement but immediately suspends payments. Barb files for spouse payments on Bill's record. Since she is also 66 she gets a $500 payment, 50% of Bill's full payment amount. That's all the Social Security they expect for the next four years.

Bill and Barb work intermittently from 66-70 to supplement their income. Since they are over FRA the Social Security is not reduced due to work.

At 70, Bill's payments are automatically triggered to start. DRCs have augmented his payment for the last four years because payments were suspended, so his payment amount is now $1,320. Barb's $500 payments continue, for total income of $1,820.

Whether Bill or Barb dies first, the survivor's payment will be $1,320 for the life of the survivor.

Figure 10.3 compares the "traditional" approach of having both file at 66 vs. the File and Suspend strategy.

Traditional approach: Bill draws 100% at 66; Barb draws 50% at 66	File and Suspend strategy: Bill Files and Suspends at 66; Barb draws 50% at 66; Bill starts payments at 70
At 66, Bill draws his own **$1,000** per month and Barb draws **$500** spousal payment.	At 66, Bill Files and Suspends, drawing **$0**. Barb draws **$500** spousal payment.
At 70, total payments = **$72,000**. Total payments of **$1,500** per month continue.	At 70, total payments = **$24,000**. Bill's payments start at **$1,320**. Barb's **$500** per month continues, for total payments of **$1,820** per month.
At 85, total payments = **$342,000**.	At 85, total payments = **$351,600**.
After first death, survivor receives **$1,000** per month.	After first death, survivor receives **$1,320** per month.

Figure 10.3. Comparison of the traditional approach of filing at 66 vs. the File and Suspend strategy, Example 1.

The break-even point in this example is 12.5 years, when Bill is 82-1/2. Note that Barb and Bill are $9,600 ahead by age 85, and the survivor gets $320 more per month for life.

Also note that Barb and Bill have a modest $1,000 Social Security payment. If yours is greater, the advantages of File and Suspend will be more.

File and Suspend: additional considerations

- You must have assets or income to bridge the four years of reduced benefits, ages 66-70. Working by either partner will not affect Social Security payments after FRA (see page 194) and could be an ideal bridge.

- If your spouse is eligible for their own Social Security, combine File and Suspend with Spousal-Only payments, described below.

- Your spouse does not have to be FRA to file on your suspended record, but at FRA, the full 50% spouse payment is available.

- As a couple, you must be expected to live past the break-even point. (Ideally, you as an individual would also reach that mark!)

- Note that, with higher monthly payments, all the ensuing COLAs would be larger dollar amounts—a nice gift for your later years.

- There's a failsafe: If "Bill" (above) dies before age 70, "Barb" can still get widow's payments augmented by DRCs up to the death month.

- Assist your SSA representative with the following citations: POMS GN 02409.100 ff and GN 02409.130 B.

File and Suspend "Contingency Fund"

One of the most remarkable features of the File and Suspend strategy is its twofold flexibility on restarting your payments.

First, you can "unsuspend" (start payments) any month up to age 70, any time you need them. At 70, your suspended payments automatically unsuspend.

Second, when you unsuspend, you can specify *any start date back to the date of suspension.* An earlier start date will trigger monthly payments plus back pay. Your suspended payments create a "contingency fund" or hedge fund that you can tap into if needed, anytime from FRA to age 70.

File and Suspend example 2

Suspended payments automatically unsuspend at age 70, and are paid at the age-70 rate. Just before age 70 you can re-assess your options and choose a different outcome:

When Bill (Example 1 above) reaches 70, he discovers that he can specify any start date for his monthly payments. He considers three options:

He could start payments effective with his original claim at age 66. He would receive a $48,000 lump sum (4 years' back pay) plus $1,000 a month for life (his original age-66 payment amount).

Or he could start payments effective with, say, age 68. He would receive a $27,840 lump sum (2 year's back pay) plus ongoing payments of $1,160 per month (his age-68 payment with 24 months' DRCs).

Or he could start payments effective with age 70. He would receive no back pay but would receive ongoing payments of $1,320 (his full age-70 payment with 48 months' DRCs).

The third option was always Bill's "Plan A," but depending on his current vs. long-term needs, Bill can choose a larger lump sum with smaller monthly payments, or a smaller lump sum with greater monthly payments. Being a long-term planner, Bill chooses to start payments at age 70 to ensure the greatest security throughout his lifetime and Barb's.

File and Suspend example 3

You can unsuspend with back pay any time from suspension to age 70. Here are Bill and Barb again from Example 1, but with this change:

At 68, tragedy strikes. Barb passes away, and Bill learns that he has a terminal illness. He decides that the whole idea of File and Suspend was to maximize payments in the long run, but now he doesn't have a long run. He wishes he had the money now, not later. In fact, he wishes he had never suspended his payments.

Bill unsuspends his payments retroactively, effective age 66. SSA immediately deposits $24,000 in Bill's bank account, representing 24 months at $1,000 per month, Bill's age-66 payment amount. He gets ongoing payments of $1,000 per month for life. The net effect is as if he never suspended payments.

File and Suspend example 4

You can suspend payments that have already been in effect:

Loretta files for Social Security at 62 because she needed the income. She gets a 75% payment.

By the time she reaches 66, her financial situation has improved. She wishes she had never taken the early Social Security and the reduced payment.

At 66, Loretta suspends her Social Security payments. She works part-time and draws down savings a bit to bridge to age 70. While suspended, her Social Security is growing at the rate of 8% per year, computed monthly.

At 70 her payments automatically resume. The payment rate is 132% of her original 75%, resulting in a 99% payment. In essence she has erased the reduction for early filing.

File and Suspend example 5

You can voluntarily suspend, unsuspend, and re-suspend, with or without back pay, like turning a tap on and off. You receive DRCs for any months payments were suspended and never paid out:

Jennifer's age-66 payment is $2,000 per month. She plans to delay Social Security until 70 to maximize future payments. But she wants to keep open the option to file for retroactive payments—she wants the Social Security contingency fund.

Jennifer files and suspends at age 66. She plans to bridge to age 70 with a combination of work and savings.

Sure enough, at age 68 she has a financial emergency and needs money quickly. She unsuspends her payments effective age 66. SSA immediately deposits $48,000 to her bank account, representing 24 months of payments at her age-66 payment of $2,000 per month.

Jennifer doesn't need the ongoing Social Security payments, so she immediately re-suspends her payments.

Her Social Security automatically resumes at 70 at $2,320 per month. That's 116% of her $2,000 age-66 payment, representing the 24 total months from age 68-70 that her payments were suspended.

"SPOUSAL-ONLY" RESTRICTED APPLICATION

Here's a way to "get paid to wait" from 66 to 70. Filing a restricted application for "Spousal-Only" payments is a way to maximize Social Security for anyone dually eligible for their own Social Security plus a spousal payment. It's particularly powerful for working couples who have reached Full Retirement Age. It also works for a divorced person eligible on their former spouse's record.

The general idea is to take a small Social Security payment at FRA and a bigger one later. To do so, you take a lower Spousal-Only benefit at FRA, and wait until age 70 to apply on your own record. By then, Delayed Retirement Credits (DRCs) will have augmented the higher payment. The aim is to use the spousal payment as a bridge to get the higher 132% payment at age 70.

Also known as "claim now, claim more later," it applies in these situations:

- Anyone who is eligible for a spousal payment (whether current spouse or former spouse) *and* would be eligible for a higher payment at age 70 on their own work record.

- Working married couples, where both are eligible for Social Security.

- The person filing for Spousal-Only payments must not have filed for a reduced payment before FRA.

- Either spouse, or both, may be working or retired after FRA.

Spousal-Only Application procedure

The procedure is as follows, assuming *you* are the one filing the Spousal-Only application:

1. For you to get a spousal payment, your spouse or ex-spouse must claim their "own" Social Security.

   a. Exception: if you have been divorced over 2 years, your ex-spouse does not need to apply.

   b. Your spouse or ex-spouse may be receiving monthly payments or be suspending payments.

   c. He or she may have applied at any age (before or after FRA).

2. At your age 66 (or more), you file for *spousal* benefits on your spouse's record.

   a. You do *not* file for your own retirement benefits. You do *not* File and Suspend your own benefits. Filing for your own benefits, even if suspended, can eliminate the spousal payments you seek.

   b. You *"limit the scope"* of the application to Spousal-Only benefits, specifically excluding retirement payments. (This is a simple checkbox in the online application if you are filing at FRA.)

3. At 70 (or before), you file for your "own" benefits. Delayed Retirement Credits have escalated your retirement payment in the background, up to 132% at age 70.

4. The new retirement payments will eliminate the spousal payments you were receiving, since your own payment is higher.

5.   Your spouse can now file for spousal benefits on your record, if that would result in a raise.

6.   The short-term effect is that the spousal payments act as a bridge to get you to age 70. The long-term effect is that the 132% payments continue throughout your life. Your surviving spouse will also get the 132% payment, no matter who survives the first death, so the higher payment will continue for the joint life of the couple.

Spousal-Only Application example 1

The Spousal-Only Application can be used by a single person who is eligible as a former spouse, as in this example, which happens to add an Undo procedure:

Bob delays his Social Security until age 66 to get a full 100% payment. He files for his own benefits at 66 and receives $2,000 per month.

Two months later Bob learns that he could have filed for spousal payments of $800 per month on his former spouse's record from 66 to 70, then switch to his own benefits at 132%, or $2,640. The problem is that his current $2,000 payments eliminate his spousal payments.

To resolve the issue, Bob withdraws his own claim and repays the $4,000 already received. The effect of this Undo is as if he never filed on his own. That opens the door to the Spousal-Only application.

Bob files a new application, restricted to Spousal-Only payments. He uses the $800 spousal payments as a bridge to get to 70. At 70 he refiles on his own record and gets $2,640 (132% of his $2,000 age-66 payment) for life.

Spousal-Only Application example 2

This strategy is particularly powerful for working couples, as in this example:

Tom and Ann both work and are eligible for their own Social Security retirement payments. They are both turning 66. Tom's full payment amount is $1,000 and Ann's is $2,200.

At 66, Ann Files and Suspends her Social Security payment of $2,200 per month. While her payments are suspended, DRCs are increasing her payment in the background.

Tom files a Spousal-Only Application on Ann's work record, limiting the scope of the application to spousal benefits only. He gets $1,100 per month as a spouse (50% of Ann's $2,200). While he draws as a spouse, DRCs are increasing his own retirement benefit every month.

At 70, Ann's payments automatically resume at $2,904 (132% of her $2,200 payment).

Also at 70, Tom files his own retirement claim. He gets $1,320 (132% of his $1,000 payment). His $1,100 spouse payments stop because he's getting a higher payment on his own record.

Whoever survives the first death will get Ann's payment of $2,904 for life.

In short, *both* Tom and Ann will get a 132% payment at 70. In addition, *one* of them will get a spousal payment from 66-70 to help bridge to 70.

Figure 10.4 compares Tom and Ann's choice between the "traditional approach" of each simply filing on their own records at 66 vs. the Spousal-Only strategy.

The bottom line is that Ann and Tom increased their total payout by $60,720 by age 85, and increased the survivor's monthly payment by $704 per month for life. Not a bad outcome for delaying full Social Security for four years, especially

Traditional approach: Each draws 100% at 66	Spousal-Only Application strategy: Tom draws 50% spousal payment at 66; both get 132% at 70
At 66, Ann draws her **$2,200** per month. Tom draws his own $1,000 plus a $100 spousal payment, making his total payment **$1,100** per month. Total couple payments = **$3,300** per month.	At 66, Ann Files and Suspends, drawing **$0**. Tom draws **$1,100** spousal payments on Ann's record.
At 70, total payments = **$158,400**. Payments of $3,300 per month each continue.	At 70, total payments = **$52,800**. Tom switches to his own $1,320 per month (132% of his $1,000). Ann's payment commences at $2,904 (132% of her $2,200). Total couple payments = $4,224 per month.
At 85, total payments = **$752,400**.	At 85, total payments = **$813,120**.
After first death, survivor continues to receive **$2,200** per month.	After first death, survivor receives **$2,904** per month.

Figure 10.4. Comparison of the traditional approach of both spouses filing at 66 vs. the Spousal-Only Application strategy, Example 2.

since the spousal payments of $1,100 per month helped them bridge those first four years.

Additional considerations

- You must be FRA or above. Under FRA, you must apply for your *own* retirement when you apply for a *spousal* payment ("deemed filing," see page 69). At FRA, deemed filing ends, opening the door to a Spousal-Only Application. In the example, Tom needs to be FRA to file the Spousal-Only Application and Ann has to be FRA to File and Suspend.

- You must have assets or income to bridge the four years of lower Social Security from age 66 to 70. The spousal payments can be part of the bridge.

- The couple should have enough life expectancy to reach the break-even point.

- Note that, with higher monthly payments, all the ensuing COLAs would be larger dollar amounts—a nice gift for your later years.

- A failsafe is in place: If Ann dies before age 70, Tom can still get widower's payments augmented by DRCs up to Ann's month of death.

- Assist your SSA representative with the following citations: POMS GN 204.004 B and GN 204.020 D.

FINDING YOUR OPTIMAL PATHWAY

If you're trying to find the optimal Social Security pathway for your individual situation, the math can be tedious. Luckily there are computer programs to run the numbers for you and give you simple step-by-step instructions for timing your Social Security.

Start with good old SSA. Start your My Social Security account at www.ssa.gov/myaccount and get your Social Security payment at FRA for you and your spouse (if married). All other planning will need this step. There are also online SSA calculators at www.ssa.gov/planners/benefitcalculators.htm if you wish to experiment with different future work scenarios like early retirement or part-time work. And of course you can get individual help on the phone or in an SSA office.

My favorite free Social Security planner is the AARP Social Security Calculator at www.aarp.org/work/social-security/social-security-benefits calculator. Input your birth dates and the benefit estimates you got from SSA, and it will advise you on your best pathway.

Also check out three private companies, http://maximizemysocialsecurity .com/, www.socialsecuritysolutions.com, and www.socialsecuritychoices.com.

They offer individual computations for a fee, and their websites will give you a good idea of how they work. Social Security Solutions has individual counseling available.

Finally, remember that Social Security is just one cog in your retirement finances. You need a strategy that takes into account your taxes, other income, work plans, savings, marital status, and life expectancy, as well as your Social Security. Only a professional financial planner can address your entire financial picture. You can search for planners at www.fpanet.org, www.napfa.org, or www.garrettplanningnetwork.com. The last one, Garrett Planning Network, lists Certified Financial Planners who are available by the hour.

Using your deeper knowledge of Social Security, especially with the specialized strategies in this chapter, you can optimize your Social Security. Using a financial professional you can optimize your entire retirement finances.

FOR MORE INFORMATION...

"When Should You Start Social Security Benefits? Do the Math!"
http://moneywatch.bnet.com/retirement-planning/blog/money-life/when-should-you-start-social-security-benefits-do-the-math/520/?tag=content;col1
or go to http://moneywatch.bnet.com/ and conduct a search for "when should you start Social Security."

"Life Expectancy Calculator"
www.ssa.gov/planners/benefitcalculators.htm, and click "Life Expectancy Calculator."

"The Social Security Claiming Guide" (e-book)
http://crr.bc.edu/special-projects/books/the-social-security-claiming-guide/
(See additional articles from the Center for Retirement Research at Boston College at http://crr.bc.edu/index.php.)

"Three Financial Do-Overs with Social Security"
www.bankrate.com/finance/retirement/3-financial-do-overs-with-social-security-1.aspx

"Retirement Planner: If You Change Your Mind"
www.ssa.gov/retire2/withdrawal.htm

"Retirement Planner: Suspending Retirement Benefit Payments"
www.ssa.gov/retire2/suspend.htm

"AARP Social Security Calculator"
www.aarp.org/work/social-security/social-security-benefits-calculator

CHAPTER ELEVEN

SOCIAL SECURITY FOR THE NEXT GENERATION

SOLVENT OR BANKRUPT?

Why should I learn about Social Security? It will be bankrupt before I retire, won't it?

Many younger workers believe that the Social Security system is bankrupt and that they'll never get a Social Security payment. "More likely to see a UFO" was one poll's finding. Fortunately, the facts are considerably brighter than that.
Here are the facts:

- Social Security is presently running a surplus, and has every year since 1984.

- Excess funds are invested safely for future needs, and earn interest.

- Surpluses are projected to continue until 2020. Then, with most Baby Boomers retired, the system will operate at a deficit, drawing from its invested funds.

- Invested funds are projected to be exhausted in 2033.

- After 2033, the system will continue to be about 77% funded for the rest of the century.

- Reforms are needed to fill the 23% shortfall, to continue to pay full benefits after 2033.

- Such reforms are now being considered. Options include cutting benefit payments, raising taxes, changing how excess funds are invested, instituting private individual accounts, providing direct government subsidies, or some mix of all of these.

Has Social Security ever faced a shortfall before?

Yes. 1983.

Headlines in 1982 stated the exact month that SSA would go broke—July 1983. The system was in a tailspin, running steady annual deficits despite Congressional attempts in 1977 and 1980 to patch up its financing.

Finally, on April 20, 1983, the 1983 Amendments to the Social Security Act were signed into law. The reforms were successful because the changes were major. On the income side, FICA taxes were increased from 5.4% to 6.2%, and more jobs were brought under the program. On the expense side, computations were lowered, retirement age was raised, some benefit categories were eliminated, and eligibility requirements were stiffened.

The result has been healthy annual surpluses since 1984, with the actual surpluses running close to the amounts forecast by the framers of the Amendments. The aim in 1983 was 50 years of solvency, and current projections say we're on track.

The accumulated surplus funds, about $2.8 trillion in 2013 and growing, are invested in U.S. Treasury bonds, widely considered the safest investment in the world.

Surpluses? I heard there were deficits starting in 2010.

In 2010, there was a slight deficit in only one of Social Security's three main income streams. If you only counted payroll tax income, it *could* be called a deficit, but that would ignore the other two income streams: interest on SSA's treasury bonds and income tax on benefits.

Income type	2012 income	% of total income
Payroll taxes	$589.5	70.1%
Interest on trust fund bonds	$109.1	13.0%
Income tax on benefits	$27.3	3.2%
General Fund reimbursements	$114.3	13.6%
Total	**$840.2**	**100%**

Figure 11.1. Sources of income for Social Security. (Dollar amounts in billions.) Virtually all of the General Fund reimbursements were due to the payroll tax "holiday" ending in 2012.

Social Security's solvency is a remarkable accomplishment in this era of troubled banks, large insurance companies in receivership, and pension plans threatened with bankruptcy. Social Security is one of the best-run financial systems in the nation and the world. Americans can take pride in this achievement, yet the success is unknown to most citizens. Social Security was financially struggling in the late 1970's and early 1980's. Even worse, there has been a massive effort since the 1990's to erode confidence in Social Security. The result is we don't recognize how financially sound Social Security really is.

What about the FICA "tax holiday" in 2011 and 2012? Didn't that reduce Social Security's revenue?

No, the shortfall was made up by general revenues transferred from the federal government to Social Security. Those transfers make up substantially all of the "General Fund reimbursements" in Figure 11.1; normally income from the General Fund is about 2.4% of Social Security's income.

WHY A SURPLUS?

Why should Social Security run a surplus instead of balancing income and expenses?

The need for building a surplus of Social Security funds is twofold. First, any financial system, if it expects to survive in the long term, needs to stay in the black. The second reason is more important, and can be summed up in two words: Baby Boom.

Before 1983, Social Security was a "pay as you go" plan. Almost as soon as the tax money came into the system, it was paid out in the form of Social Security payments. Yes, there were trust funds to hold excess money from month to month, but these contained at most a few months' worth of payments. Social Security functioned more like a pipeline than a reservoir, with tax money coming in one end and payments going out the other end in a steady stream.

But starting with the 1983 Amendments, Social Security started stockpiling funds for future retirees.

Why the change?

In a word, demographics. The "pay as you go" practice worked fine as long as there were enough workers paying taxes at one end of the pipeline to supply the payments for the beneficiaries at the other end. And back then, there were plenty of workers. In the 1940's and 50's, there were 10 to 15 tax-paying workers for every beneficiary of the brand-new Social Security system.

However, with Baby Boomers having fewer children of their own, the ratio is changing. The current ratio is 2.8 workers for every beneficiary, and in 2030, when the Baby Boom generation is retired, there will be only 2 workers for every beneficiary. Thus, it gets more and more expensive for those still working to support those on Social Security. The fact is, as Boomers retire in large numbers, they will have an unprecedented impact on *all* pension systems, Social Security included.

That is why SSA is "stockpiling" Social Security dollars now to pay for retirement benefits later. For the next two decades, SSA will act more like a reservoir and less like a pipeline, compared to its earlier years.

Many writers still call Social Security a "pay as you go" system. That ignores the large surpluses and investments of the system. The current system might more properly be called a *modified* pay as you go system.

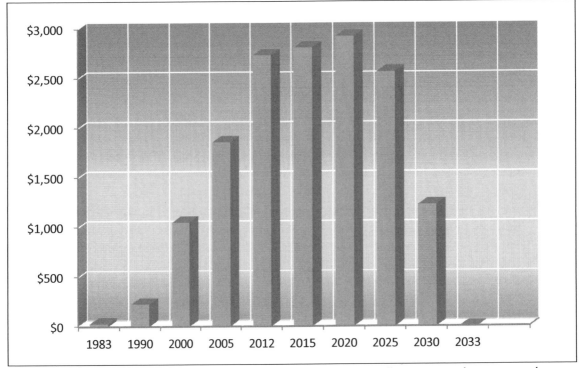

Figure 11.2. OASDI trust fund reserves. Dollar amounts in billions. Actual amounts shown to 2012, projections shown after 2012. Source: SSA Trustees Report, 2013.

AMOUNT OF THE SURPLUS

How much of a surplus is the system running each year? How long will the surplus last?

In Calendar Year (CY) 2012, the Old-Age, Survivor, and Disability Insurance (OASDI) programs cost $785.8 billion including administrative expenses, but received $840.2 billion, for a surplus of $54.4 billion. Closing balance was $2,732 billion.

The surplus was projected to dip to about $23 billion CY 2014. Then it's expected to rebound to $31 billion in CY 2018, with surpluses continuing through 2020.

The surplus is invested in two trust funds, the OASI trust fund and the DI trust fund. As noted above, the funds are invested in U.S. Treasury Bonds, considered the safest investment in the world. In CY 2012, interest income alone was $109 billion.

Figure 11.2 shows the total trust fund reserves in past years and projected reserves in future years. Note that reserves are expected to rise to a peak of about $2.9 trillion in 2020. However, don't overlook the last column, labeled 2033. The OASDI trust funds are expected to be depleted at that time, following a period of intense drawing down.

Here are some important dates for understanding Social Security's financing:

2013-2020	Expenses exceed payroll taxes.
	Payroll taxes plus interest exceed expenses.
	Trust Funds continue to grow.
2023-2033	Income from taxes and interest together no longer sufficient to pay benefits.
	Trust Fund principal is drawn down.
	Trust Funds shrinking.
2034 on	Trust Funds exhausted.
	No further interest income since principal is depleted.
	Tax income continues.
	Tax income alone is sufficient to pay about 77% of benefits

Thus, Social Security is still expected to run out of money sometime this century. If present trends and laws continue unchanged, *your* retirement may be in good shape, but our children may have another Social Security crisis similar to the one in 1983.

PROPOSALS FOR EXTENDING SOCIAL SECURITY'S SOLVENCY

What are the options for extending Social Security's solvency past 2033?

Like a family spending more than it earns, getting by with withdrawals from savings, Social Security has only three real options to reach solvency:

• Increase income (in Social Security's case, raise taxes),

• Decrease expenses (cut benefits), or

• Re-invest savings to get a better return (explore alternative investments for the Trust Funds)—really another way to increase income.

The creative and interesting part is *how* to make these changes, how to have Congress agree on a reform package, and how to make the changes acceptable to the public.

There have been numerous plans proposed to eliminate the funding shortfall:

• In 1997, the *Advisory Council on Social Security,* a bipartisan commission of experts, made a number of proposals. Most of the members agreed to expand coverage to more workers, invest part of the trust funds in the stock market, increase the number of work years in the computation, increase Full Retirement Age, and tax benefits in the same manner as pensions. Altogether, these changes would have eliminated two-thirds of the funding shortfall. The council proposed three different approaches to eliminate the last third of the shortfall.

• In 1999, the Pew Charitable Trusts conducted a massive public information and polling program, *Americans Discuss Social Security.* The most popular reforms were to raise the earnings ceiling, reduce benefits for high-income individuals, and expand coverage to more workers.

• In 2002, President Bush's *Commission to Strengthen Social Security* proposed three different plans, all based on partial privatization of the system, using individual investment accounts.

- In 2010, President Obama's *National Commission on Fiscal Responsibility and Reform,* also known as Simpson-Bowles, recommended raising the earnings ceiling, changing the benefit formula, increasing the retirement age, and expanding coverage to more workers. The report was supported by a majority of Commission members, but did not gain the supermajority needed for endorsement.

- In 2011, Congress's bipartisan *Joint Select Committee on Deficit Reduction* was formed to reduce the national debt, and Social Security reform was expected to be included in its proposals. It was unable to reach agreement and was dissolved.

- Along the way, virtually every congressional office and interest group has proposed its own plan for reform.

All of these proposals share one feature: no action was taken on any of them. Therefore, we're still on the same track laid down in the 1983 Amendments.

Analysis

Reforms are grouped around these options:

Changing the Cost of Living Adjustments (COLA). Currently, Social Security benefits are increased annually for inflation, as measured by the Consumer Price Index for Urban Wage Earners and Clerical Workers (CPI-W). Some reform plans suggest a different inflation index like the "chained-CPI" proposal, or giving COLAs smaller than the full CPI-W, like CPI minus 0.5%.

Level of monthly payments. The PIA formula could be changed to produce smaller benefits for everyone, or for targeted groups such as high earners. Alternatively, the number of work years used in the computation could be changed from the current 35 to 38 or even 40.

Retirement Age. The Full Retirement Age is currently moving from 65 to 67, with early retirement benefits still available at 62. The phase-in to 67 could be accelerated; the FRA could be moved higher than 67, e.g. 68 or 70; and/or the early retirement age could be raised beyond the current 62.

Family benefits. The current 50% computation for most spouses and children could be reduced to a lower percentage, say 40% or 33%.

Payroll taxes. The payroll tax rate, currently at 6.2% for Social Security, could be raised for everyone or for targeted groups such as high-earners. Or the taxable earnings ceiling, currently $117,000 (2014), could be raised to collect more taxes from high earners.

Coverage of earnings. Currently, about 6% of workers are outside the Social Security system, primarily state and local government workers. Covering them or new hires under Social Security would help long-term solvency. Other earnings, such as the value of employee health insurance, could also be covered by the payroll tax.

Re-investing the trust funds. Investing a modest portion of the trust funds in the stock and/or real estate markets should increase long-term returns while preserving security during market downturns.

Taxation of benefits. Currently, only part of Social Security is income-taxable, and only for higher-income retirees. More benefits could be made taxable or the income thresholds could be phased out.

Individual investment accounts. There are two kinds of individual investment accounts proposed: either a *carve-out* (replacing part of the payroll tax with a contribution to an individual account) or an *add-on* (leaving the payroll tax as-is but adding an individual account on top of it). Note that, by themselves, neither approach extends Social Security solvency. On the contrary, a carve-out will aggravate the solvency problem by reducing Social Security's income.

In practice, it's doubtful that one "fix" will be used to balance Social Security's books. There will almost certainly be a combination of tax increases and benefits cuts, as was done in 1983.

Author's Comments

Background. Social Security is just that: *social*—not individual—and *security*—not risky. With so much of retirement at risk these days, those two features should be retained in any reform package.

It's insurance, not an investment. Specifically, it's insurance with a risk pool spread over the entire working society, not an individual or a small group. That fits well with the *security* nomenclature.

Individual investment accounts. Individual accounts are the opposite of Social Security. They're not social, they're private. And they're not secure, they're risky.

Individual accounts are fine. Investment is wise. The power of compound interest is astounding. Everyone should save and invest.

However, only a fool would cancel his home insurance or health insurance and invest the premiums, because he can get a "better rate of return" by investing. The wise person buys the insurance *first* and *then* invests above and beyond the insurance.

The same applies to Social Security. It's a starting point, a secure foundation. Individuals should certainly build additional financial security atop it.

Carve-out individual accounts only weaken Social Security and compound its financing problem. Social Security has a long-term cash shortfall. You can't save it by diverting part of its funding into investment accounts. Such a move would obviously just expand the shortfall, causing bigger headaches in the near future.

Carve-out individual accounts make no sense financially, so the aim of proponents must be to shrink or dismantle Social Security on philosophical grounds. My conclusion is that any individual accounts should be funded *in addition to* Social Security (add-on), not *at the expense of* Social Security (carve-out).

I like to say that if you want an individual account, open an IRA or a 401(k). They're available here and now.

Funding Social Security. Full funding of Social Security requires a savings of 2.72% of taxable payroll (2013 Trustees Report). A remarkable document can be found at www.ssa.gov/OACT/solvency/provisions/summary.html. There, SSA actuaries list numerous individual policy proposals and evaluate the impact of each one on Social Security's solvency, in terms of a percent of taxable payroll. You can pick and choose your own reforms to save Social Security.

Below is a modest proposal, a seven-point model that fully funds Social Security for the 21st Century with no benefit cuts and a minimum of disruption. All plan numbers and savings figures are from www.ssa.gov/OACT/solvency/provisions/summary.html:

- *Raise the earnings ceiling (Plan E3.1).* This was the most popular "fix" identified by Americans Discuss Social Security and other polling. It is politically viable and could save a tremendous amount of money for the system. The ceiling can be raised to capture 90% of total compensation, as was the case in 1983, when the current ceiling was adopted. The increase would be phased in by 2023. Retirees would receive increased benefits in line with their increased contributions. Savings: 0.77% of taxable payroll; 28.3% of needed savings.

- *Increase the payroll tax rate (Plan E1.8).* An increase from the current 12.4% to 13.0% could be phased in by 2021. Nobody likes a tax increase, but this very modest increase—the employee share would be only 0.3% of payroll—makes a dramatic difference in Social Security financing. Savings: 0.53% of taxable payroll; 19.5% of needed savings.

- *Re-invest the Trust Funds (Plan G2).* This is not as popular a fix, but it is an obvious step. 40% of the funds could be put in a broad-based index of stocks between now and 2028. This option assumes a modest 5.4% return on equities. The Trust Funds would still be the most conservative pension fund around, and could weather another Great Depression. Savings: 0.44% of taxable payroll; 16.2% of needed savings.

- *Cover newly-hired state and local government employees (Plan F1).* Savings: 0.15% of taxable payroll; 5.5% of needed savings.

- *Tax Social Security as pensions are taxed (Plan H2).* This could be phased in by 2023 by lowering the existing taxation thresholds. Savings: 0.21% of payroll; 7.7% of needed savings.

- *Adjust the PIA formula (Plan B3.3).* The formula could be modified to protect lower earners and reduce benefits of higher earners. This fits well with increasing the earnings ceiling while still rewarding the higher earner with higher benefits. Savings: 0.23% of payroll; 8.5% of needed savings.

- *Increase the computation years in the formula from 35 to 40 (Plan B4.2).* This preserves the principle that benefits should be proportional to lifetime earnings. Savings: 0.46% of payroll; 16.9% of needed savings.

Remarkably, these seven reforms *by themselves* would save 2.79% of the taxable payroll, or 103% of the money necessary for *permanent* Social Security solvency. Retirement age remains the same. COLAs are not reduced. Across-the-board cuts are avoided. Cost to the government is zero. Deficit impact is positive. Changes are focused on a small number of higher-income individuals, most able to afford change. Social Security is sustainable for our children, grandchildren… basically indefinitely.

What could be simpler?

What the reader can do

Social Security will be changed in the next few years, and you will be affected. You owe it to yourself to become involved. Here are some ways you can play a role:

- Learn everything you can about Social Security. Congratulations! You've already taken a big step by reading this book. You already know more about Social Security than most people.

- Think about the value Social Security has for you, your family, and your neighbors. Is disability protection important to you? Survivor benefits?

How about spouse or child benefits? Or are retirement and Medicare most important for you?

- Talk with your family and friends about Social Security. Share this book with them to increase their understanding. Start a discussion group at work or your place of worship. Invite a speaker from SSA or AARP.

- Attend an event. Many groups are sponsoring public forums on Social Security: SSA itself, elected officials, AARP, news shows, and others. Listen to other people's ideas and polish your own.

- Use your voice. Call a phone-in talk show, write a letter to the editor, phone your Congressional representatives, send a post card to the President.

- Vote. Elect representatives who will strengthen Social Security, not weaken it.

- Elevate the debate. Don't allow misinformation like "the trust funds don't exist" or "Social Security can't work." Tell people that Social Security is valuable, strong, efficient, viable, and affordable.

Social Security's financing problems are solvable. Study after study has published plans to make the system solvent for over 75 years—straight through the retirement years of the Boomers, Generation X, Millenials, and their children.

It is perfectly reasonable to fine-tune or even redesign the system for the new century. Each generation has adapted the Social Security system for its own particular needs or desires. In the 1930s, Social Security was created as a simple pension system for selected workers and widows. In the 1940s, benefits were expanded to other family members. In the 1950s, coverage was extended and disability was added. The 1960s brought the addition of Medicare and early retirement for men. In the 70s, COLAs were written into law and benefits were expanded for former spouses. The 80s brought a landmark extension of Social Security solvency for 50 years. Now, it's time for Xers and Millenials to reshape the system for the 21st century.

The next generation needs to look at the "fine print" of reform plans, and really think about what they want their Social Security system to do.

If we do nothing, we will lose Social Security and its protections. Social Security has never been stronger or more popular. Ironically, it also has never been more threatened by those who would weaken it.

Over the past eight decades, Congress has delivered whatever changes were popular. When we speak, Congress listens. Let's make sure our voices are heard. If we are successful, we will get a Social Security system that serves us best.

For More Information...

"Trust Fund FAQs"
www.ssa.gov/OACT/ProgData/fundFAQ.html

"The 2013 OASDI Trustees Report"
www.ssa.gov/OACT/TR/2013/index.html

"Old-Age, Survivors, and Disability Insurance Trust Funds, 1957-2012"
www.ssa.gov/OACT/STATS/table4a3.html

"Operations of the Combined OASI and DI Trust Funds, In Current Dollars"
www.ssa.gov/OACT/TR/2013/lr6f8.html

"The Social Security Fix-It Book"
http://crr.bc.edu/special-projects/books/the-social-security-fix-it-book/

"Summary of Provisions That Would Change the Social Security Program"
www.ssa.gov/OACT/solvency/provisions/summary.html

"Proposals Addressing Trust Fund Solvency"
www.ssa.gov/OACT/solvency/index.html

"CBO Social Security Policy Options"
www.cbo.gov/ftpdocs/115xx/doc11580/07-01-SSOptions_forWeb.pdf

A SAMPLE RETIREMENT COMPUTATION

Our sample computation is performed for Sam Smith, who turned 62 in 2011 and is retiring in 2014 at the age of 65 and 0 months. His earnings have been comfortable for most of his life, with a few lean years due to job changes. He achieved maximum Social Security earnings in some years, with lower earnings in most years.

We will walk through Sam's Social Security computation by referring to the columns in Figure A-1. The steps are also described in Chapter 2, pages 41-55.

See Appendix E for other sources of information on Social Security computations and estimates.

Column 1 shows calendar years back to 1951, the first year for most retirement computations, and up to 2013. 2013 is the last year used for Sam's computation because it is the year before his payments begin. Any wages for 2014 will be added to the computation automatically in 2015, and so on.

Column 2 shows the maximum taxable earnings base for each year. This is the highest earnings level that can be posted to the record each year, and the ceiling for FICA taxes—FICA taxes are paid only on wages at or below this level. You can find maximum earnings for any year at www.ssa.gov/OACT/COLA/cbb.html.

Column 3 shows the national average of all wages, as tabulated by SSA for each year. This is used to determine the inflation index factor shown in **Column 4**. You can find average wages for any year at www.ssa.gov/OACT/COLA/AWI.html#Series.

Column 4 shows the inflation factor used to make earlier earnings comparable to recent earnings. It is calculated by dividing the average wage for each year into the average wage for your Base Year, the *year you attain age 60*. Sam's Base Year is 2009, so in his case, each year's inflation factor is determined by 2009's average wage of $40,711.61 (bottom of Column 3). Average wages for later years will not affect Sam's computation.

The inflation factors are "locked in" at the year you turn 60. These same factors would be used to compute Sam's payment even if he first filed for Social Security in 2015 (age 66), no matter how much inflation drove up average wages in the interim. The inflation factor "lock-in" is illustrated in Column 4 by the

Column 1	2	3	4	5	6	7	8
Year	Max. Earnings Base	Average Wage	Inflation Index Factor (2009 elig. yr.)	Sam's Actual Earnings	Sam's Indexed Earnings	High 35 Years	Comp. Earnings
1951	$3,600	$2,799.16	14.5442240	$0.00	$0.00	L	$0.00
1952	$3,600	$2,973.32	13.6923069	$0.00	$0.00	L	$0.00
1953	$3,600	$3,139.44	12.9677936	$0.00	$0.00	L	$0.00
1954	$3,600	$3,155.64	12.9012213	$0.00	$0.00	L	$0.00
1955	$4,200	$3,301.44	12.3314705	$0.00	$0.00	L	$0.00
1956	$4,200	$3,532.36	11.5253287	$0.00	$0.00	L	$0.00
1957	$4,200	$3,641.72	11.1792258	$0.00	$0.00	L	$0.00
1958	$4,200	$3,673.80	11.0816076	$0.00	$0.00	L	$0.00
1959	$4,800	$3,855.80	10.5585378	$0.00	$0.00	L	$0.00
1960	$4,800	$4,007.12	10.1598180	$0.00	$0.00	L	$0.00
1961	$4,800	$4,086.76	9.9618304	$0.00	$0.00	L	$0.00
1962	$4,800	$4,291.40	9.4867899	$0.00	$0.00	L	$0.00
1963	$4,800	$4,396.64	9.2597097	$0.00	$0.00	L	$0.00
1964	$4,800	$4,576.32	8.8961458	$0.00	$0.00	L	$0.00
1965	$4,800	$4,658.72	8.7387974	$0.00	$0.00	L	$0.00
1966	$6,600	$4,938.36	8.2439535	$600.00	$4,946.37	L	$0.00
1967	$6,600	$5,213.44	7.8089726	$600.00	$4,685.38	L	$0.00
1968	$7,800	$5,571.76	7.3067774	$650.00	$4,749.41	L	$0.00
1969	$7,800	$5,893.76	6.9075785	$1,000.00	$6,907.58	L	$0.00
1970	$7,800	$6,186.24	6.5809943	$1,200.00	$7,897.19	L	$0.00
1971	$7,800	$6,497.08	6.2661396	$4,000.00	$25,064.56	L	$0.00
1972	$9,000	$7,133.80	5.7068617	$6,000.00	$34,241.17	L	$0.00
1973	$10,800	$7,580.16	5.3708114	$8,000.00	$42,966.49	H	$42,966.49
1974	$13,200	$8,030.76	5.0694592	$5,500.00	$27,882.03	L	$0.00
1975	$14,100	$8,630.92	4.7169491	$9,200.00	$43,395.93	H	$43,395.93
1976	$15,300	$9,226.48	4.4124747	$9,300.00	$41,036.02	L	$0.00
1977	$16,500	$9,779.44	4.1629797	$10,000.00	$41,629.80	L	$0.00
1978	$17,700	$10,556.03	3.8567160	$6,000.00	$23,140.30	L	$0.00
1979	$22,900	$11,479.46	3.5464743	$12,000.00	$42,557.69	L	$0.00
1980	$25,900	$12,513.46	3.2534255	$13,000.00	$42,294.53	L	$0.00
1981	$29,700	$13,773.10	2.9558785	$15,000.00	$44,338.18	H	$44,338.18
1982	$32,400	$14,531.34	2.8016418	$20,000.00	$56,032.84	H	$56,032.84
1983	$35,700	$15,239.24	2.6714987	$22,000.00	$58,772.97	H	$58,772.97
1984	$37,800	$16,135.07	2.5231753	$25,000.00	$63,079.38	H	$63,079.38
1985	$39,600	$16,822.51	2.4200675	$28,000.00	$67,761.89	H	$67,761.89
1986	$42,000	$17,321.82	2.3503079	$31,000.00	$72,859.54	H	$72,859.54
1987	$43,800	$18,426.51	2.2094043	$28,000.00	$61,863.32	H	$61,863.32
1988	$45,000	$19,334.04	2.1056960	$31,000.00	$65,276.57	High	$65,276.57
1989	$48,000	$20,099.55	2.0254986	$33,000.00	$66,841.45	H	$66,841.45
1990	$51,300	$21,027.98	1.9360685	$35,000.00	$67,762.40	H	$67,762.40
1991	$53,400	$21,811.60	1.8665119	$40,000.00	$74,660.47	H	$74,660.47
1992	$55,500	$22,935.42	1.7750540	$45,000.00	$79,877.43	H	$79,877.43
1993	$57,600	$23,132.67	1.7599183	$50,000.00	$87,995.92	H	$87,995.92
1994	$60,600	$23,753.53	1.7139183	$55,000.00	$94,265.51	H	$94,265.51
1995	$61,200	$24,705.66	1.6478657	$61,200.00	$100,849.38	H	$100,849.38
1996	$62,700	$25,913.90	1.5710337	$62,700.00	$98,503.81	H	$98,503.81
1997	$65,400	$27,426.00	1.4844166	$65,400.00	$97,080.85	H	$97,080.85
1998	$68,400	$28,861.44	1.4105883	$67,000.00	$94,509.42	H	$94,509.42
1999	$72,600	$30,469.84	1.3361281	$68,000.00	$90,856.71	H	$90,856.71

Column 1	2	3	4	5	6	7	8
Year	Max. Earnings Base	Average Wage	Inflation Index Factor (2011 elig. yr.)	Sam's Actual Earnings	Sam's Indexed Earnings	High 35 Years	Comp. Earnings
2000	$76,200	$32,154.82	1.2661122	$52,000.00	$65,837.83	H	$65,837.83
2001	$80,400	$32,921.92	1.2366110	$51,000.00	$63,067.16	H	$63,067.16
2002	$84,900	$33,252.09	1.2243324	$51,000.00	$62,440.95	H	$62,440.95
2003	$87,000	$34,064.95	1.1951173	$52,000.00	$62,146.10	H	$62,146.10
2004	$87,900	$35,648.55	1.1420271	$55,000.00	$62,811.49	H	$62,811.49
2005	$90,000	$36,952.94	1.1017150	$58,000.00	$63,899.47	H	$63,899.47
2006	$94,200	$38,651.41	1.0533021	$61,000.00	$64,251.43	H	$64,251.43
2007	$97,500	$40,405.48	1.0075764	$63,000.00	$63,477.32	H	$63,477.32
2008	$102,000	$41,334.97	0.9849193	$65,000.00	$64,019.75	H	$64,019.75
2009	$106,800	$40,711.61	1.0000000	$65,000.00	$65,000.00	H	$65,000.00
2010	$106,800	$41,673.83	1.0000000	$65,000.00	$65,000.00	H	$65,000.00
2011	$106,800	$42,979.61	1.0000000	$67,000.00	$67,000.00	H	$67,000.00
2012	$110,100	$44,321.67	1.0000000	$68,000.00	$68,000.00	H	$68,000.00
2013	113,700	N/A	1.0000000	$69,000.00	$69,000.00	H	$69,000.00
2014	117,000	N/A	N/A	N/A	N/A	N/A	N/A

Figure A-1. Retirement computation example (Sam Smith).

inflation factor "1.00000" posted for every year from 2009 on. It will continue at 1.00000 indefinitely. In other words, there is no further inflation indexing of *wages* after age 60. But the Social Security *benefit* is adjusted for CPI inflation, as shown below (see pages 260 and 262).

The inflation index factors, and the entire computation dependent upon them, are updated each year for those turning 60. A second retiree, Ms. Jones, who turned 60 in 2012, would have different, higher inflation index factors for every year because they would be compared to the *2012* average wage, which was higher than that of 2009.

You can find the indexing factors for any year at www.ssa.gov/OACT/COLA/awifactors.html. Note that the chart there is tied to the year of eligibility (age 62) rather than the Base Year (age 60).

Column 5 shows Sam's actual earnings. Usually, Sam's earnings were below the Social Security maximum. However, in 1995-1997, his earnings were above the maximum. In practice, only earnings up to the maximum would be posted to SSA's records and used in the computation.

Column 6 displays Sam's *indexed earnings*. These are simply his actual earnings (Column 5) or maximum earnings (Column 2), whichever is lower, multiplied by the inflation index factor for each year (Column 4), to account for inflation.

Column 7 is an analysis of Column 6, searching out the 35 years with the highest indexed earnings. The 35 high years, also called the "computation years," are labeled "H." Low years are labeled "L." The low years are sometimes called "dropout years" because they will not be used in the computation. Note that the computation years do not have to be continuous years, as shown by 1973 being an "H" computation year surrounded by "L" years, and 1974 being an "L" year surrounded by "H" years.

Column 8 is a transcription from Column 6 of the earnings from the 35 highest years. These are the "computation earnings" from the computation years. It is these earnings which determine Sam's full payment at his Full Retirement Age, called his Primary Insurance Amount (PIA).

Benefit Computation

Computation of Average Earnings
Dividend:...$2,435,501.96
Divisor Months (35 years x 12 months):................................. 420
AIME: **$5,798**

Computation of full retirement payment
(See text)
Age 62 PIA (2011):... **$2,072.00**
January 2012 COLA (3.6%):...$2,146.50
January 2013 COLA (1.7%):...$2,182.90
January 2014 COLA (1.5%):...$2,215.60
2014 PIA:.. **$2,215.60**

Computation of reduced retirement payment
Reduction Months.. 12
Reduction Factor:... 0.93333
Benefit before rounding: $2,067.80
Monthly Payment:... **$2,067.00**

Figure A-2. Sam Smith's payment computation

Benefit Computation

Computation of Average Earnings
Dividend:...$2,435,501.96

Figure A-2 details Sam's computation. The first figure, his "dividend," is the sum of all indexed earnings from his best 35 years—the sum of Column 8. As can be seen, Sam earned over $2.4 million in his career, after accounting for inflation.

> **Divisor Months (35 years x 12 months):** 420

The "divisor months" converts Sam's lifetime dividend into a monthly earnings figure. The 420 months shown are the number of months in the 35 computation years (35 x 12 = 420).

> **AIME:** **$5,798**

Dividing the dividend by the divisor months results in Sam's "AIME," or Average Indexed Monthly Earnings. As the name indicates, this is Sam's average monthly earned income after the inflation index is factored in.

> **Age 62 PIA (2011):** **$2,072.00**

The Average Indexed Monthly Earnings (AIME) figure is the basis for the computation of Sam's age 66 full payment amount (his PIA), as of his age 62. Every PIA is determined by a three-stage computation based on the AIME. Sam's computation, based on his year of eligibility, looks like this:

1. 90% of first $749 of AIME   = $674.10
                                             (Max $674.10)

2. Plus 32% of next $3,768 of AIME   = $1,205.76
                                       (Max $1, 205.76)

3. Plus 15% of AIME above $4,517 ($1,878 x 0.15)   = <u>192.15</u>

The result is rounded down to the nearest dime. The sum of stages 1, 2, and 3 is the full payment amount at Full Retirement Age, age 66 in Sam's case, *as computed at age 62.* This is his *age 62 PIA.*

4. Sum of 1, 2, and 3 (rounded down)   = $2,072.00

Notice the figures which govern this computation. On the left are the *90%, 32%, and 15% multipliers.* These percentage multipliers stay the same from year to year. Next are the *$749 and $4,517* figures (the $3,768 is the difference between the two). These figures are called the "bend points" in the Social Security computation. They determine *where* the percentage multipliers apply, and how much of your AIME you receive in your Social Security payment. The bend points are updated each year to account for inflation. The bend points used in your computation are the ones in effect the year you turn 62.

You can see that rewards for a low AIME are high (90% return) while rewards for a higher AIME taper off (32% and 15% returns). The 90%, 32%, and 15% multipliers are the mechanism used to give low-income workers a faster payback, while retaining higher payment amounts for high-income workers.

January 2012 COLA (3.6%):	$2,146.50
January 2013 COLA (1.7%):	$2,182.90
January 2014 COLA (1.5%):	$2,215.60
2014 PIA:	**$2,215.60**

Next, Sam's Age 62 PIA is adjusted for inflation to a "current" PIA for the year he first draws benefits. In this case, Sam's first benefit is at age 65—three years after his Age 62 PIA. Each January, his PIA will earn the COLA (Cost Of Living Adjustment) based on the inflation rate, whether or not he was actually drawing a payment.

Adding the three COLAs makes his 2014 PIA $2,215.60, after again rounding down each step to the next lower dime.

Computation of reduced retirement payment	
Reduction Months	12

The last few lines in Sam's benefit computation determine his reduced payment for being younger than his Full Retirement Age. If he enrolls in his birth month at age 65, he will have 12 "reduction months" because he is 12 months younger than his FRA of 66.

Reduction Factor:	0.93333

The reduction factor is computed as follows:

- For the first 36 months of early eligibility, each reduction month causes a payment reduction of 5/9 of 1% (0.00556).
- Each additional early eligibility month causes a reduction of 5/12 of 1% (0.00417).

With 12 reduction months, Sam's total reduction for early retirement is 6.667%, dropping Sam's payment to 93.333% of his full payment amount (PIA).

Benefit before rounding:	$2,067.80

The reduction factor of 0.93333 times Sam's full payment amount ($2,215.60) makes Sam's benefit amount $2,067.80.

Monthly Payment: **$2067.00**

Sam's actual monthly payment is rounded down to the next lowest *dollar*. Thus, Sam's monthly payment at age 65 will be $2,067.00.

Not included in this example are Medicare premiums. Since Sam is retiring at age 65, he also files for Medicare Parts A and B and pays a Part B premium of $104.90. This is deducted directly from his Social Security payment, reducing his net payment to $1,962.10.

SOCIAL SECURITY FACTS AND FIGURES

SOCIAL SECURITY'S BUDGET

SSA's budget is one of the biggest in the world. Figures for income, expense, and assets for Social Security programs in 2012 are as follows (all figures are in billions):

	Income	Expenditures	Trust Fund Assets
OASDI	$840	$786	$2,732
Medicare A	243	267	220
Medicare B	294	307	67
Total	**1,377**	**1,360**	**3,019**

The SSA and Medicare budgets are actually separate. Social Security alone is the biggest item in the 2014 federal budget, ahead of the Department of Defense. If Social Security and Medicare were an independent nation, it would have one of the world's largest national budgets, and be ranked thirteenth in the world according to GDP, between Australia and Spain. And with over $3 trillion in assets, SSA is one of the world's largest investors.

With annual expenditures over $1.3 trillion, Social Security plus Medicare spend about $113 billion per month, $3.7 billion per day, or about $155 million per hour. This works out to about $43,000 per second. At the same time, the combined trust funds are growing at a rate of $17 billion per year, or $47 million per day.

www.ssa.gov/policy/docs/statcomps/supplement/2013/4a.html#table4.a3
www.ssa.gov/policy/docs/statcomps/supplement/2013/8a.html#table8.a1
www.ssa.gov/policy/docs/statcomps/supplement/2013/8a.html#table8.a2
www.socialsecurity.gov/OACT/TRSUM/index.html

SOCIAL SECURITY BENEFICIARIES

58.2 million individuals receive a Social Security payment each month—over one in six Americans (February 2014). The beneficiaries fall into the following categories:

Retired workers	47.2 million
Spouses of retirees	2.3 million
Children of retirees	0.6 million
Survivors of deceased workers	6.2 million
Disabled workers	8.9 million
Spouses of disabled workers	0.2 million
Children of disabled workers	1.9 million
Total OASDI beneficiaries	58.2 million

In addition, there are about 8.4 million SSI beneficiaries.

www.ssa.gov/policy/docs/quickfacts/stat_snapshot/index.html
www.census.gov/main/www/popclock.html

SSA: THE AGENCY

There are about 64,000 employees of SSA, in Field Offices, Program Service Centers, Teleservice Centers, and Headquarters facilities.

The 1,263 Field Offices cover every major community in the U.S. Their mission is to serve as the face-to-face meeting point between the agency and the public by processing claims, inquiries, and reports of change, all in a neighborhood office setting.

The six Program Service Centers are organized to keep records and issue payments, and to process behind-the-scenes workloads such as record corrections. In addition to the six regular PSCs, an Office of Disability Operations serves as a PSC for all disability payments, and an Office of Foreign Operations serves as a PSC for all overseas operations such as payments to foreign residents.

The 30 TeleService Centers handled 79 million calls in 2012, or about 316,000 calls per workday. These calls range from general inquiries and requests for Social Security numbers to filing claims.

SSA Headquarters (located in Baltimore) and its ten Regional Offices (located in major cities throughout the country) coordinate the activities of all branches of the agency and attend to administrative functions such as budgeting, hiring, and training.

The agency's staffing level has dropped from 70,758 total work years to 64,601 from 2010 to 2013, resulting in a lean operation with very low overhead. In 2012, Social Security administrative costs were $6.3 billion, or about 0.80% of total expenses (0.75% of income). By comparison, overhead can run 20% or more in private insurance companies, and 10% to 20% in large charitable organizations. The average mutual fund has a 1.5% overhead.

www.ssa.gov/policy/docs/statcomps/supplement/2013/2f1-2f3.html
www.ssa.gov/policy/docs/statcomps/supplement/2013/4a.html#table4.a3

SOCIAL SECURITY CLAIMS, FY 2012

The following claims were filed in Fiscal Year 2012:

Retirement & Survivor	5.0 million
Disability	3.4 million
SSI	3.0 million
Total claims	13.4 million

That is about 53,000 claims per workday, or over 42 claims per field office per workday.

In addition, the SSA 800 telephone network received 79 million calls, with an average wait time of 4.9 minutes to reach a live representative

www.ssa.gov/policy/docs/chartbooks/fast_facts/2013/fast_facts13.html#contributions
www.ssa.gov/policy/docs/statcomps/supplement/2013/2f7.html

SOCIAL SECURITY TIME LINE

8/14/1935   Social Security Act signed into law. Only industrial workers are covered, with retirement benefits available only at 65.

1/1937   First Social Security taxes collected; 1.0% of first $3,000 earned.

1939   Survivor benefits, spouse benefits, and child benefits added.

1/1940   First Social Security monthly benefits paid.

1951	Work coverage extended to farm labor, domestic service, and some self-employed workers.
1955-56	Work coverage extended to military service, self-employed farmers and most professionals.
1956	Disability benefits added for ages 50-64. Early retirement at 62 available to women.
1960	Disability benefits added for those under 50.
1961	Early retirement at 62 available to men.
1965	Divorced wife benefits added. Work coverage extended to medical doctors.
7/1965	Medicare coverage begins.
1/1974	SSI benefits begin.
6/1975	Automatic cost-of-living adjustments begin.
1977	Divorced husband benefits added.
1/1984	Up to 50% of benefits includable in taxable income. All newly-hired federal employees, plus the President, Vice-President, and members of Congress, are covered by Social Security.
1/1994	Up to 85% of benefits includable in taxable income.

www.ssa.gov/history/
www.ssa.gov/policy/docs/statcomps/supplement/2013/2a20-2a28.html

2014 REFERENCE DATA

CONTACTING SOCIAL SECURITY

Web: www.socialsecurity.gov or mirror site www.ssa.gov
Telephone: (800) SSA-1213
TTY: (800) 325-0778

Toll-free telephone is staffed workdays from 7 a.m. to 7 p.m. in the time zone you call from. Recorded message service at all other hours.

CONTACTING MEDICARE

Web: www.medicare.gov
Telephone: (800) MEDICARE (800-633-4227)
TTY: (877) 486-2048

FICA TAX RATES

Social Security and Medicare taxes (2014 earnings ceiling: $117,000)

Paid by employee	7.65%
(6.20% Social Security, 1.45% Medicare)	
Paid by employer	7.65%
Paid by self-employed individual	15.3%

Medicare only taxes (On earnings over $117,000)

Paid by employee	1.45%
Paid by employer	1.45%
Paid by self-employed individual	2.90%

Work Credit/Quarter Of Coverage

Minimum earnings to achieve one quarter of coverage: $1,200

Earnings Limits While Enrolled

Under FRA (age 66):	$15,480/year ($1,290/month) Deduction = 1/2 of excess earnings
Turning FRA:	$41,400/year ($3,450/month) for months prior to birthday only. Deduction = 1/3 of excess earnings
FRA and up:	No earnings limit.

Medicare Facts

Part A premium

With 40+ Work Credits	$0
With 30-39 Work Credits	$234.00/month
With under 30 Work Credits	$426.00/month

Part B premium	$104.90/month - $335.70/month (See Figure 6.1, p. 131)
Part A deductible	$1,216/benefit period
Part B deductible	$147/year

Benefit Payments

Total cash benefits paid (2012)	$775 billion

Individual monthly benefits (2014):

Maximum for age 66 retiree	$2,642
Average retired worker	$1,294
Retired couple, both receiving benefits	$2,111
Aged widow(er) alone	$1,243
Widowed parent & 2 children	$2,622
Disabled worker	$1,148

www.ssa.gov/OACT/FACTS/
www.ssa.gov/policy/docs/statcomps/supplement/2013/highlights.html
www.medicare.gov/your-medicare-costs/costs-at-a-glance/costs-at-glance.html
www.ssa.gov/pressoffice/factsheets/colafacts2014.html

CRITICAL AGES

Birth
- Receive Social Security number (automatic if US-born). Page 210
- Eligible for Social Security child's payments. Pages 63, 70
- Eligible for SSI payments if disabled and needy. Page 220

16
- Parent's Social Security payments stop when youngest child reaches 16. Pages 63, 66, 88, 89

18
- Child's Social Security payments stop unless child is in elementary or high school, or disabled. Pages 63, 71, 88, 93
- Disabled individual can get SSI without counting parent's income and resources. Page 220

19
- Child's Social Security payment stops even if in elementary or high school, unless disabled. Pages 63, 71, 88, 93

22
- Must be disabled by age 22 to receive Disabled Adult Child Social Security payments. Page 117

50
- Eligible for Social Security payments as a Disabled Widow(er) (reduced payment amount). Page 116

60	• Eligible for Social Security payments as a Widow(er) (reduced payment amount). Page 88
	• Remarriage after 60 does not bar Social Security Widow(er)'s payments. Pages 87, 89
62	• Eligible for early Social Security retirement or spousal payments (reduced payment amount). Pages 38, 63, 68
65	• Eligible for Medicare. Page 128
	• Eligible for SSI Aged payments. Page 219
65-67	• Full Retirement Age (FRA). Exact FRA, currently 66, is determined by birth year. Page 51
	• Eligible for unreduced Social Security retirement, spousal, or widow(er)'s payments. Pages 51, 63, 67, 88, 91
	• Maximum spousal and widow(er)'s payments. Pages 67, 91
	• Earned income no longer reduces Social Security payment. Page 200
	• Retirement payments automatically increase if payments were withheld due to work (ARF). Page 204
	• Able to suspend payments voluntarily to receive Delayed Retirement Credits (DRCs). Page 232
	• Able to draw "Spousal-Only" payments without applying for retirement payments. Page 237
70	• Maximum retirement payments. P. 53
	• Voluntarily suspended payments automatically resume. P. 233

TAXATION OF SOCIAL SECURITY BENEFITS

BACKGROUND

Part of your Social Security payments may be income-taxable if you have outside income such as a pension, dividends, or interest. See page 205 for background information.

The following worksheet will help you estimate how much of your Social Security will be included in your taxable income. Use actual IRS worksheets for tax filing.

TAX ESTIMATOR WORKSHEET

Estimator: How much of my social security benefits are taxable?
(Tax Returns Filed in 1995 and Later)

1. Your Social Security Benefits   _____(1)

2. 50% of Line 1   _____(2)

3. Your gross income[A]   _____(3)

4. Your tax-exempt interest income   _____(4)

5. Sum of Lines 2, 3, and 4   _____(5)

6. Your adjustments to income[B]   _____(6)

7. Is amount on Line 6 less than Line 5?
    If No, stop. None of your Social Security is taxable.

    If Yes, subtract Line 6 from Line 5   _____(7)

1. If you are:
    Married filing jointly, enter $32,000

    Single, enter $25,000

    Married filing separately and lived apart
    from spouse all year, enter $25,000   _____(8)

    (If married filing separately and lived with spouse
    for part of year, skip lines 8-15. Multiply
    line 7 by 0.85 and enter result in line 16.
    Then go on to Line 17.)

2. Is the amount on Line 8 less than the amount on Line 7?
    If No, Stop. None of your Social Security is taxable.

    If Yes, subtract Line 8 from Line 7   _____(9)

3. If married filing jointly, enter $12,000
    If single enter $9,000
    If married filing separately and lived apart
    from spouse all year, enter $9,000   _____(10)

4. Subtract Line 10 from Line 9. If zero or les, enter 0   _____(11)

5. Enter the smaller of Line 9 or Line 10   _____(12)

6. Enter one-half of Line 12   _____(13)

7. Enter the smaller of Line 2 or Line 13   _____(14)

8. Multiply Line 11 by 0.85. If Line 11 is zero, enter 0   _____(15)

9. Add Lines 14 and 15   _____(16)

10. Multiply Line 1 by 0.85   _____(17)

11. Enter the smaller of Line 16 or 17. _____(18)

LINE 18 = TAXABLE BENEFITS. This amount would be included in your taxable income on your Form 1040.

NOTE A.   Income BEFORE subtracting itemized deductions and personal exemptions. Include all income from Form 1040, "Income" block, right-hand column.

NOTE B.   Include adjustments in Form 1040, "Adjusted Gross Income" block. Do not include student loan interest deduction, tuition and fees deduction, or domestic production deduction.

DESCRIPTION: Starting with tax returns filed in 1995, up to 85% of Social Security benefits must be included in taxable income. The 85% rule applies to marrieds with over $44,000 income and singles with over $34,000. Up to 50% of benefits are taxable for marrieds with income from $32,000 to $44,000, and for singles with income from $25,000 to $34,000.

Note that Line 18 is *not* the amount of tax you must pay on your Social Security. It is simply the amount of your Social Security to be included *in your taxable income* on your Form 1040. It would then be taxable at your tax rate.

You can prepare a computer spreadsheet to perform these computations. You can then use it to compare various income scenarios for you.

Source: www.irs.gov/pub/irs-pdf/i1040.pdf

EXAMPLES OF TAX COMPUTATIONS

Example 1: Single Person James Johnson

Assumptions:

Social Security	13,400
Gross Income	$6,000
Non-taxable interest income:	5,000
Income adjustments	0

Computation:

(1-6)	½ Social Security	$6,700
	+Gross Income	+6,000
	+ Non-Taxable Interest	+5,000
(7)	Total	$17,700

(8)	IRS Base Amount (for individual)	25,000
(9)	Line 8 is greater than Line 7, no Social Security is taxable	0

Example 2: Single Person Mary Smith

Assumptions:

Yearly Social Security	13,400
Gross Income	$12,000
Non-taxable interest income:	10,000
Income adjustments	0

Computation:

Using the worksheet above, Line 18 =	$1,850

Therefore, $1,850 of Mary's Social Security is included in her taxable income on her IRS Form 1040. The remaining $11,550 of her Social Security is tax-free.

Example 3: Married Couple John and Marsha

Assumptions:

Yearly Social Security	$22,000
Gross Income	$20,000
Non-taxable interest income:	15,000
Income adjustments	0

Computation:

Using the worksheet above, Line 18 =	$7,700

Therefore, $7,700 of John and Marsha's Social Security is included in their taxable income on IRS Form 1040. The remaining $14,300 of their Social Security is tax-free.

Example 4: Married couple Bill and Barbara

Assumptions:

Yearly Social Security	$36,000
Gross Income	$43,000

Non-taxable interest income: 26,000
Income adjustments   0

Computation:
Using the worksheet above, Line 18 = $30,600

Therefore, $30,600 of John and Marsha's Social Security is included in their taxable income on IRS Form 1040. The remaining $5,400 of their Social Security is tax-free.

SOURCES OF SOCIAL SECURITY INFORMATION AND MATERIALS

ITEM	HOW TO FIND	NOTES
SSA Telephone	(800) SSA-1213	Information, publications, claims.
SSA Website	www.ssa.gov	General information, on-line publications, benefit estimates, claims, and research.
"My Social Security" personal account	www.ssa.gov/myaccount	Anytime access to earnigs record and benefit estimates. For those on Social Security, online address changes, benefit verification letters, and more.
Apply for Social Security benefits	www.ssa.gov/applyonline/ or (800) SSA-1213	Apply for Social Security retirement, spouse's, survivor's, or disability payments.
Online Social Security Estimates	www.ssa.gov/estimator/	Instant benefit estimates. • You input identifying data to access the estimator. • Past earnings are automatically included but not posted. • You can alter the retirement date and future earnings fields to model various retirement scenarios.
Social Security Statement	www.ssa.gov/myaccount	See "My Social Security Account" above.
Online Social Security publications	www.socialsecurity.gov/pubs/englist.html	Access to all SSA publications.

ITEM	HOW TO FIND	NOTES
Social Security Benefit Calculators Home	www.ssa.gov/OACT/anypia/index.html	Links to all benefit calculators: • Retirement Estimator (at link immediately above) • Quick Calculator (rough estimate based on current earnings) • Online Calculator (you input past and future earnings; you need Social Security Statement—below—for past earnings) • Detailed Calculator (downloadable "AnyPIA" program) • WEP Calculator
AARP Social Security calculator	www.aarp.org/work/social-security/social-security-benefits-calculator.html	Help with when to apply, especially to optimize timing for married couples.
Medicare Hotline & Website	(800) 633-4227 TTY (877) 486-2048 www.medicare.gov	General information on Medicare including costs, deductibles, etc.
Medigap Plan Finder	www.medicare.gov/find-a-plan/questions/medigap-home.aspx	Computer assistance to select Medigap, Part C, or Part D plans tailored to your needs and budget.
Parts C & D Plan Finder	www.medicare.gov/find-a-plan/questions/home.aspx	
Information on • **Medicare coverage** • **Supplemental insurance** • **Long Term Care Insurance**	Your state Insurance Commissioner • Find in www.shiptalk.org • "A Shopper's Guide to Long-Term Care Insurance" free order form at https://eapps.naic.org/forms/ipsd/Consumer_info.jsp	Non-biased publications, information, seminars, counseling on Medigaps, Medicare Advantage plans, Part D drug plans, employer or union plans, and LTC insurance.

GLOSSARY OF SOCIAL SECURITY TERMS

Bold face indicates a cross-reference—more information can be found in the glossary under that reference. Also see the index (following this glossary) for further information.

A

AIME: Average Indexed Monthly Earnings. The average monthly earnings of a worker's computation years. The computation years are normally the worker's best 35 years after adjusting for inflation.

ALJ: Administrative Law Judge; a judge who presides over **appeals** at the **Hearing** and **Appeals Council** levels.

Appeal: An administrative process to review an adverse decision from Social Security.

Appeals Council Review: The final level of **appeal**, following a **Hearing**. The Appeals Council is a panel of three **ALJs**.

Applicant: The person actually signing the application for Social Security benefits. May be different from the **claimant**, as when a parent applies for a child claimant.

Approved Charge: The dollar amount approved by Medicare for a medical procedure.

Assignment method of payment: An agreement by a medical **provider** to charge no more than the Medicare **approved charge** for a medical procedure.

Auxiliary benefits: Social Security payments to auxiliaries—people other than the worker. Referred to in this book by the terms **family benefits** and **survivor benefits**.

C

Claimant: A person for whom a Social Security claim is filed. See **Applicant**.

Coinsurance: A portion of a medical bill that must be paid by the patient, typically expressed as a percentage of the total bill. See **Co-payment**.

COLA: Cost Of Living Adjustment. An increase in cash payments to account for inflation. Social Security COLAs are paid in January.

Co-Payment: A portion of a medical bill that must be paid by the patient, typically expressed as a flat dollar amount. See **Coinsurance**.

COBRA (Consolidated Omnibus Budget Reconciliation Act of 1985): the law which requires limited continuation of employee health insurance after leaving employment.

Covered work: Employment or self-employment which is covered by Social Security—subject to Social Security taxes and posted to the earnings record.

CR: Claims Representative. A Social Security representative trained to process claims and other complex work.

Credits: See **Work Credits**

Currently insured: Status of a worker who dies or becomes disabled before earning enough work credits to be **fully insured**, but who does have 6 work credits out of the 13 calendar quarters ending in death or disability. Currently insured status allows limited **survivor payments** and **ESRD** Medicare.

Custodial care: Nursing care providing personal assistance with dressing, eating, bathing, etc. Distinguished from **skilled nursing care**.

D

DDS: Disability Determination Service. The government agency which determines whether a claimant meets the definition of disability, typically a state department of health.

Deductible: A dollar amount set by Medicare which must be paid by the beneficiary before Medicare benefits can begin. For **Medicare Part A,** the hospital deductible is $1,216 per benefit period; for **Medicare Part B,** the deductible is $147 per year (2014).

Dependent benefits: See **Family benefits**.

DI: Disability Insurance

DIB: Disability Insurance Benefit. Disability payments made to a worker on his or her own record.

Direct deposit: Sending a Social Security payment by wire transfer directly into a bank account, rather than sending a paper check by mail.

Disability: A medical condition which prevents or will prevent the performance of **Substantial Gainful Activity** for at least 12 months or until death.

DRC: Delayed Retirement Credit. A bonus added to a retirement payment because the worker delays eligibility until after the **Full Retirement Age**.

Dual entitlement: Simultaneous entitlement on two different work records, e.g. as a worker in one's own right and as the spouse of another worker.

E

Earnings record: The record of all **covered work** performed by a worker.

Eligible: Meeting all legal factors of entitlement except for filing a valid claim. A person may be eligible for payment, but not **entitled**, because he or she has not yet filed for benefits.

Enrollment periods: Specified time periods for enrolling in Medicare or supplemental insurance.

Entitled: Literally, receiving title to (ownership of) payments. This means that a person meets all legal requirements for benefit payments, including filing a valid claim. See **Eligible.**

ESRD: End Stage Renal Disease. Severe kidney disease requiring dialysis treatment or transplant, and qualifying for ESRD Medicare.

F

Family benefits: Payments made to a living spouse, former spouse, or child on the work record of a living worker.

Family Maximum: A maximum payment amount available to an immediate family under one earnings record. Applies to both **family benefits** and **survivor benefits**.

FICA: Federal Insurance Contributions Act. Refers to the 6.2% Social Security tax on wages, and often refers to the 1.45% Medicare tax as well.

FRA: Full Retirement Age. The age at which a retiree can receive 100% benefits (100% of the **PIA**). Currently 66, but scheduled to rise to 67.

Fully insured: Status of a worker who has sufficient **Work Credits** for unrestricted retirement, disability, or survivor payments.

H

Hearing: The second level of administrative appeal, after **Reconsideration** and before **Appeals Council Review**.

HI: Hospital Insurance; same as **Medicare Part A**. Also means Health Insurance, especially when used with the acronym **OASDHI** or **RSDHI** to describe SSA's programs.

HMO: Health Maintenance Organization. A pre-payment group medical practice providing medical services through its own (or contracted) hospitals, clinics, etc. Services typically include a flat **Co-payment**.

I

Indexing: Adjusting for inflation. Indexed wages are wages adjusted for inflation.

Insured Status: A worker's status of meeting or not meeting the work requirements for receiving payments, as measured in **Work Credits**.

L

LTC: Long-Term Care. Usually refers to custodial care given at home or in an institution such as an adult family home or assisted care facility. LTC can also include respite care or other ancillaries. Also refers to insurance that pays for such care.

M

Maximum earnings: The maximum amount of earnings subject to Social Security taxes. Also known as *taxable earnings ceiling.*

Means testing: Requiring low income or resources for eligibility, as with public assistance programs. Social Security is not means tested, while **SSI** is.

Medicaid: A medical program for low-income individuals; part of the public assistance program. Included with **SSI** entitlement.

Medicare card: A card issued by Medicare indicating entitlement to **Medicare Part A** and/or **Part B**. It provides your claim number for processing medical claims.

Medicare Part A: The hospital insurance portion of Medicare, primarily covering hospital and **Skilled Nursing** bills.

Medicare Part B: The medical insurance portion of Medicare, covering physicians' services and other medical bills.

Medigap insurance: Private medical insurance intended to supplement Medicare's coverage, filling Medicare's "gaps."

Monthly earnings test: A **Retirement test**, used in the first year of retirement, which considers the retiree's earnings month by month rather than annually.

O

OASI: Old-Age and Survivor Insurance. Archaic acronym for SSA's original insurance programs. Also OASDI, Old-Age, Survivor, and Disability Insurance; and OASDHI, Old-Age, Survivor, Disability, and Health Insurance. See **RSDHI**.

P

PIA: Primary Insurance Amount. The 100% payment level yielded by a retirement, disability, or survivor computation. The PIA is the basis for payment computations for everyone entitled to benefits on a given earnings record (e.g. the worker, spouse, children, survivors, etc.). It is the amount of retirement benefits payable at **FRA** (Full Retirement Age).

Provider: As used by Medicare, a hospital, nursing facility, physician or other entity providing medical services.

Q

QC: Quarter of Coverage. Archaic term for a **Work Credit** on a worker's earnings record.

QMB Program: The Qualified Medicare Beneficiary program, which pays Medicare deductibles and premiums for low-income individuals.

R

Reconsideration: The first level of administrative **Appeal**, after an initial determination and before a **Hearing**.

Representative payment: Payment of Social Security benefits to a representative payee rather than directly to the beneficiary, because the beneficiary is incapable of managing money.

Retirement Test: A test to determine if a retirement claimant or beneficiary is truly retired. Retirement benefits can be paid only if work activity is below the limits of the retirement test.

RIB: Retirement Insurance Benefit. A retirement payment from SSA.

RRB: Railroad Retirement Board. The agency which processes claims and payments for railroad retirees.

RSDHI: Retirement, Survivor, Disability, and Health Insurance. Acronym describing SSA's insurance programs. Also RSI or RSDI, as appropriate. Archaic reference: **OASI**.

S

SGA: Substantial Gainful Activity. A specified threshold of work activity defining whether a medical impairment is a **disability**. SGA is usually measured by dollar earnings level, but can also be measured by work hours.

Skilled Nursing care: Nursing care providing at least 4 hours per day of highly skilled therapy such as physical therapy.

SMI: Supplemental Medical Insurance. Same as **Medicare Part B**.

SR: Service Representative. A Social Security representative skilled in processing new information to existing Social Security payment records, and with expertise in Medicare.

SSA: Social Security Administration. The government agency which administers the Social Security and **SSI** programs.

SSB: Social Security Board. The original name for what later became the Social Security Administration.

SSI: Supplemental Security Income. A public assistance (welfare) program, administered by **SSA**, providing **Medicaid** and cash payments to needy aged, blind, and disabled individuals.

SSN: Social Security Number.

Substantial services: Work limit used in the **Monthly retirement test** for self-employed individuals. Over 45 hours of work per month in a trade or business is considered substantial. Over 15 hours per month can be substantial if performed in a highly skilled occupation.

Survivor benefits: Payments made to a living spouse, former spouse, child, or parent of a deceased worker.

T

TSR: TeleService Representative. An **SR** specially trained in telephone interviews.

W

Work Credit: The basic unit of work used to establish eligibility for Social Security benefits. For example, 40 work credits are required for retirement benefits. One work credit is posted to a worker's earnings record for each $1,200 earned (2014), up to a maximum of 4 per year.

Workers' compensation: A program paying benefits to workers disabled because of job-related injuries.

INDEX

Bold face indicates a figure/illustration

☆ ABOUT THE AUTHOR ☆

Andy Landis is one of the nation's foremost authorities on Social Security and Medicare, in demand nationwide as an author, speaker, and consultant.

Andy has guided tens of thousands to abundant retirements while working at the Social Security Administration, AARP, multi-national corporations, and his own practice, Thinking Retirement.

Through Thinking Retirement, Andy educates both individuals and financial professionals through live workshops, books, articles, webinars, and professional education courses.

In addition to *Social Security: The Inside Story,* he is the author of *When I Retire,* providing a simple way to plan a fulfilling retirement life. He is a regular blogger for the *Wall Street Journal's* "MarketWatch" site. On TV, he has appeared on Fox Business News and PBS, and is a frequent guest on radio.

Andy lives in Seattle with Kay, keyboards, camper, computers, cars, and sometimes kids.

Follow Andy and Thinking Retirement on Facebook. Learn more at www.andylandis.biz.

39498900R00166

Made in the USA
Lexington, KY
25 February 2015